SOUTHERN LITERARY STUDIES

Louis D. Rubin, Jr., Editor

METAMORPHOSES OF THE RAVEN

METAMORPHOSES

OF THE RAVEN

Literary Overdeterminedness
in France and the South Since Poe

JEFFERSON HUMPHRIES

LOUISIANA STATE UNIVERSITY PRESS
BATON ROUGE AND LONDON

DESIGNER: Joanna Hill
TYPEFACE: Linotron Trump
TYPESETTER: G&S Typesetters

Publication of this book has been assisted by a grant from the Andrew W. Mellon
Foundation.

LIBRARY OF CONGRESS CATALOGING IN PUBLICATION DATA

Humphries, Jefferson, 1955–
    Metamorphoses of the Raven.

    (Southern literary studies)
    Bibliography: p.
    Includes index.
    1. Poe, Edgar Allan, 1809–1849, Raven.   2. Poe, Edgar Allan, 1809–1849—
Influence.   3. Ravens in literature.   4. Birds in literature.   5. French literature.   6. American literature—Southern States—History and criticism.
7. Literature, Comparative—American and French.   8. Literature, Comparative—French and American.   9. Symbolism in literature.   I. Title.   II. Series.

PS2609.H85   1985   811'.3   84-14321
ISBN 0-8071-1185-6

For Wallace Fowlie
et pour Michel Wallace

CONTENTS

To turn the symbolizing into the symbolized, to regain pure
language fully formed in the linguistic flux, is the tremendous
and only capacity of translation. In this pure language—which
no longer means or expresses anything but is, as expressionless
and creative Word, that which is meant in all languages—all
information, all sense, and all intention finally encounter a stra-
tum in which they are destined to be extinguished.

—WALTER BENJAMIN
"The Task of the Translator"

"Why, when you go to Lima-Peru or Berlin-Germany or Geneva-
Switzerland or even" —one waits, suspended, to see if it will
come and it does—"Paris-France, they've all heard about
Alabama."

—GEORGE WALLACE
Quoted in *Wallace*
by Marshall Frady

Lost, is it, buried? One more missing piece?

But nothing's lost. Or else: all is translation
And every bit of us is lost in it
(Or found . . .)
. . . .
And in that loss a self-effacing tree
Color of context, imperceptibly
Rustling with its angel, turns the waste
To shade and fiber, milk and memory.

—JAMES MERRILL
"Lost in Translation"

PREFACE

This work is an essay in the true sense of *try*, first attempt.
My experiment in these pages has been to develop and apply (for
me the two have not remained discrete) a new idea of literary
history methodologically grounded in linguistic, semiotic, and
psychoanalytic theory, a literary history that ascribes primacy
neither to literature nor to history, nor, I hope—and here is the
real danger—to myself. My goal has not been to compile a catalog of French writers who have had some contact, personal or
literary, with American southerners and vice versa. That would
have partaken of the sort of taxonomic, historical tradition in
critical scholarship that I have been trying to go beyond.

On one hand, I have wanted to elucidate a relation between
two languages and literary cultures usually ignored by the English departments whose province it is to study and teach southern literature, and whose bias toward Anglo-American 'moral',
'historical', and 'organic' critical discourses, and a concurrent
antipathy for Continental methodologies, have kept them from
acknowledging some basic characteristics of southern literary
tradition. That very blindness has not infrequently afflicted the
authors themselves, imbued as they so often are with English-
speaking prejudice—no less real for being often unconscious.

On the other hand, I have discovered in the relations between
French and southern literatures a hyperbole of the dialectic of
literariness. Hence the frequent theoretical digressions in the
text, though in fact they have as legitimate a claim to constitute
the text's mainstream as the rest. A glossary of critical and
rhetorical terms is appended in the hope of making this volume
accessible to as wide an audience as possible, perhaps including
some readers who have heretofore shunned anything calling itself 'theoretical' or brandishing such forbidding epithets as 'overdetermination'. If I could gain and keep the attention of even a

few such readers by an effective demonstration of my wish to be understood, my greatest hope in writing this book would be fulfilled.

I should perhaps say a word or two about the use in these pages of what will doubtless strike some as jargon. There is a difference, albeit subtle, between obscurity and difficulty. To avoid the former must be counted among the greatest virtues of any scholar or writer, but to shrink from new and (at first, apparently) arcane terms is to blind oneself to new concepts. Let us not confuse the shock of the new with an aversion to the obscure. A new terminology, a new word, long or short, may be the only access we have to a new way of thinking about language or literature or human endeavor. The story is often told of Picasso's reply to a distinguished gentleman who could not see the point of his *Demoiselles d'Avignon*. "Do you understand Chinese?" he is supposed to have asked the man, who replied that he did not. "But it can be learned," came the answer. My goal in this book has certainly been to show why the 'language of literary language' is worth learning and to make it as accessible as it can be, and also to participate in it, to expand my own knowledge of it. The value of the rhetorical and otherwise technical terms contained herein is to render accessible the means of literature, the 'how' of it, rather than to deal only with its effects, with the 'content' that a reader must generate from the text as he reads it. As Paul de Man has written, "Technically correct rhetorical readings may be boring, monotonous, predictable and unpleasant, but they are irrefutable. . . . They are, always in theory, the most elastic theoretical and dialectical model to end all models and they can rightly claim to contain within their own defective selves all the other defective models of reading-avoidance, referential, semiological, grammatical, performative, logical, or whatever."[1]

A note on translations. In the case of excerpts from a novel or poem, I have always given the original and a translation. Transla-

1. Paul de Man, "The Resistance to Theory," in *The Pedagogical Imperative*, Yale French Studies No. 63 (1982), 20.

tions are my own except when otherwise noted. In quoting expository prose, I have given only English in the body of the text, except where the French is needed to make or support a point. Where the translations of such expository French are mine, as is usually the case, I have included the original texts in the footnotes. Whether to use a published translation or my own has been dictated first by availability and second by my sense of whether translations observed aspects of the original that I wished to emphasize.

Surely many readers will disappointedly note the absence of their favorite French or southern writer and bridle at the inclusion of some they might have omitted. I have chosen the texts and authors best suited to nourish my progress, and implicit in my argument is that the progress is not, cannot be, finished. I hope that others will apply my model to other authors, even to intercultural symbioses other than the one discussed here.

ACKNOWLEDGMENTS

All my friends have contributed to this work if simply by indulging my obsessive behavior while writing it. Many colleagues were generous beyond all expectation with ideas, advice, and sympathy. Among the latter, I would be remiss not to single out Barbara Johnson and John Hollander at Yale; Adelaide M. Russo and Lewis P. Simpson of Louisiana State University; Beverly Jarrett of Louisiana State University Press; and C. Carroll Hollis of the University of North Carolina. Their support and counsel were, like grace, far greater than their object merited, both unforeseen and indispensable. I will not venture to assert that these individuals have succeeded in redeeming this volume, but if they have not, it is not for lack of Herculean efforts but rather for my not having followed their advice as closely as I should have. Thanks also are due my copy editor, Shannon Sandifer, without whose efforts the manuscript would have been much the poorer.

I gratefully acknowledge permission to reprint the following: Yves Bonnefoy, "Jean et Jeanne," and excerpts from "Lieu de Combat," in *Poèmes*, copyright © 1978 by Mercure de France, and from "L'Acte et le lieu de la poesie," in *L'Improbable*, copyright © 1980 by Mercure de France, reprinted by permission of Mercure de France. Pierre Reverdy, "Figure delayée dans l'eau," in *Main d'Oeuvre, poèmes 1913–1949*, copyright © 1949 by Mercure de France, reprinted by permission of Mercure de France. Excerpts from William Styron, *The Long March*, copyright © 1952 by William Styron, copyright renewed 1980, reprinted by permission of the Harold Matson Co., Inc. Excerpts from Flannery O'Connor, "The Displaced Person," copyright 1954 by Flannery O'Connor, reprinted from her volume *A Good Man Is Hard to Find and Other Stories* by permission of Harcourt Brace Jovanovich, Inc. Excerpts from Reynolds Price,

"The Annual Heron," in *Vital Provisions*, copyright © 1982 by Reynolds Price, reprinted with the permission of Atheneum Publishers and Harriet Wasserman Literary Agency, Inc. Excerpts from James Merrill, from "Lost in Translation," in *Divine Comedies*, copyright © 1976 by James Merrill, reprinted with the permission of Atheneum Publishers. Excerpts from *Mystery and Manners* by Flannery O'Connor, selected and edited by Sally and Robert Fitzgerald, copyright © 1961, 1969 by the Estate of Mary Flannery O'Connor; from *The Message in the Bottle* by Walker Percy, copyright © 1958, 1975 by Walker Percy; from *Collected Poems, 1919–1976* by Allen Tate, copyright © 1952, 1953, 1970, 1977 by Allen Tate, copyright 1931, 1932, 1937, 1948 by Charles Scribner's Sons, copyright renewed © 1959, 1960, 1965 by Allen Tate; reprinted by permission of Farrar, Straus and Giroux, Inc. Excerpts from Georges Bataille, *Le Mort*, © 1967 by Société Nouvelle des Editions Jean-Jacques Pauvert, reprinted by permission of Société Nouvelle des Editions Jean-Jacques Pauvert. Excerpts from Julien Green, "Leviathan," © 1929 by Editions du Seuil, and from "Autobiographie," in *Oeuvres complètes*, © 1963 by Bernard Grasset, Publishers, both reprinted by permission of Editions du Seuil. Excerpts from William Faulkner, "L'Apres-midi d'un Faune," in *William Faulkner: Early Prose and Poetry*, compiled and edited by Carvel Collins, © 1962 by Little Brown and Company, reprinted by permission of Carvel Collins. Excerpts from Paul Valéry, *Leonardo Poe Mallarmé*, copyright © 1972 by Princeton University Press, reprinted by permission of Princeton University Press and Routledge and Kegan Paul. Excerpts from William Faulkner, *As I Lay Dying* (Vintage, 1964), © 1930, renewed 1957 by William Faulkner, from *The Sound and the Fury* (Vintage, 1954), © 1929, renewed 1956 by William Faulkner, and from "A Rose for Emily," in *Collected Stories of William Faulkner* (Random House, 1950, reprint Vintage, 1977), © 1934, 1950 by Random House, Inc.; from Robert Penn Warren, "Two Poems About Suddenly and a Rose," © 1966 by Robert Penn Warren, and from "Evening Hawk," © 1975 by Robert Penn Warren, both in *Selected Poems, 1923–1975* (Random House, 1976); from Barry Hannah, *Ray* (Al-

fred A. Knopf, 1980, reprint Penguin, 1981), © 1980 by Barry
Hannah; reprinted by permission of Random House, Inc., and
Alfred A. Knopf, Inc. Michel Leiris, "Le plongeoir de Narcisse,"
and excerpts from "Glossaire j'y serre mes glosses," and "Mar-
rons sculptes pour Miro," all in *Mots sans mémoire*, © 1969 by
Editions Gallimard; excerpts from Paul Valéry, "Le Cimetière Marin," in *Charmes*, and "Petite lettre sur les mythes," in *Variété*,
both included in *Oeuvres*, © 1957 by Editions Gallimard; excerpts from Jean-Paul Sartre, "Sartoris," and from "La tem-
poralité chez Faulkner," both in *Critiques littéraires (Situations
I)*, © 1947 by Editions Gallimard; excerpts from René Char,
"Feuillets d'hypos" in *Fureur et Mystère*, © 1967 by Editions
Gallimard; Robert Desnos, "Le dernier poème," in *Domaine
public* and excerpts from "J'ai tant rêvé de toi," in *Corps et
Biens*, included in *Domaine public*, © 1953 by Editions Gallimard; excerpts from Paul Eluard, "Par une nuit nouvelle," in *La
vie immediate*, included in *Oeuvres complètes*, © 1968 by Editions Gallimard; from Saint-John Perse, "Images à Crusoé," in
Eloges, suivi de La Gloire des rois, Anabase, Exil, © 1960 by
Editions Gallimard; excerpts from Francis Ponge, "Notes pour un
coquillage," in *Le Parti pris des choses, suivi de Poèmes*,
© n.d. by Editions Gallimard; reprinted by permission of Editions Gallimard. Diagrams from Shoshana Felman, "On Reading
Poetry: Reflections on the Limits and Possibilities of Psychoanalytical Approaches," in *The Literary Freud: Mechanisms of
Defense and the Poetic Will*, edited by Joseph Smith (Yale University Press, 1980), copyright © 1980 by the Forum on Psychiatry and the Humanities of the Washington School of Psychiatry;
reprinted by permission of Shoshana Felman.

Chapter IV has appeared previously, in slightly different form, as
"The Cemeteries of Allen Tate and Paul Valéry: The Ghosts of
Aeneas and Narcissus," in *Southern Review*, XX (January, 1984).
Chapter VI has appeared previously, in slightly different form, as
"The Raven Re-versed" in *Maieutics: The Journal of the Centre
for Theory in the Humanities and Social Sciences* (York Univer-
sity, Downsview, Ontario, Canada, October, 1984).

METAMORPHOSES OF THE RAVEN

INTRODUCTION

The root of *interpretation* (*interpretatio*) means 'translation'.
The English *translate* comes from the Latin verb *transfero*, by
way of the past participle *translatus*; the French *traduire* goes
back to the related Latin *traduco*. Both Latin words mean 'to
carry or lead over'. The literal meaning of these roots is the
actual transportation of some cargo from one place to another.
Transfero can also mean 'to copy', 'to defer', or 'to put off'. The
issue involved in translation is always, sooner or later, what is
being carried or transported. What is the cargo, and where is it?
We assign it the name *original*, giving the literally spatial meaning of *transfero* a chronological inflection. The cargo is not so
much a thing, an object, as an intention, a moment of genesis,
embodied by the text. Every time we speak of originals, we lend
credence to a deific view of writing in which every author cre-
ates his text as surely and in as unproblematic a fashion as the
Creator in saying *"Fiat lux."* A cosmogonic view of art implies a
fall. From the original to the translation, vitiation occurs. In the
carrying over, some of the cargo is spilled; substituted for the
original is an inferior copy, a replica in figurative language. What
was supposed to be *trans*ferred is in fact *de*ferred, from the Latin
defero, 'to bring *down*' or 'to carry *away*'.

If the view of the original as Logos, a totalization of word and
being, of signifier, signified, and referent, were more than a
myth, there would be only one text and one language, and no
need of translation. The act of translation reflects the same need
as the evolution of the word itself: the necessity of deferment, of
an endless repetition of the passage across, in order to keep alive
the belief that a cargo, an original, does or did exist. If we stop
and look for it, we find that in fact the original is not totalized
with its object, its purported cargo, and does not achieve an
identity of being. What a literary original can be said to do is

sustain credence in itself, to fuel endless passages, or defer-
ments, while a lesser work would have been seen through. Still,
what is the original text but a translation from thought language
to written language? And thought language translates the written, the spoken, and the visual, imagistic originals that have
been read, heard, and seen before. The source, if it can be called
such, is the phenomenon of signification itself. Signification,
which includes images as well as words (words are, after all,
images, and images are signs, too), is a dialectic of translation in
which signs signify by varying ratios of resemblance and difference, all with reference to the hypothetical ur-text of language,
which has no positive being but is the dialectic of resemblance
and difference. Nevertheless, unless the illusion of a positive
origin or signified is sustained, for an instant at least, signification does not occur. That illusion cannot alter the fact that any
act of perception is an act of translation, of carrying over, and
that there is in fact no cargo, no end but the act itself. There are
no originals, no predecessors, and no anxieties of influence, only
good translations (those that can sustain repeated crossings) and
bad ones (those that cannot), whether we are talking about the
literal case of rendering from one language to another, or the
ongoing literary tradition within one language. This is, as Mallarmé and Poe have written, in the nature of the language—at
least in the nature of language as they and we know it. Here is
Mallarmé:

> Languages being imperfect by being several, the supreme one is
> lacking: thinking being writing without accessories nor whisper-
> ing but the immortal word still silent, the diversity, on earth, of
> idioms keeps anyone from saying the words which otherwise
> would find themselves, by singular coinage, as the truth itself
> materially. . . . —*Only*, be it known, *verse would not exist*: it
> philosophically remunerates for the failing of languages, superior
> complement.[1]

1. Stephane Mallarmé, *Oeuvres complètes*, ed. Henri Mondor and G. Jean-
Aubry (Paris, 1945), 363–64. "Les langues imparfaites en cela que plusieurs,
manque la suprême: penser étant écrire sans accessoires, ni chuchotement mais

And here is Poe:

> My general proposition, then, is this: —*In the Original Unity of the First Thing lies the Secondary Cause of All Things, with the Germ of their Inevitable Annihilation.*
>
> . . . .
>
> Let us begin, then, at once, with that merest of words, "Infinity." This, like "God," "spirit," and some other expressions of which the equivalents exist in all languages, is by no means the expression of an idea, but of an effort at one. It stands for the possible attempt at an impossible conception. Man needed a term by which to point out the *direction* of this effort—the cloud behind which lay, forever invisible, the *object* of this attempt. A word, in fine, was demanded, by means of which one human being might put himself in relation at once with another human being and with a certain *tendency* of the human intellect. Out of this demand arose the word, "Infinity"; which is thus the representative but of the *thought of a thought.*[2]

Plato goes even further, saying that the "failing of languages" is in the nature of human experience.

> What other way can there be of knowing them [things] except the true and natural way, through their affinities, when they are akin to each other, and through themselves? For that which is other and different from them must signify something other and different from them.[3]

We know things through their likeness to other things ("through their affinities") and through their difference from other things ("through themselves"). Perception, then, or at least linguistic perception, is necessarily ironic, a permanently repeated distanc-

---

tacite encore l'immortelle parole, la diversité, sur terre, des idiomes empêche personne de proférer les mots qui, sinon se trouveraient, par une frappe unique, elle-même matériellement la vérité. . . . —*Seulement, sachons n'existerait pas le vers*: lui, philosophiquement rémunère le défaut des langues, complément supérieur."

2. Edgar Allan Poe, *Works* (New York, 1979) 185–86, 200.

3. Plato, "Cratylus," in *The Collected Dialogues*, ed. Edith Hamilton and Huntington Cairns (Princeton, 1961), 472.

ing, parabasis,[4] carrying over, recopying, refiguration, a perpetual deferment of the signified, which is shown to be only a somewhat different sort of signifier. Jacques Lacan has elaborated the consequences, if not more thoroughly, more usefully for my purposes, than anyone else.

> Between the two chains . . . those of the signifiers in relationship to all the ambulatory signifieds which are in constant circulation because they are always in a process of transposition [*glissement*], the 'pinning down' I speak of, or the *point de capiton*, is mythical, for no one has ever been able to pin a signification on a signifier; but on the other hand what *can* be done is to pin one signifier to another signifier and see what happens. But in this case something new is invariably produced . . . in other words, the surging forth of a new signification.[5]

"To pin one signifier to another signifier and see what happens," that is my purpose here in pinning French and southern literature together, after the example of so many French and southern writers themselves. Because it is grounded in the very same idea of translatedness, of which it is my purpose to study a particular instance, an adapted and modified Lacanian paradigm will provide a theoretical framework for the readings that follow.

It is my premise here that the nineteenth century in America and in France witnessed the emergence of a new kind of literary consciousness, grounded in a sense—sometimes retrospective or latent—of its own translatedness. Edgar Allan Poe founded an

4. This refers to Schlegel's definition of irony as "permanent parabasis," parabasis, in Classical Greek drama, being that moment when the chorus would step forward, remove their masks, and speak in the author's name—a distancing of the work from the work within the work. The fact that the text in question, a dramatic one, would be performed rather than read silently, does not compromise or modulate the irony in the least but rather, if anything, increases it. The chorus remove their masks, as though to speak in their own behalf, and proceed to act under the guise of not acting, recite as though speaking spontaneously. See Friedrich Schlegel, *Kritische Friedrich-Schlegel-Ausgabe*, ed. Ernst Behler (Paderborn, W. Germany, 1963), 85.

5. From an unpublished seminar, cited by Anthony Wilden, in Jacques Lacan, *Speech and Language in Psychoanalysis*, trans. and ed. Wilden (Baltimore, 1981), 274.

other literature, a literature of 'carried-overness', within the dominant literary culture of America, that of the Northeast. To contest his own dependence and derivativeness and to undermine the eastern canon, Poe exposed the idea of original as mythic, partly by intent and partly by accident, that is, by a circumstantial collusion of signifiers, those constituting his temperament and those constituting his age. In his works, he enacted the essential translatedness and nonintegrity of textuality, again at least as much by accident as by will, making incongruence and the grotesque (the innately semiotic tension of logic and illogic) characteristic of his stories and poems. He did not so much deliberately lose the northern original as realize that he was losing it whether or not he chose to, grounding his poetic principle in an ethos and a mythos of loss which the Civil War confirmed as peculiarly southern and from which Faulkner and the Fugitive poets would conjure the phoenix of Southern Literature.

At the same time, Baudelaire and Mallarmé in France found themselves balked by the originary monolith of romanticism. From Poe they extracted, or thought they extracted, the latent power of translatedness to dissolve such predecessors. In the process, both Poe's English, inscribing an extreme tension within itself, and the French of Baudelaire and Mallarmé, which modulated even as it reflected that tension, gained something as they lost, as the tension of each was magnified or modulated by the other, enacting a *mise en abîme* of translatedness, a loss of loss in which each was transmogrified. My project here is to trace some of the ways in which French and southern writing are nourished by the idea of translatedness, how texts repeat the primal tension of trans-Atlantic deferral, the loss of the allegorical originals of northern literature and of romanticism, in allegories both spatial and temporal, synchronic and diachronic. I do not mean to imply that Emerson and Hugo should be read as necessarily and causally antithetical to Poe and Baudelaire, far from it. The earlier writers' status as origin or precursor is purely a function of the later writers' need to be seen (by themselves or modern readers) as different. How Emerson and Hugo appear to us 150 years later inevitably contaminates our idea of the way they appeared to Poe and Baudelaire. For Poe and Baudelaire as we are able to construe them, Emerson and Hugo were allegorical names of Origin and of Precedence, which needed to be allegorically lost.

Often, allegories of loss and translatedness imitate translation itself, centering on tropes of tropes—birds, ravens for instance, which, like colors and flowers, are always pure signifiers, unanchored in any signified, any original, and yet inciting endless efforts to translate their significance. If along the way, poets of translatedness engage in mimocentric, logocentric mythologizing, positing origins, as Baudelaire and Mallarmé do with Poe, it will be a different sort of origin that is really identical with the dialectic of signification. Of course, for any sort of origin to be thought, there must be the momentary error of thinking it as though it positively existed, as we will see in Baudelaire's maudlin and mendacious apotheosizing of Poe.

History, in this context of translatedness, is not the signified, but simply another signifier, another symptom of the cultural unconscious. Literary texts are not seen in a causal relation but rather as involved in a dialectical contamination, variously associated, misconstrued, and illuminated by resemblances and differences that, if looking back to a common original, look back to it not as an object, a totalized entity, a Logos, but as the beginning of a self-conscious translatedness in literature, rather as the Lacanian ego looks to the unconscious, knowing fully well that whatever name, whatever shape is momentarily ascribed to it, none is correct and yet all are necessary.

In one sense, what is being described here is an invention of the unconscious, or rather one of its avatars or symptoms. Repeated allusion to Poe by such Freudian theorists as Marie Bonaparte and Lacan himself attest to the fact. That the theorists should be French while the writer is American reveals a crucial aspect of the unconscious: it is translatedness, a perpetually repeated transit and deferment that is its own object. In addition to the meanings already alluded to—'to carry or lead over', 'to copy', 'to put off', 'to defer'—*transfero*, the root of *translate*, could also mean 'to use a word figuratively'. The conventional usage of *translate* uses figuratively all of the other meanings, figural and literal, of the root word; that is to say, the use of *translate* in the conventional, modern sense to mean the rendering of one language into another applies one of *transfero*'s figural meanings ('to use a word figuratively') to all of the others and uses all of the word's meanings according to one of them, in a figurative way, to describe the carrying over from language to language. Or, we could derive the modern meaning first and apply it to the other meanings to obtain, 'to use a word figuratively'. The same process would occur, except that we would be enacting the latter meaning as we generated it, translating within the language from figure to figure rather than from one language to another. The difference between 'to render one language into another' and 'to use a word figuratively' is merely one of extent. The order in which 'carry over' is carried over to generate all its figurative meanings does not matter; there is no causal relation among the various derivations. They are all generated by tautology: translation ('to carry over') being translated ('used figuratively') as translation ('the rendering of one language into another'). The same signifier, applied to itself ('carried over') generates all the other signifiers, ciphered in one word.

What we see here is a maddeningly radical instance of what Quintilian called the trope of transumption, or metalepsis, "a figure of a figure," as Harold Bloom calls it.[6] It is a kind of rhetorical syllogism of the kind 'x is like y, and y is like z, therefore x is like z,' y being the intermediate step or metalepsis, the object of allusion, which is itself omitted. Here is the example cited by Quintilian: "*Cano* ['to sing'] is a synonym for *canto* ['to recite' or 'incant'] and *canto* for *dico* ['to indicate' or 'say'], therefore *cano* is a synonym for *dico*, the intermediate step being provided by *canto*." That metalepsis turns on two kinds of synonymity, a morphological and phonemic one between *cano* and *canto*, and a semantic one between *canto* and *dico*. It depends on an overdetermination of sound and sense. As

6. Harold Bloom, *A Map of Misreading* (New York, 1975), 102.

John Hollander writes: "We might translate the whole sequence into modern English by saying *sing* (for Milton or Pope or Wordsworth) means 'say,' which means 'write,' which means, for us today, 'type,' (with the operative pun that implies that typing is a type and thereby, an antitype, of writing)."[7] We will see, in the course of this study, how often poetic effects rely on a metalepsis governed by such overdetermination of sound and sense. The synchronic effect is frequently overlaid with a historicocultural overdetermination, comprising the diachronic aspect of the sound and the sense that are overdetermining each other, the inflection that past use, poetic and otherwise, has given to each. Thus John Smith, in his *The Mysterie of Rhetorique* (London, 1657), describes metalepsis most aptly and charmingly as what happens "when divers Tropes are shut up in one word."[8] Metalepsis, to resume, might be described as an elliptical surfeit of signification, or an elliptical overdeterminedness. Quintilian is uneasy with metalepsis, as he is with catachresis, which is also referred to as *abusio*, 'a false use of tropes'. Catachresis is similarly overdetermined, but not so elliptical.

The reason for Quintilian's discomfort with transumption may be that the trope does omit the middle term, which is supposed to ground it, and therefore innately permits fallaciousness, like syllogisms, even though in specific cases it may not be fallacious. X may be like y, and y may be like z, but this need not imply a likeness between x and z. The properties linking x to y may be entirely different from those linking y to z. At the opposite extreme, the trope dissolves into tautology, as in the case of the modern meaning of translation: x is like x_1, x_1 is like x_2, therefore x is like x_2, or more precisely, x generates x_1, which is then applied to x to give x_2. This case is more gravely fallacious, for in it the grounding is never there to be omitted; the grounding, the original, is identical with the other two terms, and thus lost before the troping begins, creating a hyperbole of signification.

7. John Hollander, *The Figure of Echo* (Berkeley, 1981), 135. The previous quotation from Quintilian is cited by Hollander.
8. Cited *ibid.*, 146–47.

Throughout this study, we will see how catachresis, the less potent sibling of metalepsis, recurs as a hyperbole of figurative language.[9] Metalepsis, as it occurs in the etymology and in the act of translation, is an even more radical trope of a trope, because in addition to being overdetermined, it omits the middle term. The Greek root of metalepsis, *metalambanô*, means not only 'to exchange' or 'to take in a new way' but '*to understand*'.[10] Metalepsis enacts, in hyperbolic fashion, the misprision and tautology of signification—understanding—which this study will seek, paradoxically and tautologically, to understand, that is, to repeat.

"To transume," says Harold Bloom, "means 'to take across.'"[11] Quintilian says that "it is the nature of metalepsis to form a kind of intermediate step between the term transferred and the thing to which it is transferred, *having no meaning in itself*, but merely providing a transition" (emphasis mine).[11]
In the case of translation, it is language, the word *translation* itself, which is at once the intermediate step, the term transferred, and the thing to which it is transferred—with, of course, a slightly different inflection at each stage, an inflection obtained by doubling the word on itself. The word is its own cargo; to apply translation to language as we conventionally do is to take 'taking across' across, to use (figuratively) the word that means 'to use figuratively'. It is to translate translation into translation. What happens when we translate a word from one language to another? Something very similar. Translation occurs as a linguistic metalepsis: *une vache* refers to a large bovine domestic animal, designated in English by the word *cow*, hence we say that *vache* is 'cow'. The metalepsis is effected by our common mental picture—imagistic signifier—of a cow. Translation in practice always hovers between the two extremes of the ideal (for purposes of fidelity) tautology and the fallacious syl-

9. See *ibid.*, 140: "Erasmus likens transumption to catachresis" and 141: "The older rhetorics might associate this with catachresis, or abusio, a wrenching of sense hovering between the brilliant and the disreputable."
10. *Ibid.*, 133.
11. Bloom, *A Map of Misreading*, 102.

logism. It substitutes one signifier (one substitution) for another by the mediation of a third, and therefore is a trope of troping.

In the practice as in the etymology of translation, the cargo, the signified, is the object of a radical irony, a movement of self-displacing displacement. What is at stake is nothing less than the nature of literature, of language, and, indeed, of human experience in the wake of Freud's discovery of the unconscious and Lacan's description of it as the locus of substitution of the signifier, as translation.

In this study, I am dealing with a specific symptom of the Western cultural unconscious: the fact of a recurring symbiosis between French and southern writers. Of course, the unconscious is bound to exceed the specificity of the symptom and of my specific analyses of it. My premise is, as Shoshana Felman has written, that

> the discourse of literary history itself points to some unconscious determinations which structure it but of which it is not aware. . . . Literary history, or more precisely, the critical discourse surrounding Poe, is indeed one of the most visible ("self-evident") *effects* of Poe's poetic signifier, of his text. Now, how can the question of the peculiar effect of Poe be dealt with analytically? My suggestion is: by locating what seems to be unreadable or incomprehensible in this effect; by situating the most prominent discrepancies or discontinuities in the overall critical discourse concerning Poe, the most puzzling critical contradictions, and by trying to interpret those contradictions as symptomatic of the unsettling specificity of the Poe-etic effect, as well as of the necessary contingence of such an effect on the unconscious.[12]

My concern here extends beyond Poe, focusing not exclusively on his text's effect in critical discourse but on the recurrence of that effect, as the symptom of translatedness, in literary texts in France and the South, in French and English. The phenomenon

---

12. Shoshana Felman, "On Reading Poetry: Reflections on the Limits and Possibilities of Psychoanalytical Approaches," in Joseph M. Smith (ed.), *The Literary Freud* (New Haven, 1980), 147.

most fortuitously happens to coincide with a literal, historical
interdependence between the two literary and linguistic cultures—making it a symptom that might be described, after the
example of translation, as a linguistic, a historical, and a literary
metalepsis, which together compose a metalepsis of metalepses,
or an elliptical overdetermination of three elliptical over-
determinations.

In my exploration of the phenomenon, Poe, or an effect associated with Poe that the title of this work ciphers as the 'Raven'
for reasons which will be apparent in Chapter 2, is the middle
term of the metalepsis, the metalepsis itself, the trope of translation, of translatedness, alluded to by the others, (un-)grounding
them and omitted by them, repressed, even as it is alluded to.

I. PROLOGUE

Since Poe, there has existed a remarkable and persistent affinity between the French and southern literary communities. The French today still wonder why Americans are not as anxious as they to acknowledge Poe's greatness.[1] The story is told by Simone de Beauvoir that during a tour of America she never once heard an American intellectual list Poe among his country's great literary figures. She concluded that Americans must have thought he was a French writer.[2]

Often in the twentieth century, Catholicism has been a prominent common denominator in this intercultural, interlinguistic phenomenon, especially in such southern writers as Walker Percy, Flannery O'Connor, Allen Tate, and Caroline Gordon, and such French writers as Jacques Maritain and Julian Green (who, in an uncanny historical coincidence, combines a southern heritage with a French education and upbringing). But the exchange has been as much secularly philosophical as religious. It was Sartre and Malraux, after all, along with Maurice Coindreau, the great French interpreter of the South, who brought about the European apotheosis of Faulkner. And Walker Percy credits Sartre with awakening him to existentialism and phenomenology.[3] Such is Percy's debt to French philosophy that an interviewer could ask him, with reason, "Why weren't you influenced by American writers?"[4]

But Catholicism and existentialism are only specific instances

1. See Patrick F. Quinn, *The French Face of Edgar Poe* (Carbondale, 1957).

2. Simone de Beauvoir, *America Day by Day*, trans. Patrick Dudley (New York, 1953).

3. John Carr (ed.), *Kite-flying and Other Irrational Acts: Conversations with Twelve Southern Writers* (Baton Rouge, 1972), 39–46; see Stanley D. Woodworth, *William Faulkner en France (1931–1952)* (Paris, 1959).

4. Carr (ed.), *Kite-flying and Other Irrational Acts*, 42.

of this phenomenon. We find such writers as Fred Chappell, not especially religious or steeped in philosophy, winning a prize from the académie française, for example. Chappell, indeed, is far more admired in France than he is in America outside the South. Chappell himself has said that "Poe, Flannery O'Connor, it seems to me, get the most out of the form I like. They have the kind of perfection I'd like to achieve. That's one of the reasons my books go to France. *My novels aren't very American novels. Poe is not a very American writer*" (emphasis mine). What he has in common with Poe and O'Connor is not just the formal and thematic economy of which he is speaking here, but the surreal, the grotesque. Shelby Foote has gone so far as to wonder if indeed some southern fiction has not begun to parody itself, its grotesqueness. Chappell prefers to see this affinity for the grotesque as a kind of deranged, hyperbolic phenomenology. "It takes an awful lot of nerve to say that the guy is really out of his mind: 'Normal people like me, man, we know better.' I would never be able to say that about anybody. I get along well with guys who think they're Napoleon." Chappell has put his finger on the characteristic rhetoric of a great deal of southern fiction, particularly that which the French have tended to admire. Yet for Chappell, it is not grotesque, as it has so often appeared to the northern critic who would read it simply as poorly executed realism; for Chappell and many another southern writer, it *is* realism, hyperrealism: "This is all exaggeration and hyperbole, but it is pretty good scientific theory too. You find this in the works of Whitehead and Russell. . . . You know, our old notion of what is real ain't got nowhere to go."[5]

Flannery O'Connor explains the southern writer's penchant to grotesquerie as a phenomenon of loss, of a sense of displacement, exile, unwholeness. "It is when the freak can be sensed as a figure for our essential displacement that he attains some depth in literature." It is because of the southern intellectual's sense of displacement and defeat that he favors hyperbole over controlled mimesis. "When Walker Percy won the National

5. *Ibid.*, 225, 233.

Book Award, newsmen asked him why there were so many good Southern writers and he said, 'Because we lost the War.' He didn't mean by that simply that a lost war makes good subject matter. What he was saying was that we have had our Fall. We have gone into the modern world with an inburnt knowledge of human limitations and with a sense of mystery which could not have developed in our first state of innocence—as it has not sufficiently developed in the rest of our country."[6] It is just such a rhetoric of loss and displacement, hyperbole and catachresis,[7] that has so often placed the southern writer at odds with the northern critic and the northern writer who, since Hawthorne and until recently, have tended to make somewhat different demands of literature.

    There is another reason in the Southern situation that makes for a tendency to the grotesque and this is the prevalence of good

6. Flannery O'Connor, *Mystery and Manners*, ed. Sally and Robert Fitzgerald (New York, 1969), 45, 58–59.

7. Pierre Fontanier, in his classic work *Les Figures du Discours* (Paris, 1977), 77, 213, consigns catachresis to a kind of no-man's ground, neither literal nor figural but partaking of both. Catachresis is seen here as abuse, as ex-tension, a kind of tension exceeding the bounds of what is "proper signification." In the second quotation, it is described as a kind of necessary metalepsis, or substitution of a substitution, the same sort of rhetorical gesture of which *translation*, in the Introduction herein, is seen to be a hyperbole. But, as with translation, the sign substituted is substituted for an idea that is in effect created by the act of substitution; the *idée nouvelle* referred to by Fontanier cannot be represented semiotically except by the arbitrary and illogical substitution for it of another sign, a previous substitution. The central term, the metalepsis that grounds the trope and is dropped from it here, would be the pure Idea, uncontaminated by any involvement with signification—such an Idea is always necessarily omitted—it can neither be known, nor thought, nor described. Fontanier's own language points to this fact: if the "new idea," the signified of the catachresis, can be described as an idea, then it *does* have a previous signifier of its own. What he describes can only hold true if the new idea is realized, created, by the arbitrary and illogical substitution of a substitution (a figure) for a semiotic nullity. Catachresis is not literal because it offends the logic of signification; that is, it arbitrarily, without regard for semiotic affinity, substitutes sign for sign, contradicting a prior semiotic distinction, for instance, between the act of speaking and the act of stabbing, when Hamlet says, "I will speak daggers to her" (see Richard A. Lanham, *A Handlist of Rhetorical Terms* [Berkeley, 1968], 212). Yet it is not

Southern writers. *I think the writer is initially set going by liter-ature more than by life.* When there are many writers all employ-ing the same idiom, all looking out on more or less the same social scene, the individual writer will have to be more than ever careful that he isn't just doing badly what has already been done to completion.

. . . .

The Southern writer is forced from all sides to make his gaze extend beyond the surface, beyond mere problems, until it touches that realm which is the concern of prophets and poets. When Hawthorne said that he wrote romances, he was attempt-ing, in effect, to keep for fiction some of its freedom from social determinisms, and to steer it in the direction of poetry. I think this tradition of the dark and divisive romance-novel has com-bined with the comic-grotesque tradition, and with the lessons all writers have learned from the naturalists, to preserve our South-ern literature for at least a little while from becoming the kind of thing Mr. Van Wyck Brooks desired when he said he hoped that our next literary phase would restore that central literature which combines the great subject matter of the middlebrow writers with the technical expertness bequeathed by the new critics and which would thereby restore literature as a mirror and a guide for society.

For the kind of writer I have been describing, a literature which mirrors society would be no fit guide for it, and one which did manage, by sheer art, to do both these things would have to have recourse to more *violent* means than middlebrow subject matter and mere technical expertness.[8] (emphasis mine)

This is not to say that the average southern writer, indeed any southern writer, eschews realism altogether, but rather that he or she seeks "to exhaust the concrete" rather than to reflect it.

---

figural either, because it does not substitute *for* anything. It substitutes a sub-stitution for a semiotic nullity: "une idée nouvelle qui elle-même n'en avait point [de signe] ou n'en a plus d'autre."
8. O'Connor, *Mystery and Manners*, 45–46.

There is in much of the writing to come out of the South since Poe a rhetoric that goes against the American grain and even against the grain of the English language, which the French poet Yves Bonnefoy has described as Aristotelian. That is, the English language has sufficient lexical and phonemic inventory, aided by the factor of syllabic stress, to undertake the project of naming the world, without the need or the inevitability in French, with its lack of stress and more limited phonemic scale and vocabulary, of more obviously figurative, formal strategies of representation. Each word and phoneme in French must bear a greater burden of signification and figuration. *Cul* means 'ass' and *sac* means 'bag' but *cul de sac* is much more likely to mean 'dead-end street' than 'ass of a bag'. What ought to be catachresis ('ass of a bag') is , in the most conventionally literal sense, brazenly metaphorical. There is the more literary example of *rime equivoquée*, as in these lines by Theodore de Banville: "Dans ces meubles laques, rideaux et dais moroses, / Danse, aime, bleu laquais, ris d'oser des mots roses." Such an effect would be quite impossible in English and is completely untranslatable on account of mutually reinforcing factors of stress and morphological diversity. So by describing French as Platonic, Bonnefoy points to the greater potential for figurative ambiguity that is built into the language.[9]

Thus, when a poet writes *loss*, a Frenchman is likely to read the word *perte* as not only descriptive of some real loss, not only as a specific historical phenomenon (the Civil War), but also as Loss, with myriad poetic and metaphysical connotations. Even the word *South* is more allusive, more densely and yet more vaguely, indeterminately metaphorical for the French. Simone de Beauvoir writes: "I thought: I am going down South, that is fascinating. And I wondered if there would still be the same attraction on the other side of the equator. Here the word 'South' had a more pathetic sound than elsewhere. It meant the tragic war described by Faulkner and Caldwell, the land of slavery and

9. This observation was made by Bonnefoy in his graduate seminar at Yale University in the fall of 1977 and has not, to my knowledge, appeared in print. The lines from Banville are cited in Hollander, *The Figure of Echo*, 32.

hunger." Even in the physical presence of the very place, the word remains a pathetic sound, in the French sense of *moving*, involving pathos, richly metaphorical, poetically historic—thickly redolent of Baudelairean contrasts and of enslavement and hunger, both spiritual and fleshly, in a setting of languid splendor—because the South's history, for a Frenchman, is nothing but metaphysic, poetry, literature, a magnificently lugubrious cipher. It is not only due to the otherness of the history itself, to a Frenchman, but also to the otherness of the language. De Beauvoir goes on to say that "realism easily takes on the false colors of poetry when exported from one country to another," speaking specifically of the transposition from English to French.[10] All of this powerfully suggests that a change will occur in the figurative language of a poem (or a novel) as it is translated. The history of literary relations between France and the South would seem to imply that if something is lost in translation, there is something gained as well. In the mirror of French, the southerner seems often to have been able to see his best face, a face less salient in English, and his fellow countrymen in the North have been able to discern what otherwise might have eluded their view altogether. How might this occur?

There is, to begin with, a historical affinity between France and the South that is precisely the ethos of loss. Since Napoleon's defeat at Waterloo, France has been humiliated militarily three times: in 1870, 1914, and 1940. The last defeat and occupation left scars that are still not entirely healed, evidenced by the fact that only recently has the government allowed the film *Le Chagrin et la Pitié* to be shown on French national television. The French poet has his own reasons for writing the word *perte* and his own experience with which to read the word when he encounters it in someone else's poem. Of course, in translation, a Frenchman is more likely to think of his country's own occupation and defeat than of the South's, or if he knows of the American Civil War, to understand it in terms of the wars of which he has had more immediate knowledge and of a European

10. Beauvoir, *America Day by Day*, 86–87, 56.

literary thematic of war and loss. This will be true whether he reads a translation or the original language; the problem of translating a poem "correctly" suggests the problem of reading it "correctly" in the first instance. Reading, after all, is a sort of translation into one's own codes of experience, literary and real. Each for his own reasons, the Frenchman is likely to listen when the southerner speaks of loss, and vice versa. The northerner, at least prior to Vietnam, had less reason to listen. Yet often, through the voices of Frenchmen, he has heard. What is it precisely that the language does to reveal the southerner's case so strongly in French?

We might begin by considering the ethos of loss or defeat in the context of Platonic, neo-Platonic, and Aristotelian philosophies, following Bonnefoy's analogy. Plato would have banned from his perfect Republic a poetry that merely reflects reality, for to him the Good, the Beautiful, and the True are not evident in the world of appearances, which imperfectly imitates the Ideal, divine archetypes. In this view mimetic poetry mediates what is already mediated and vitiated. The approach to divine forms must be through Beauty, through the love it inspires, the nostalgia for Ideal Form which it suscitates, and the sense of having *lost* these forms, of not having direct access to them. Poetry must subvert the mimetic function of language in order to rend the real, do violence to it, to create a sense of loss that is the only means by which the Ideal may be apprehended.[11] The theosophical dualism and consequent nihilism latent in such an Ideal philosophy was developed by Greek Gnosticism and repressed by such neo-Platonists as Plotinus.[12]

Cratylus depicts an exhaustive debate on the nature and origin of language. In it we find that Plato, too, in his characterization of Socrates, identifies the significative function of language as a miscarriage, a defeat, and an ongong loss, having nothing what-

11. See *Princeton Encyclopedia of Poetry and Poetics* (Princeton, 1974), 619–21; Eric A. Havelock, *Preface to Plato* (Cambridge, 1963); Paul Friedlander, *Plato: An Introduction*, trans. Hans Meyerhoff (Princeton, 1969), 59–84; Julia Annas, *An Introduction to Plato's Republic* (Oxford, 1981), 217–71, 336–43.
12. See Hans Jonas, *The Gnostic Religion* (Boston, 1958), 270–81.

ever to do with historical phenomena. As a purely metaphysical phenomenon, language *is* loss, error.

> SOCRATES: Let us return to the point from which we digressed. You were saying, if you remember, that he who gave names must have known the things which he named. Are you still of that opinion?
>
> CRATYLUS: I am.
>
> SOCRATES: And would you say that the giver of the first names had also a knowledge of the things which he named?
>
> CRATYLUS: I should.
>
> SOCRATES: But how could he have learned or discovered things from names if the primitive names were not yet given? For, if we are correct in our view, *the only way of learning and discovering things is either to discover names for ourselves or to learn them from others* [emphasis mine].
>
> CRATYLUS: I think that there is a good deal in what you say, Socrates.
>
> SOCRATES: But if things are only to be known through names, how can we suppose that the givers of names had knowledge, or were legislators, before there were names at all, and therefore before they could have known them?
>
> CRATYLUS: I believe, Socrates, the true account of the matter to be that a power more than human gave things their first names, and that the names which are thus given are necessarily their true names.
>
> SOCRATES: Then how came the giver of names, if he was an in-spired being or god, to contradict himself? For were we not saying just now that he made some names expressive of rest and others of motion? Were we mistaken?
>
> CRATYLUS: But I suppose one of the two not to be names at all.
>
> SOCRATES: And which, then, did he make, my good friend—those which are expressive of rest, or those which are expressive of motion?
>
> . . . .
>
> But if this is a battle of names, some of them asserting that they are like the truth, others contending that *they* are, how or by

what criteria are we to decide between them? For there are no other names to which appeal can be made, but obviously recourse must be had to another standard which, without employing names, will make clear which of the two are right, and this must be a standard which shows the truth of things.

. . . .

But if that is true, Cratylus, then I suppose that things may be known without names?
CRATYLUS: Clearly.
SOCRATES: But how would you expect to know them? *What other way can there be of knowing them, except the true and natural way, through their affinities, when they are akin to each other, and through themselves? For that which is other and different from them must signify something other and different from them* [emphasis mine].
CRATYLUS: What you are saying is, I think, true.
SOCRATES: Well, but reflect. Have we not several times acknowledged that *names rightly given are the likenesses and images of the things which they name?*[13] [emphasis mine]

The only way of knowing "things" is through their likenesses and images, which are names, either linguistic, ideational, or imagistic signifiers. The thing itself is nothing but the idea of itself, its image and name. What is perception but translation from image to name to idea, endlessly and in whatever order, among whatever oddly concatenated permutation of these codes and their myriad subcodes?

Socrates, in Plato's *Symposium*, argues that Love, Eros, is not only "the consciousness of a need for a good not yet acquired or possessed" but for a good, an object, that by its very nature is discontinuous with desire, its Other:

Everyone . . . who feels desire, desires what is not in his present power or possession, and desire and love have for their object

13. Plato, *Collected Dialogues*, 471–73. See Gérard Genette, *Mimologiques, Voyage en Cratylie* (Paris, 1976).

things or qualities which a man does not at present possess but which he lacks.

· ·

Love exists only in relation to some object and . . . that object must be something of which he is at present in want.[14]

· ·

Love is in love with what he lacks and does not possess.[15]

It must be remembered that Eros, in its highest manifestation, aims not at individuals but at the Ideal, Truth and Beauty. The desire to know is not at all different in kind from concupiscence. Aristophanes, in the same dialogue, recounts a myth of genesis that describes mankind as the rupture and fragmentation of a primal totality, an irremediable loss of perfect self-sufficiency.

In the first place there were three sexes, not, as with us, two, male and female; the third partook of the nature of both the others and has vanished. . . . Secondly, each human being was a rounded whole.

· ·

Man's original body having been thus cut in two, each half yearned for the half from which it had been severed.

· ·

Each of us then is the mere broken tally of a man.[16]

Desire for a primal state of inconceivable wholeness conditions all human endeavor. All such myths of totality remain partial, fragmentary—names. As they reflect the desire to know, the highest sort of desire, they, like Eros, bely the totality toward which they strain, with which desire in all its avatars must ever be discontinuous. Experience is the perpetual production of like-nesses, copies, of which no original may be located or logically postulated. Knowledge occurs in the transposition and flux from one state of likeness to another, one frame of naming to another, even, hyperbolically, one language to another.

14. Walter Hamilton, introduction to *The Symposium*, by Plato (New York, 1951), 19.

15. Plato, *The Symposium*, 77–78.

16. *Ibid.*, 59, 61, 62.

Plato also believed in the contradictory function of poetry as teacher, as a pillar of social morality. It is that aspect of Plato's thought that Aristotle pursues with his theory that art is superior to history because it is "more universal." But Aristotle sees the universal and the particular as a totality: "By the universal, I mean how a person of a certain type will on occasion speak or act, according to the law of probability or necessity." So the poet is a *faber*, not a *vates*, a describer and a transcriber, not a visionary and not merely a translator of translations: "the poet or 'maker' should be the maker of plots rather than of verses, since he is a poet because he imitates, and what he imitates are actions."[17] For Aristotle, there is no difficulty locating the original from which literary copies derive; it is 'action'. Knowledge is a function of action, not of perpetual flux, translation, or naming. We might say that Mr. Van Wyck Brooks, as Flannery O'Connor referred to him, was carrying on the Aristotelian tradition. More recently, in *On Moral Fiction*, the novelist John Gardner provides an example of Aristotelianism so accusatorily hyperbolic as to suggest an emperor's panic as he hovers on the brink of realizing his nudity, as if Mr. Gardner himself were astonished at the implications of his own works of fiction, which, if moral or realistic at all, are most ambiguously so.

The Platonic strain in French poetry is best known to us today through the avatars of symbolism: Baudelaire, Mallarmé, Rimbaud. The error that one is always tempted to make in reading the works of these poets is to turn the symbol into an encoded mimesis—a movement toward possession and totalization of the Truth in the thing which has simply been rendered more complex and satisfying to the effete by a deliberate use of arcane vocabulary and bizarre syntax. That approach considers the poem as a puzzle to be solved, or an open box, for which one need only locate the proper size of lid in order to "close it up."[18] The results of such efforts are often interesting and instructive,

17. Aristotle, *On Poetry and Music*, trans. S. H. Butcher (Indianapolis, 1956), 13.
18. I am thinking here of Michael Riffaterre, *Semiotics of Poetry* (Bloomington, 1978); see, for instance, p. 149.

and to the extent that reading cannot ever entirely separate itself from gestures toward closure, however subtle or cleverly concealed, no reader can claim to eschew such strategies entirely. But the symbolist impulse is not one of deliberate difficulty, nor of tortured mimesis. It aims not to totalize the thing, to possess it, but in the Platonic sense to lose it, to make of the poem not a meaning but a loss, a misplacement of sense, of appearance, of the thing, through the achievement of a beauty of form and sound in language to give us a sense of loss, of absence, which intimates the Ideal. Yves Bonnefoy, as he writes of Rimbaud, speaks for his own poetic tradition and language.

> Our senses speak only of our place of exile. To recover *the true life*, the veil of the senses must first be rent. This is the true function, a negative one, of hallucinations and *deliriums*. And thus here is suggested, beyond physical aspects forced to destroy each other, the possibility of a supreme encounter which is, this time, the Vision.
>
> . . . .
>
> Thus the *unknown* is both light and rhythm, our only true act, a *rapture*; and in any case the violent denial of language in its rational uses.
>
> For are these not connected with the world of appearances? Do they not merely describe our sensory constructions: which are precisely the occultation of being? They are not *of the soul, for the soul*, that much is sure. Yes, but it remains true . . . that this darkened language of ours still contains a spark. . . . When Baudelaire evokes the Swan it is in order to resuscitate human presence in a place where nothing remains but pretense and shadows.

When he speaks of "casting off the burden of sense appearances," Bonnefoy refuses the error of reading Rimbaud as any sort of arcane mimesis, albeit of Ideal actions, realities, and sees instead the poet's abnegation of possession, his embracing of loss that reaches beyond absence into the realm of free-floating, objectless desire, which aims not to totalize, to possess, to solve, but only to celebrate itself, to pursue itself, taking itself as its own object. "And I believe I have thus defined the ambition of the *songs of nothingness*—poems that Rimbaud was soon to write—but as well of an entire tradition of poetry without any explicit philosophy, that of the simplest songs, those we so willingly call in French 'transparent' when we understand that they almost burn up the dim veil of our senses."[19]

How does the literary grotesque find a place in this tradition? The word *grotesque* comes from the Italian *grotta*, 'cave' (suggesting already, coincidentally but fortuitously, Plato's celebrated cave of the senses).[20] The words *grotesco* and *la grotesca* described a particular style of ornamental painting that apparently became known and practiced in Italy soon after the birth of Christ. The style was condemned by such critics as Vitruvius for offending Aristotelian versimilitude.

> All these motifs taken from reality are now rejected by an unreasonable fashion. For our contemporary artists decorate the walls with monstrous forms rather than reproducing clear images of the familiar world. Instead of columns they paint fluted stems with oddly shaped leaves and volutes, and instead of pediments arabesques, the same with candelabra and painted edicules, on the pediments of which grow dainty flowers unrolling out of roots and topped, without rhyme or reason, by figurines. The little stems, finally, support half-figures crowned by human or animal heads. Such things, however, never existed, do not now exist, and shall never come into being.[21]

But in fact what was offensive about the style for Vitruvius was the aporia within the very word *verisimilitude* to which it pointed—*veri-*, 'truth', and *similitude*, 'likeness'. A likeness of truth is an image of truth, an illusion of truth—false truth. The grotesque is a *mise en cause* not only of verisimilitude and the mimetic principle that enforces it, but of truth and the knowledge of it as Aristotle conceived them. The truth of appearances

19. Yves Bonnefoy, *Rimbaud par lui-même*, trans. Paul Schmidt (New York, 1973), 48−49, 49−50.
20. Plato, *Republic*, trans. Desmond Lee (New York, 1974), 316−35.
21. Quoted in Wolfgang Kaiser, *The Grotesque in Art and Literature*, trans. Ulrich Weisstein (New York, 1966), 20.

is only apparent to us through the likeness of it that our senses provide—the false truth of similitude. The grotesque implies that all perception is delirium, hallucination. Mimesis cannot countenance that concept without becoming a rather nihilistic, gnostic Platonism. For the Aristotelian, then, the grotesque is an aporia, offensive, an outrage to good taste. To the gnostic Platonist, it is a rhetoric of irony, of permanent parabasis, constant displacement and dispersal of the poet's and the poem's voice, a self-contradiction, a tension, a rhetoric that is above all aware of its own bankruptcy, of having lost the Truth. It knows the Ideal only by mourning the loss of it, only as what exceeds it, as absent and unnameable. But when it gives up on knowing, then mourning becomes celebration. In the relations between France and the South, a dialectic of linguistic likenesses has occurred in which we might look to discover just such odd, crepe-bedecked frolicking.

II. POE-ETICITY

One ought to begin with a prototypical instance of interlinguistic transfusion from which a model might be extracted. In this case, there can surely be no doubt about whose work that ought to be. Poe, to this day, remains a figure of both admiration and mockery. Aldous Huxley, W. H. Auden, T. S. Eliot, Henry James, along with many critics, notably Yvor Winters, have shown his narrative and prosody, and the theories by which he attempted to justify them, as at best provincial and at worst ludicrous—grotesque.[1] But Poe has become part of the American canon and, through the criticism of such modern southerners as Allen Tate, inseparable from the traditions of southern literature.[2] As an American poet, he is thought of more as *interesting*, an aberration, a perverse anachronism, than as someone for younger writers to emulate.[3] And an anachronism he is, in the fullest sense of the word: temporally as well as poetically out of place, severely paradoxical, however studied.

Poe, as much as any writer in the nineteenth century, worked to shape a southern literary identity. That he should have conceived himself as southern in the first place is somewhat grotesque: he was born in Boston and signed his first collection of poems as "a Bostonian." Yet his early identification with the North was a necessary first step toward a sense of it as other. It was Poe, long before the Civil War, long before any actual loss, who set down the southern poetic as one of loss, defeat, bereave-

1. See Julian Symons, *The Tell-Tale Heart* (New York, 1981), 178, 197–98, 240; Eric W. Carlson (ed.), *The Recognition of Edgar Allan Poe* (Ann Arbor, 1966); Robert Regan (ed.), *Poe* (Englewood Cliffs, 1967); Quinn, *The French Face of Edgar Poe*, 11.
2. Allen Tate, "Our Cousin, Mr. Poe," in Regan (ed.), *Poe*, 38–50.
3. Symons, *The Tell-Tale Heart*, 199.

ment. His work—the ethos that it embodies and its relation to the southern history that follows—is a legitimate *mise en cause* of the causal conventions of history, and it is entirely appropriate that Poe, whose theory so often followed his poetic practice of deriving cause from effect, should have effected such a reversal— one more aspect of his multifaceted grotesqueness.

That grotesqueness is characteristic of everything about Poe, his life no less than his work. His intellect constantly enacted aporias of the visionary and the practical that are reflected in his poems as a fantastic thematic and a rigid, absurdly factitious prosody and in his stories as a mimesis of the supernatural combined with the detective story's fetishistic mania for logic and deduction. Julian Symons has gone so far as to say that Poe's mind embraced a revulsion for American materialism, which he wished to project entirely onto the evil North (anticipating the agrarian movement), and an obsession with the very technicality of that materialism. "Part of Poe wished to preserve poetry as a sacred mystery; another part wanted to demonstrate that the whole thing was a technical problem, which could be solved as one solves a cryptogram. These two parts might be termed Visionary Poe and Logical Poe. It was Visionary Poe who conceived the poems, but Logical Poe who wrote them."[4]

Just as the literary being of Poe is itself a tension of these two alterities, it is the occasion of a tension in American letters: that between North and South. The literary fact of Poe as southern comes into being in a dialectic with not one but two othernesses: the North, an essentially symmetrical other, and a third, heterogenous, mediating term, French symbolism. The specificity of Poe's southernness (otherness with respect to the northern, dominant literary strain) is brought about largely *a posteri-*

---

4. *Ibid.*, 177. To get some idea of Poe's sense of himself as southern, see his review of "The South Vindicated from the Treason and Fanaticism of the Northern Abolitionists," in *Complete Works of Edgar Allan Poe*, Virginia ed. (New York, 1979), VIII, 265–74. For his antipathy to the Bostonians, see "Boston and the Bostonians," *Complete Works*, XIII, 1–12.

ori, by the mediation of his French readers. Schematically, the dialectic could be described this way:

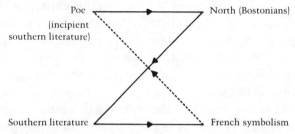

The model is loosely inspired by Lacan's Schéma L, to which it bears some structural resemblance. The major contribution of Lacanian theory to this model of literary history is the idea of the symbolic order, which is structured like language.[5] In my paradigm it is language, and it operates like translation. Generally speaking, the model works in this way: we may posit whatever literary entity we please as (X). The line from (X) to the heterogenous Other is the axis of the symbolic, structured like language.

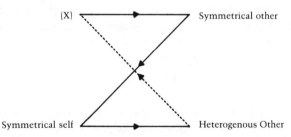

The paradigm is at once simpler and more subtle than it may appear, in my adaptation of it as well as in the original prototype of Lacan. For the latter, it describes the self as a dialectic of desire, comprising four poles. The first is the hypothetical self prior to psychological structure, shapeless, a lump of libido. Through the mediation of its own image, in a mirror, say, it

5. See Jacques Lacan, *Ecrits* (2 vols.; Paris, 1966), I, 66; Lacan, *Speech and Language in Psychoanalysis,* 106–108; J. Laplanche and J.–B. Pontalis, *The Language of Psychoanalysis,* trans. Donald Nicholson-Smith (New York, 1973), 210, 439–40.

begins to know itself—as a dialectic of resemblance and difference, identity and otherness—in terms of what it is, which is
defined relative to what it is not. Thus, the axis from the second
and third poles, from symmetrical other to symmetrical self (my
terminology, not Lacan's), represents the dialectic of the imaginary—in the sense of having to do with images, the relation
between the specular other and the specular self. The symmetrical, specular self is precipitated by the apprehension of its
counterpart, the symmetrical other, and yet the inverse statement is equally valid, that the symmetrical other is precipitated
by the structuring of the self as a dialectic, its constitution of
itself as an ego. It is not possible to reduce the dialectic to a
causal relation. It does not describe a progression with a beginning and an ending, which is closed and totalized. It describes
precisely the untotalizable.

The fourth term is unlike all the rest. It is the unsymmetrical
Other, the locus of the unconscious, the id, which for Lacan is
structured like language—that is, signifying differentially, each
sign defined by its difference from and resemblance to other
signs, virtually rather than positively and not admitting of even
the illusion of totalization. The heterogenous Other defines the
possibilities of what the self may say, do, and think. The Other
is not a totalizable 'thing'; it never even appears to be one. It is
rather the language in which the self, as a sort of text, is articulated to itself and to other selves. Lacan ascribes various names,
qualifications, and properties to the Other: "locus of the signifier," "locus of the Word"; sometimes it even refers to one or
both parents, not as persons, but as symbols.[6] The Other is in
fact the unnameable, the possibility of language, of the self's
language, and of the discourse of consciousness. And as the possibility and origin of the dialectic, it necessarily exceeds the
language and the dialectic. If it could be named, encompassed, or
fixed, not only would the Other become mediated and therefore
no longer Other, but the possibility of the dialectic would be
obliterated, just as Socrates, in *The Symposium*, says that the

6. Lacan, *Speech and Language in Psychoanalysis*, 263–70.

object of Eros must be discontinuous with Eros, unsymmetrical. Every name ascribed to the Other is at best provisional, at worst naive and erroneous, and in all instances somewhat provisional and somewhat erroneous in varying degrees of each. But analysis, understanding, knowledge, reading, and literature as we know them can come into being only through such provisional errors along the axis from (X) to the Other, the axis of the symbolic. Desire cannot exist without an object, and thus to exist it must engage in the dialectic conditioned by and grounded in the absolute Otherness that every symmetrical other, as image, provisionally names, and of which every specific heterogenous Other is a symbol, a cipher. That pure Otherness is the possibility of images, names, and symbols, the possibility of desiring and knowing. In the ongoing relay, dialectic of desire that the self is, the Other is chimera, is flux, a succession of shapes and images, names, all of which are true and none of which is final. The frustration in dealing with such a dialectic is in wanting to immobilize and totalize it, to arrest the flux. But the flux is precisely the possibility of wishing to immobilize it, of being frustrated by it. As Barbara Johnson has put it in her discussion of Lacan's "Séminaire sur la lettre volée": "'Undecidability' can no more be used as a last word than 'destination.' 'Car,' said Mallarmé, 'il y a et il n'y a pas de hasard.' The 'undeterminable' is not opposed to the determinable; 'dissemination' is not opposed to repetition. If we could be sure of the difference between the determinable and the undeterminable, the undeterminable would be comprehended within the determinable. What is undecidable is whether a thing is decidable or not."[7] What is essential to keep in mind is that every reading, every act of understanding, is both provisional and erroneous, including the one reflected in this statement.

The schematic is particularly suited to the interlinguistic, intercultural phenomenon described here, which is grounded in an ethos of loss and the grotesque. It is a peculiar variant of Pla-

7. Barbara Johnson, *The Critical Difference* (Baltimore, 1981), 146.

tonic gnosticism because it views the author and the text not as objects but as dialectical tensions. Two things ought to be clearly understood before proceeding, however. One is that the efficacy of this paradigm in no way depends on such a literal discrepancy of language as that between French and English. Translation may occur in many ways, between media whose difference is minute (dialects of the same language, for example, or different literary movements within one tradition) or very great (as that between French and English, or even greater, between time and language—the translation of the former into the latter is history). History is simply one of the dialects of the symbolic; it has no necessary priority over the others. It should also be noted with care that the coincidence of French and southern literary traditions, of French and southern historical experiences, is my point of access to this model, a privileged, hyperbolic point of access, but by no means the only one. What is occurring in the interaction of Poe with French symbolism is the primal scene of an ongoing exchange between two cultures that has nourished both and in which certain catholic aspects of literariness become especially visible.

From the French perspective, the dialectic would be reversed. The literature, taking its immediate past, romanticism, as symmetrically inverted other, would constitute itself as symbolism through the heterogenous foreignness of Poe himself, the grotesque southerner.

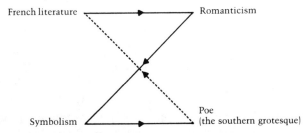

On the more abstract, linguistic level, what is involved here is the dialectic of the being of language itself, between mimesis and symbol or allegory.

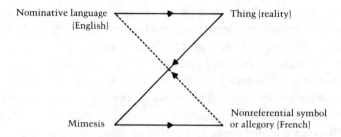

And yet it is French, the more ideal, Platonic language, that is also realizing itself through a dialogue with the mimetic English.

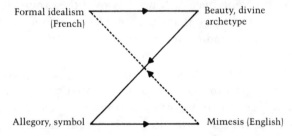

Of course, it is immediately apparent, in the model as well as in its application, that the labels "Aristotelian" and "Platonic" applied to French and English are somewhat arbitrary, and each language can be read in either mode. The distinction itself is a function of the symbolic order and therefore must inevitably be arbitrary even as it is suggestive, just as language, discourse, any sign, must be.

This paradigm describes language and literature as semiotic parabasis, as displacement and self-substitution, making language necessarily ironic. The literary, linguistic self *is* desire, and desire as a rhetoric is parabasis, a dialectic of projection and introjection. Thus desire is synonymous with self-displacement, dispersal, loss. The dialectic of desire by which a self of whatever kind is constituted is a dialectic in which that self is always being forced to look for itself outside of itself, to follow after itself, never catching up. The model of that self equates becoming with losing. So that if loss, defeat, and bereavement are motifs that frequently arise in the articulation of a symbolic discourse, it should surprise no one; for the very concept of the symbolic, of language, of literariness, is grounded in a metaphysic of loss, a rhetoric of parabasis, in which any specific concept of loss is *lost*—including the very model itself—displaced, following after an otherness. Once we have recognized the dialectic, we cannot justify arresting it. The duality of language as sign, as signifier and signified (implied by both the denominative and the symbolic models of language) has already preordained the dialectic, and in making the concept of the symbolic possible, has already determined the agenda of objects it can address and conclusions it may reach. The model itself generates its own inadequacy, loses itself in its own becoming. If language is loss, then any historical ground of affinity, that between France and the South, for example, is imaginary. That may make my paradigm appear as so much sophistry, but it is no more so than any model of literary language that takes account of the sign's duality (which implies the third term: signifier, signified, *referent*), the descriptive and referential function of language. It is more forthcoming, at least, than to use a model that would pretend to arrest the dialectic by which poeticity, literariness, is generated, and so totalize its object with itself, exempt itself from itself, from the implications of its own reflexivity.

This dialectic describes both a tautology and an aporia, which are resumed by the concept of the grotesque. Poe's intellect, to return to Symons' characterization, embraced just such a contradiction. Poe believed that the composition of poetry or narrative ought to be governed by an order as severe as that of music. Part of that order was a rigid adherence to the principle of mimesis, which parodies the didacticism he so abhorred in northern writers. He concludes an early review thus:

> The author avers upon his word of honor that in commencing this work he loads a pistol, and places it upon the table. He further states that, upon coming to a conclusion, it is his intention to blow out what he supposes to be his brains. Now this is excellent. But, even with so rapid a writer as the poet must undoubtedly be,

there would be some little difficulty in completing the book under thirty days or thereabouts. The best of powder is apt to sustain injury by lying so long "in the load." We sincerely hope the gentleman took the precaution to examine his priming before attempting the rash act. A flash in the pan—and in such a case—were a thing to be lamented.[8]

Such a vicious and hilarious enactment of the mimetic fallacy went hand-in-hand with his belief of poetry that "no point in its composition is referable either to accident or intuition. . . . the work proceeded step by step, to its completion with the precision and rigid consequences *of a mathematical problem*" (emphasis mine).[9] The task which Poe sets poetry is precisely Mr. Van Wyck Brooks's hopeful archetype: the composition of a poem that will "suit at once the popular and the critical taste." Yet this seeming slavishness to materiocentric mimeticism and popular culture is really nihilism of the most vehement species—it means, like Flannery O'Connor, to use the concrete so thoroughly as to exhaust it. "Inspired by an ecstatic prescience of the glories beyond the grave, we struggle by multiform combinations among the things and thoughts of Time to attain a portion of that Loveliness whose very elements perhaps appertain to eternity alone."

As Symons paraphrases, "It was not so much in as '*through* the poem, or *through* the music' that eternity could be glimpsed."[10] Poetry could not approach truth as a positive reality, as the didactic literature of the North attempted to do. Instead, it had to turn the mimetic and didactic, the referential (unpoetic) function of language against itself, thereby inducing a state of vision that would exceed the significative economy of language. This 'ecstasy' has nothing to do with Truth. "In enforcing a truth, we need severity rather than effervescence of language. We must be simple, precise, terse. We must be cool,

8. Symons, *The Tell-Tale Heart*, 180.
9. E. H. O'Neill (ed.), *The Complete Poems and Stories of Edgar Allan Poe, with Selections from His Critical Writings* (New York, 1967), II, 979, 1026.
10. Symons, *The Tell-Tale Heart*, 175.

calm, unimpassioned. In a word, we must be in that mood which, as nearly as possible, is the exact converse of the poetical."[11]

Thus, properly, a poem had to be about *nothing*; it had to enact the failure of positively conceived truth and the stultification of mimesis, of materiocentrism and didacticism, of literary morality. Symons calls this "a self-evident absurdity," and many before him have said as much.[12] Considered within the orthodoxy of Aristotelian aesthetics, it surely is. But Poe is talking about using the means of mimesis, the English language, to subvert its ends, the Aristotelian imitation of an action. His concept of the poem, indeed of literature, is an aporia of means and ends, a cryptogram that, though absolutely rigorous, is not to be solved but *dis*solved. It uses the means and media of life to create the effect of death. It shows death as undoing, nothingness, the disfiguration and dissolution that are implicit in every act of figuration and solution, just as life is no more than death-by-degrees and "the things and thoughts of Time" no more than temporal figures for timelessness, totality, eternity—their heterogenous Other.[13]

Poe's work is bound to offend the orthodox English-speaking sensibility in the same way that *la grotesca* exasperated Vitruvius, by pointing to the simplemindedness of the very idea of verisimilitude. Less often, it will appeal to sensibilities who succeed in suppressing either Poe's visionary side, making of him a meticulous craftsman of intricate verbal machines, or his logical side, making of him a morbid lunatic, pure and simple. The French, however, were able to read Poe the way he wanted to be read, all the more so because they completely misunderstood him. As often a linguistic as a biological misprision, that misunderstanding is hyperbolically illustrated by Baudelaire's dedication of a translation of one of Poe's stories to Maria Clemm, the latter's aunt and mother-in-law: "Goodbye,

11. O'Neill (ed.), *The Complete Poems and Stories of Edgar Allan Poe*, 1025.
12. Symons, *The Tell-Tale Heart*, 176.
13. See Jean Laplanche, *Vie et Mort en Psychanalyse* (Paris, 1970), translated by Jeffrey Mehlman as *Life and Death in Psychoanalysis* (Baltimore, 1976).

madame; among the different greetings and formulas of complimentation which may conclude a missive from one *soul* to another *soul*, I know of only one for the sentiments to which you
inspire me: *goodness, godness*." The editor writes that "Baudelaire meant to play on the words, but his insufficient knowledge
of English betrayed him: *Goodness* is a swearword completely
out of place under the circumstances, *godness* is a barbarism for
godliness and in any case has no place here."[14] *Goodness, godness*—in English the words mean nothing in that context, signify nothing but a miscarriage of language in its everyday usage.
Thus they mean everything in relation to Poe; they sum up his
poetic of the grotesque, of mimesis against itself, of loss and
defeat deliberately elected. Had the error been brought to his
attention, Baudelaire himself might have been able to point out
its faithfulness to Poe's literary intentions, no less real for being
inadvertant.

So Poe's work, as it based itself critically and poetically in an
ethos of loss and defeat (in the etymological sense of *dé-faire*, 'to
undo'), anticipates the myth of the Civil War, exposing it as gratuitous and yet necessary: the poetic of loss, as southern, pre-
dates it, and yet the war was necessary to historically enact that
poetic. But it could only enact it by being a lost cause from the
start. And so it was, to many southerners, an effort doomed to
failure, deserving to fail, indeed *needing* to fail, and not only all
the greater, the nobler, for embracing futility, but great and noble
only because it embraced futility—the means of victory used to
subvert the end of it. So, through that defeat was southern literary culture to take on a life it had not had before and to even-
tually dwarf and engulf that of the rest of America. As Allen
Tate would write in his "Elegy" to Jefferson Davis:

14. Charles Baudelaire, *Oeuvres Complètes*, ed. Marcel Ruff (Paris, 1968):
"Adieu, madame; parmi les différents saluts et les formules de complimentation
qui peuvent conclure une missive d'une *âme à une âme*, je n'en connais qu'une
aux sentiments qu'inspire votre personne: *goodness, godness*" (318). "Baudelaire a voulu jouer sur les mots, mais sa connaissance insuffisante de l'anglais l'a
trahi: *Goodness* est un juron tout à fait déplacé en l'occurrence, *godness* est un
barbarisme pour *godliness* et de toute façon n'a pas sa place ici" (318).

What did we gain? What did we lose?
....
Our loss put six feet under ground
Is measured by the magnolia's root;
Our gain's the intellectual sound
Of death's feet round a weedy tomb.[15]

Again, the defeat, and history in general, assume a symbolic significance that must not be mistaken for a causal one. "Thus it is," writes Jacques Lacan, "that if man comes to thinking the Symbolic order, it is because he is caught in it from the first in his being."[16] "These laws are precisely those of Symbolic determination. For it is clear that they are anterior to all actual enactment of chance, as it is evident that we must judge according to its adherence to these laws whether an object is proper or not to be used in obtaining a series, still in this case symbolic, of instances of chance: whether to qualify, for instance, a coin for this purpose, or that object admirably denominated die."[17] And further: "The Symbolic function presents itself as a double movement within the subject: man makes an object of his action, but only in order to restore to this action in due time its place as a grounding. In this equivocation, operating at every instant, lies the whole process of a function in which action and knowledge alternate." Thus my analysis occurs on this same level of the symbolic and is subject to the same analogy with language. It is conditioned by what it describes, is involved tautologically with its object, a relation that precludes any possibility of exhaustiveness, closure, conclusion, or 'correctness'. My pretense here is not to truth but rather to rigor. "For exactitude is to be distinguished from Truth, and conjecture does not ex-

15. Allen Tate, *Collected Poems, 1919–1976* (New York, 1977), 177.
16. Lacan, *Speech and Language in Psychoanalysis*, 106–107.
17. Lacan, *Ecrits* I: "Mais ces lois sont précisément celles de la détermination symbolique. Car il est clair qu'elles sont antérieures à toute constatation réelle du hasard, comme il se voit que c'est d'après son obéissance à ces lois, qu'on juge si un objet est propre ou non à être utilisé pour obtenir une série, dans ce cas toujours symbolique, de coups de hasard: à qualifier par exemple pour cette fonction une pièce de monnaie ou cet objet admirablement dénommé dé" (74).

clude rigorous precision. And even if experimental science gets its exactitude from mathematics, its relationship to nature does not remain any less problematic."[18]

Baudelaire's unknowing but total misrepresentation of the life of Poe is well known. The article "Edgar Allan Poe, sa vie et ses ouvrages," which appeared in 1852, was based almost entirely on two articles by John M. Daniel and John M. Thompson that had appeared in the *Southern Literary Messenger* a few years before. Daniel, with whom Poe had come close to dueling, was most partisanly southern. He despised the Northeast, which, in the persons of Rufus Wilmot Griswold, James Russell Lowell, and Nathaniel Parker Willis, he blamed for the failure of Poe's literary reputation during his lifetime.[19] It is in Daniel's consciously southern eyes that Poe becomes an object of mythology as a southerner. Daniel saw Poe as the archetype of the southern aristocrat—brilliant, well-born, cultivated yet drawn irresistibly to dissipation in all its forms—an aristocrat in a democracy, spurned by his countrymen because he was superior to them and because he told them truths they did not wish to hear.[20] So Baudelaire would write that "Edgar Poe was thus raised in a noble affluence, and received a complete education." In his endorsement of all these lies, however, Baudelaire contributed im-

18. Lacan, *Speech and Language in Psychoanalysis*, 48, 49.

19. Symons, *The Tell-Tale Heart*, 166–67; Baudelaire, *Oeuvres complètes*, 319; W. T. Bandy, "New Light on Baudelaire and Poe," *French-American Literary Relationships*, Yale French Studies No. 10 (1952), 65–69; Henry Blumenthal, *American and French Culture, 1800–1900: Interchanges in Art, Science, Literature, and Society* (Baton Rouge, 1975), 211–17. Bandy, in his introduction to Charles Baudelaire, *Edgar Allan Poe, sa vie et ses ouvrages* (Toronto, 1973), writes that the evidence is strong that "Baudelaire had a firsthand acquaintance with only a very small part of Poe's writings. Among the major works he had almost certainly not laid eyes on were 'The Raven' (and most of Poe's other poems), *Arthur Gordon Pym*, *Eureka* and still more important, the critical essays on poetry and aesthetics, including 'The Philosophy of Composition.' Baudelaire was therefore indebted to Daniel, not merely for providing him with information on Poe's life and personality, but also for something equally, if not more crucial: a broad, if vicarious, view of Poe's work" (xxxiii).

20. Symons, *The Tell-Tale Heart*, 166–67; Baudelaire, *Oeuvres complètes*, 319–36.

mensely to the apotheosis of Poe as the other of American letters, the founder of a new order of literariness that conceived itself in opposition to the dominant strain, that of the East. "His countrymen find him scarcely American, and yet he is not English." What set Poe and the new literature apart was their negativity. "If you talk with an American, and if you speak to him about Mr. Poe, he will admit his genius; willingly, even, perhaps he will be proud of it, but he will finish by saying, in a superior tone: 'But myself, I am a positive man.'"[21]

Thus it is with the greatest irony that we must read such statements as this by Baudelaire: "All of Edgar Allan Poe's stories are, so to speak, biographical. One finds the man in the work." The aporia implicit in literary history is thus unwittingly stated: the work is in the man. Where is the man? Why, in the work. The man, as Baudelaire conceived him, was as much a fiction as the work and was the more so for not being acknowledged as such. So we are faced with a tautology, an equation comprising nothing but variables. Nevertheless, Baudelaire the critic, entirely blind to its insolubility, proceeds to solve the equation by an absolutely arbitrary assignation of values. A second version of Baudelaire's essay, described by a modern French editor as revised and corrected, does not substantially alter the initial misprision. It speaks of Poe's "quasi-miraculous intelligence" and of his family as "one of the most respectable of Baltimore," which could hardly have been less accurate. Poe's grandfather, a spinning-wheel maker, had come from Ireland, himself the grandson of a tenant farmer. Baudelaire refers to him as "General" Poe, whom Lafayette held in esteem. In fact, David Poe's rank in the American Revolution was major. John Allan, who adopted Poe, was not "a wealthy merchant," but plainly, if com-

---

21. Baudelaire, *Oeuvres complètes*: "Edgar Poe fut ainsi élevé dans une belle aisance, et reçut une éducation complète" (321). "Ses compatriotes le trouvent à peine' Américain, et cependant il n'est pas Anglais" (321). "Si vous causez avec un Américain, et si vous lui parlez de M. Poe, il vous avouera son génie; volontiers même, peut-être en sera-t-il fier, mais il finira par vous dire avec un ton supérieur: Mais moi, je suis un homme positif" (320).

fortably, middle-class.[22] The source of much of the misinformation was Poe himself. He was as assiduous in the cultivation of his own myth as in the composition of any poem.[23] Poe did not receive the education and upbringing of a wealthy aristocrat any more than he ever went to Greece or Russia, though both of Baudelaire's essays repeat the popular myths that he did. All of this only underlines Poe's importance for France and for southern literary consciousness. The equation of his life and work, if it contained nothing but variables, nevertheless arranged them in such a way that Baudelaire could complete the circuit. In Poe he found "ce monstre délicat," "mon semblable,—mon frère," the Other who allowed him to achieve his own literary being.[24]

The element of the detective story and the rigors of plot and logic in Poe's work are well known. The 'mathematicality' would not seem odd at all if it were not intertwined so inextricably with a sense of the ineffable. That is what makes Poe's work an equation missing the necessary term for its solution, and it is that quality which makes it a generative matrix for French and for southern writers, indeed for any writer who chooses to address it, as shown in the results obtained recently by Lacan and Derrida. Barbara Johnson has described this quality of Poe as that of "a literary text that both analyzes itself and shows that it actually has neither a self nor any neutral metalanguage with which to do the analyzing."[25] Gaston Bachelard has interpreted Poe as "the poet of darkened water, water which is stagnant, heavy, and dead. It *absorbs* life, drains it away." By a chiasmus of symbolic rhetoric, water becomes for Poe "that

22. *Ibid.*: "Tous les contes d'Edgar Poe sont pour ainsi dire biographiques. On trouve l'homme dans l'oeuvre" (321). "Une intelligence quasi miraculeuse"; "une des plus respectables de Baltimore"; "un riche négociant" (321).

23. Symons, *The Tell-Tale Heart*, 3–4.

24. Baudelaire, *Oeuvres complètes*, 43.

25. Johnson, *The Critical Difference*, 110. One of the most famous French treatments of Poe is Marie Bonaparte, *Edgar Poe, étude psychanalytique* (3 vols.; Paris, 1958), translated by John Rodker as *The Life and Works of Edgar Poe: A Psychoanalytic Interpretation* (London, 1949). This was one of the first serious applications of Freudian theory to literature. Bonaparte was a disciple of Freud, and though her analysis is rather reductively literalist by today's standards, it

which drinks."[26] John Porter Houston has written of this odd, paradoxical quality as a "poetic device that assumes great importance in certain modern poems, especially monologues: this is the covert plot, or allusion to a complex of actions and circumstances of which the reader is given only a part. The effect is found in 'Ulalume' and other pieces by Edgar Allan Poe."[27]

Houston, most instructively, applies the model to one of Verlaine's sonnets, "famous for its obscurity," and to the frequent recourse of critics to biography as a solution to the poem's cryptic allusions. "Most of the commentary this sonnet has received," he writes, "consists in the *invention* of anecdotes about Verlaine, Rimbaud, Mathilde Verlaine, and Madame Rimbaud *mère*" (emphasis mine). Houston goes on to say that "the bankruptcy of the biographical method still prevalent in French studies could not be more complete."[28] It is also true that the bankruptcy of method, of reading ("Hypocrite lecteur! mon semblable"[29]) at all, much less of analyzing the text, is what is exposed here. Having pointed a finger of blame at perpetrators of the mimetic fallacy, Houston, most amusingly and very much

---

remains a critical landmark and is certainly highly significant as yet one more instance of the nourishment of French intellect by Poe, following in the steps of Mallarmé and Valéry and preceding Lacan and Derrida.

26. Quinn, *The French Face of Edgar Poe*, 24–25; Gaston Bachelard, *L'Eau et les rêves* (Paris, 1942).

27. John Porter Houston, *French Symbolism and the Modernist Movement: A Study of Poetic Structure* (Baton Rouge, 1980), 54. Julian Symons has noted this quality of Poe's work with particular reference to the criticism it tends to engender. Symons describes the works themselves as a catachresis of mimetic detail and allegorical indeterminacy; perhaps it is because of this very quality— and it is this quality which makes Poe "the absolute literary case" (Mallarmé)— that, as Symons says, the theories "do not enhance the effect of the story. They do not so much explain it as explain it away. This is partly because vagueness of meaning combined with particularity of detail mark Poe's finest work, and any attempt to clarify that vagueness runs the risk of damaging a story. It is also, however, because Poe only partly knew what he was doing. In the end it is impossible to ignore his life in dealing with his art, because the two were impenetrably interwoven." Symons, *The Tell-Tale Heart*, 238. See also David Ketterer, *The Rationale of Deception in Poe* (Baton Rouge, 1979).

28. Houston, *French Symbolism and the Modernist Movement*, 55.

29. Baudelaire, *Oeuvres complètes*, 43.

after the fashion of Poe himself, proceeds to perpetrate it himself: "The two men Rimbaud and Verlaine, incidentally, are not known [as the invented anecdotes allege] ever to have been in a barn with one or the other of the women."[30]

The fallacy of the biographical method is to establish history as the signified of symbolic language rather than as a dialect of it. To view the text as purely referential leads to a trivializing literalism that is perhaps more obviously narrow nowadays than its inverse fallacy: to view the text entirely in isolation, attributing to language a primacy that the biographers reserve for history. The inverse fallacy leads not so much to triviality as to obscurity, but it is in its own way just as literal and just as narrow. My own method, insofar as it treats history like language, is guilty of that fallacy. The point I wish to make is that once language has contemplated itself as language, there is no real choice but to embrace the fallacy. To avoid it, we would have had to purge our consciousnesses of language, and that is not, for now, in the offing. Reading and perception, generally, are arbitrary inasmuch as they are grounded in language, an arbitrary system of names assigning sounds to visual images. And language is fallacious insofar as it forgets its own arbitrariness, the aporia latent in its project of imitating the real and in its duality (present to both eye and ear, a sign and a sound referring to something else and yet an image in itself of itself). It is fallacious, too, insofar as we attempt to totalize the model and say: Here is the truth about this poem or this event or this person. We cannot discover anything that is not already implicit in the method we use to discover it—including the method and the model themselves, whether they are linguistic or historical, textual or biographical—unless it is the discovery of the very fraudulence, the bankruptcy, the conflagration and dissolution (progressive and asymptotic defeat and loss), which are nothing more or less than reading, as a hyperbolic exemplar of perception. It was, in fact, that very discovery which Baudelaire and Mallarmé made in Poe, and though they may not have realized

30. Houston, *French Symbolism and the Modernist Movement*, 54–55.

all of its implications, it is indelibly inscribed in their poetry. It is not only appropriate, but perhaps inevitable, that they should have made such a discovery in a poet who wrote in another language. It is the *missing term* that incites the equation's solution, invites reading, and it is only by filling it in with an arbitrary value that reading occurs, *translating* absence into presence.

The New York *Tribune* of April 28, 1877, said of Mallarmé that "it is to him that Americans are indebted for the Poe sonnet." Joseph Halpern writes that "in 1877, Mallarmé, 'le pur et séraphique Mallarmé' (Dujardin), appears to have turned his thoughts to America rather frequently." Certainly it ought not to surprise us that this was because of Poe. "He was then interested in becoming a correspondent for an American newspaper, he was awaiting publication of his translation of Poe, and he produced for American consumption the following, astonishing, 'word for word' translation of his 'Tombeau d'Edgar Poe,' complete with notes:"

> But, in a vile writhing of a hydra, (they) once hearing the Angel[3]
> To give[4] too pure a meaning to the words of the tribe,
> They (between themselves) thought (by him) the spell drunk
> In the honourless flood of some dark mixture.[5]
>
> Of the soil and the ether (which are) enemies, o struggle!
> If with it my idea does not carve a bas-relief
> Of which Poe's dazzling[6] tomb be adorned,
>
> (A) Stern block here fallen from a mysterious disaster,
> Let this granite at least show forever their bound
> To the old flights of Blasphemy (still) spread in the future.[7]

. . . .

[3] the Angel means the above said Poet
[4] to give means giving
[5] in plain prose: charged him with always being drunk
[6] dazzling means with the idea of such a bas-relief
[7] Blasphemy means against Poets, such as the charge of Poe being drunk[31]

31. Joseph Halpern, Introduction to *Mallarmé*, Yale French Studies No. 54 (1977), 5–6.

A most queer and comical instance of self-mutilation, this. That Mallarmé did not hesitate to perform it attests to an assumption of writing as reading, poetry as its own translation, an incitement to completion that always fails, sometimes soberly, sometimes movingly, sometimes ludicrously. The missing term which suscitates our lust for closure, the desire to read, to rewrite, is irrevocably missing.

Insofar as French readers since Baudelaire have mistaken the specter of Poe for that missing term and generated from it the view of literary textuality as necessarily grotesque, they are justified in calling Poe, as Mallarmé did, "this exception, in effect, and the absolute literary case."[32] So Valéry begins his praise of Poe's "Eureka"—and he has been virtually the only serious writer to praise it so highly in any language—by saying of mystics that "one can hardly speak ill of them, for what one finds in their work is only what one brings to it." He was not speaking of Poe, yet what he proceeds to derive from "Eureka" (the thesis of which is that "in the original unity of the first thing lies the secondary cause of all things, with the germ of their inevitable annihilation") consigns Poe and everything read or thought to the status of fabulous origin. Experience and knowledge (reading) force us to assume a totality that precedes and exceeds us and them, which by its precedence and excess throws us into the secondary, vitiative acts of reading and perception. And yet, to carry on, to 'understand', we must 'invent', assume such impossible totalities beyond us.

> We are besieged by what is remembered, what is possible, what is imaginable, calculable, all the combinations of our ideas in all degrees of probability, in every phase of precision. How can we form a concept of something that is opposed to nothing, rejects nothing, resembles nothing? If it resembled something, it would no longer be the whole. If it resembles nothing . . . And, if this totality is equivalent in power to one's mind, the mind has no hold over it. All the objections that rise against an active infinity,

32. Mallarmé, *Oeuvres complètes*, 531: "Il est cette exception, en effet, et le cas littéraire absolu."

all the difficulties encountered when one attempts to draw order out of multiplicity, here assert themselves. No proposition can be advanced about this *subject* so disordered in its richness that all *attributes* apply to it. Just as the universe escapes intuition, in the same way it is transcendent to logic.

As for its origin—IN THE BEGINNING WAS FABLE. It will be there always.

We are derived from totality; therefore it is inconceivable to us. We are its antithesis, entropic beings—readers. The totality toward which we strive in reading the world is inconceivable except as the origin of its consequences: loss, annihilation, entropy. It *is* the absolutely asymmetrical Otherness toward which every textual and perceptual dialectic strains and falls short of. We experience it by losing it, in fables of origin, fables of meaning. Here is Valéry again: "As for the idea of a beginning—I mean an absolute beginning—it is necessarily a myth. Every beginning is a coincidence; we must picture it as some sort of contact between all and nothing. In trying to think of it, we find that every beginning is a consequence—every beginning *completes* something." [33]

"Such as unto himself at last eternity changes him." So commences Mallarmé's translation of Poe into literary mythology. Eternity is as inconceivable as totality and to us looks and sounds like the idiom of death, the Other of our lives of entropic reading. So Poe becomes Poë(te), a fabulous origin, suscitating "with a naked sword / His century terrified not to have known / That Death was triumphant in this strange voice!" ("Le Poëte suscite avec un glaive nu / Son siècle épouvanté de n'avoir pas connu / Que la mort triomphait dans cette voix étrange!") Poe the drunken liar has become an allegory of poeticity, a voice of death, of Otherness, of lostness which suscitates loss in turn; Poe the man, drunk and mendacious, has been stripped of his alcohol, his lies, and his flesh, leaving only a skeletal blade of words, a blade that is a voice—not death, the absolute Other,

33. Paul Valéry, *Leonardo Poe Mallarmé*, trans. Malcolm Cowley and James R. Lawler (Princeton, 1972), 162, 175–76, 172.

totality, but its voice, one of its names, infested and invested by it.

Mallarmé addresses himself to the dead man Poe, conceiving his poem, his fable, in the symbolic idiom of death.

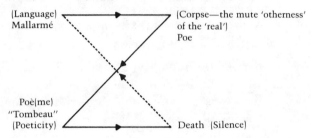

Language addresses itself to the mute thing, names it (imitates it, if you wish), and so becomes literary, a poem. It can only address its own being from the vantage point of death, the inconceivable Other. That is, it cannot resolve the issue of its own being, cannot dialogue with silence, but only allegories of silence, fables of origin—allegories, then, of its own inadequacy, or bankruptcy. Literature henceforth enacts an endlessly repetitious failure, reaching backwards in time to engulf the first word chanted by the first poet. And literary historians can only enact, in their own way, the failures of such repetitions or the repetitions of such failures. "But it is the glory of man to waste his powers on the void, and it is something more than that. Often such crack-brained researches lead to unforeseen discoveries. The role of the nonexistent exists; the function of the imaginary is real; and we learn from strict logic that *the false implies the true.* One might say that the history of thought could be summarized in these words: *It is absurd by what it seeks, great by what it finds.*"[34]

In *American Hieroglyphics*, John T. Irwin has shown how symbol grows out of and depends on a questing after antithetical origin toward which it always strains and from which it must always hold back.[35] His reading of *Arthur Gordon Pym* is a bril-

34. *Ibid.*, 170.
35. John T. Irwin, *American Hieroglyphics* (New Haven, 1980).

liant demonstration of that thesis. He holds the actual origin of the linguistic symbol in American literature to be the Egyptian hieroglyph, though for Irwin the hieroglyph itself becomes a symbol, a fabulous origin; it becomes a cipher for a hypothetically ideal language that would be totalized with being, sign and referent integrated, and for the antithetical self prior to the splitting of self-consciousness in the mirror-stage. The process of self-realization/self-differentiation is for Lacan a myth of origin in the same sense; the mirror-stage can with greater logic be seen as a symptom of an always anterior sense of self-as-other than as the actual origin or cause of it.[36] Irwin's argument concerning the nature of symbolism in American literature groups Poe together with northern writers such as Whitman, Emerson, Thoreau, Hawthorne, and Melville, and yet his book suggests a marked difference between Poe and these writers. Poe accounts for the eleven chapters in the book that make up by far the most convincing demonstration of its thesis in every respect. Irwin devotes five chapters, by contrast, to Emerson, Thoreau, Hawthorne, and Melville together, and these writers do not lend themselves nearly so well to his approach. None is inevitably led to surmise that there is indeed something exemplary about Poe that he does not share with the other writers, northerners all, and that this exemplary quality could not therefore, in the nineteenth century, properly be located in the mainstream of American letters. It remains only to point out that Irwin, in his brilliant use of Champollion's discovery of the Rosetta stone and of the hieroglyphic in generating his own myth of origin, repeats Poe's own postulations in "Eureka" and *Pym*, reads him and understands him brilliantly, only by repeating him and by an apparent blindness to the repetition. Irwin's fable of origin, centering around the hieroglyphic, is another version of the voyage to the abyss, the quest for the source, that is his object of study—one more instance of the text appearing to determine, and be determined by, the reading. The reason Irwin does not

36. See Gary Lee Stonum, "Undoing American Literary History," *Diacritics*, XI (1982), 2–12.

immediately see that may be his attempt to keep his study entirely on this side of the Atlantic and to place Poe in the mainstream of the northern tradition. However, his allusion to Champollion's discovery that re-created, as it were, an entire lost culture through the possibility of translation, points not only to my own undertaking but to the tautological transumption, troping of trope, involved in his reading of Poe. The hieroglyph, imagistic sign, as it feigns a visual resemblance to and identity with the thing named and strays from that resemblance, playing upon it, enacts, after all, the dialectic of language described above in this schema.

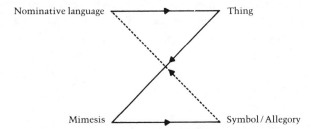

Such schemas are my own hieroglyphics of origin.

A similar approach can be taken with a particular poem by Poe, its English 'origin' with its *hypocrite lecture*, its French *semblable*. I have chosen "The Raven," not only because it is the best known of Poe's poems in France and America, but also because birds, like colors, are always hyperbolic instances of figuration, tropes of tropes. They are infinitely suggestive and irreducible to any specific signification.

It is very easy to make fun of "The Raven" in English, to mock its clanky rhythm and incessant rhymishness, coupled with a preposterously melodramatic content: a large and homely black bird sententiously croaking the word *nevermore* to a gentleman alone in his library at night, mournful over having lost someone "nameless," whom he nevertheless refers to as Lenore. It is possible, and perhaps even likely, that there is a metalepsis at work in the Raven's refrain. In Latin a raven says not, as in English, "caw," but, more like the German "kra," *cras*, 'tomorrow'. So that *nevermore* tropes the Latin, negates it; *cras*

provides the transumptive link between the noise made by a
raven and "nevermore." The French symbolist transumption of
Poe and "The Raven" has completely crowded out the allusion
by the metalepsis of translation, making *nevermore* into a symbol rather than a metalepsis.[37]

It must be added that the author himself contributed to the
possibility of this unknowing metalepsis of a metalepsis by
glossing his own poem as he did. In describing the poem's composition, Poe confirms our worst suspicions, that he not only
followed a technique much like that of Madison Avenue admen
in selecting the name *Lenore* and the refrain of *nevermore* and
in the use of such vocabulary as *yore* and *forevermore* but that
he meant to. In "The Philosophy of Composition" the logical
Poe insists that poems must be conceived like detective stories,
with a minimum of spontaneity. A reasonable argument can be
made that Poe's theory of poetics is actually a manual for media
salesmen, a primer of ear-bending for apprentice shysters, with
its grave admonitions against losing the reader's attention by
droning on too long. The tone of the poem and its content had to
be governed by beauty, which was necessarily sad as well
as brief. *Nevermore* made a suitable refrain because it was
sonorous, not to mention sad, and rhymed with a great many
other sad and sonorous words such as *implore, forevermore,* and
yore. But it would have been too ridiculous, even for Poe, to
place this refrain in a human mouth. What was needed then was
some beast gifted with speech but not reason, so that it would
not know how foolish it sounded. It might have been a parrot,
but parrots are not lugubrious-looking birds. A raven would suit
much better: large, black, and ugly. There could be no question
of subject. "The death of a beautiful woman," wrote Poe, "is
unquestionably the most poetical topic in the world."[38]

With the detective story rigor of "The Purloined Letter," the
narration is ordered thus:

37. The observations in the previous paragraph and this one come from re-
marks made to me by Paul de Man and John Hollander, respectively.
38. O'Neil (ed.), *The Complete Poems and Stories of Edgar Allan Poe,* 982.

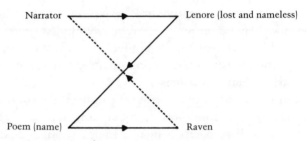

The problem we immediately encounter is, according to strict Lacanian theory, inevitable and irremediable, endemic, but one which for purposes of reading must, erroneously, be solved: the virtual impossibility of any sort of symbolic articulation between narrator and Raven. The bird is an incongruity, a blank term, the missing solution to the crime. We might spell *raven* backwards and get *nevar*, rhyming with Levar, which though sounding very much like the name of a science-fiction hero can be read as consonant with *never*. But that engages no dialectic. It merely repeats what the raven says. We might hear *rave*, and *rav-ishing* or consider the archaic sense of *raven* as 'to plunder or pillage', with similar results. How can we connect the raven with raving and pillaging and erotism? We could, if we could ally him with the nameless lost Lenore *and* the narrator. We would need to discover in him an identity with both, to reconcile act (raving, ravishing, pillaging) with object (the deceased Lenore), language (raving) with movement (pillaging), object raven with verb raven.

Mallarmé's translation of the poem is in prose, denuded of all the trappings of verse, of its entire *raison d'être* for Poe. One cannot blame Mallarmé for this, though the logical Poe probably would have. It would be quite impossible to sustain any pretense of rendering the poem's content into French *and* of keeping the rhyme. The raven has become a *corbeau*, as French has only one word to designate all members of the genus *Corvus*, among which English distinguishes the crow from the raven. The latter is a larger and less common bird of North America and is specifically a species indigenous to Europe and Asia, and not to the

United States. So that, translating back to English, *corbeau* gives us two words: raven and crow. Logical Poe chose the bird for its grand and exotic ugliness and its association in many folk traditions with ill fortune, and because its name was a two-syllable word containing the consonant *r*, which he wished to repeat as often as possible. So the French translation has without question "plundered" and "pillaged" his poetic intentions beyond recognition. It has changed not only the bird but the form of the text from verse to prose, altering its texture toward that of narrative.

The translation has also altered the poem's figurative structure in a most fortuitous fashion, without meaning to. *Corbeau* is in French phonetically overdetermined in a way that the English raven is not, but ought to be, for purposes of interpretation. Hearing it spoken, we would have to judge from context whether it was one word or two: *corbeau* or *corps beau*, 'beautiful body' or 'corpse', or *cor beau*, 'beautiful horn'. A horn is a mute object that may be made by a musician to 'speak' the language of music. But *cor* can also signify the musician himself. The raven is an emblem of this tension—no more understanding of his own words than if he were lifeless, yet making them, by his own voice and volition, alive. So a poem dumbly repeats as we 'play' it, read it to ourselves. We are named by it as we name it, repeat its naming. The beautiful body (or corpse) is thus played by the desiring subject as a musician blows notes from a horn; desire is like reading, like writing, and like the making of music—all of these activities demand a silent other to articulate themselves to themselves, to name themselves in symbolic language. The word *raven* is more overdetermined than some in English, but only when combined with the French *corbeau* is it overdetermined enough. The phonemic equivocation of *corbeau* turns a grotesque, though suggestive, metaphor into sublime metalepsis and completes the poem's circuit, revealing the raven as encompassing all of the three other poles of the dialectic without totalizing them. Here is a schematic rendering of this overdeterminedness:

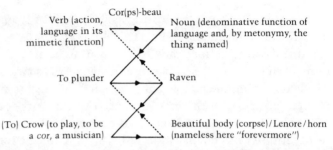

The act of plundering, ravishing, becomes a simile for making a noise (language spoken by a bird that cannot understand it, music coaxed from a mute, lifeless object), a simile for language in its paradoxicality, its grotesqueness. Its poeticity, aseity, is inseparable from its mimetic, active, functional aspect. Along with the lost Lenore, the Raven becomes a metonym of death, particularly of death as beautiful, within an ethos of necrophilia, loss, and bereavement. And yet he is also a figure of the narrator, of active desire (Eros) that is coincident with mourning and that is, as Laplanche has shown, nothing but the tension within death, Thanatos. The Raven thus emerges as an emblem of the chiasmus of the narrator and Lenore, his loss, Eros and Thanatos, desire and death. If we compare this dialectical matrix with the previous one derived from Mallarmé's "Le Tombeau d'Edgar Poe," it is easy to see that the two parallel one another, and it is possible to substitute freely from one to the other.

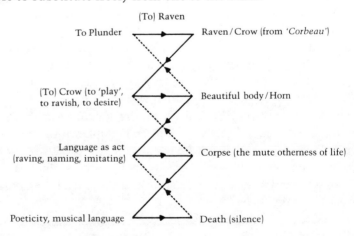

Language is indeed, in its interpretive function, an act of pillaging that is directed at its own poeticity. We cannot read or interpret the text without damaging it as a text that is not referential or metalingual but *poetic*, which refers to nothing but itself.[39] We can also see, reading from bottom to top on the right side of the matrix, that the object of the poem is, by increments, more and more repressed, occulted, in figurative metonyms. Death becomes a corpse, then a beautiful body that might be alive or dead, and finally a raven. The symbolic language (diagonal axis from lower right to upper left) tells us that the poem, literary language, sublimates a desire that is specifically physical (to plunder or ravish) and directed toward another body, a beautiful one. Yet it also reveals a tension, an ambivalence within that desire which is expressed, and repressed, in the poem's figurative structure. The beautiful body (metonym of Platonic Beauty, which may only be apprehended as lost, absolutely Other) after which the narrator (and the reader) lust, which arouses them to an interpretive tumescence, is death. Thanatos is the stasis to which Eros tends; Eros is only a tension defined in relation to that hypothetical stasis (Thanatos). The ultimate end of desire is possession, totalization, immobilization of its object—death. And insofar as desire is gratified by a reduction in the tension that defines it, it seeks not only the end of others, other desires, but of itself.[40] Language in its literary use, analogically, is a tension of referentiality and aseity, communication or speech act and pure musicality, sound. This tension *is* overdetermination, and without it we cannot read literarily at all. The tension is expressed in an endless variety of dialectics of symbolic language. A word is a sign in the ear and in the eye, and for both it signifies something else as well as only itself.

According to Freudian and Lacanian theory, it is to just such

39. These terms are borrowed from Roman Jakobson, "Language and Poetics," in Seymour Chatman and Samuel Levin (eds.), *Essays on the Language of Literature* (Boston, 1967). The *poetic* is language "for its own sake;" the *metalingual* refers to language that is inscribed in a certain code or codes of language; the referential is language in its usual, "communicative" function. For Mallarmé's translation of *The Raven*, see Mallarmé, *Oeuvres complètes*, 190–93.

40. See Laplanche, *Vie et mort en psychanalyse*.

instances of overdetermination that the analyst must address himself.[41] The grotesque, as we have seen, has the effect of over-determining mimesis: it confronts us with a rupture between the text and its pretended project (referentiality). Such overdeter-minations are the object of psychoanalytic reading, the possibil-ity of it. It is just this sort of overdetermination, on the broader plane of culture, that has been occurring between France and the South since Poe. We have seen in "The Raven" that translation from English to French is more than a simple one-to-one decod-ing of words. What happens when French is translated into En-glish is that many literal and figurative translations are possible because each French word is more overdetermined than any En-glish counterpart, as, for instance, when *corbeau* generated crow as well as raven, beautiful body and beautiful horn (horn-player). This is true in spite of the unusual extent to which *raven*, for an English word, is already overdetermined. In general, French con-denses, English disperses. What that suggests is the grotesque-ness of the word *literal* applied to translation. Translation is only a hyperbolic illustration of what happens whenever we un-dertake to decode, to interpret, to read, a text.

Let us look back for a moment at Mallarmé's translation of his "Le Tombeau d'Edgar Poe."[42] His overdetermination here con-firms the link between death, violence, and language that was suggested by that poem as well as by "The Raven." By some truly occult mental calculus, his French *glaive* has become an English 'hymn'—an instrument of violence turned into a musi-cal sacrament of words. This might be suggested by such figur-ative uses of *glaive* as *le glaive de la loi*, but no other translator would dare take such liberty. Swords do not sing; unlike ravens, they do not even talk, and there is nothing necessarily religious about them. We could not ask for a translator more familiar with the author and the author's intentions than the author himself. What we get from him is at best puzzling. The implications, for

41. See Laplanche and Pontalis, *The Language of Psychoanalysis*, 292–93; Lacan, *Ecrits*, I, 111–208; Lacan, *Speech and Language in Psychoanalysis*, trans. Anthony Wilden.
42. Mallarmé, *Oeuvres complètes*, 70.

reading as well as for translation, are serious indeed. And what is at stake is nothing less than the very nature of symbolism as such. There are many instances, equally striking, in this translation: *triompher* becomes 'extolled', *plus pur* becomes 'too pure', *proclamèrent* becomes 'thought', *nue* becomes 'ether', *calme* turns into 'stern', and *noir* into 'old'. Mallarmé's poem becomes rather grotesque in his own English. It is not his fault; English cannot enact the formal and figurative strategies of French. Poe might have been trying to make it do so, and if he was, he made an important discovery even as he failed. I would not doubt that Mallarmé, who was after all an English teacher (though by most accounts not a very good one), knew perfectly well how ludicrous his poem had become in English and perhaps even sought to make a virtue of necessity by rendering it more grotesque than it need have been. Such overdetermination is the very soul of poeticity.

We witnessed in "The Raven" a particularly dramatic example of poetic overdetermination. A grotesque and apparently gratuitous, absurd metaphor in English is revealed in French, by the use of interpretive techniques more suited to French than to English (phonemic overdetermination), as sublime metaphor, but only at the price of an extreme equivocation between several possible referents and signifieds. What we have, then, is a case of metalepsis, what Harold Bloom calls the "trope of tropes," the trope of the poetic sublime.

> The trope of metalepsis . . . is a trope-reversing trope, a figure of a figure. In a metalepsis, a word is substituted metonymically for a word in a previous trope, so that a metalepsis can be called, maddeningly but accurately, a metonymy of a metonymy.
>
> Quintilian, in defining metalepsis and in giving it the Latin name transumption, deprecated the trope and said it was good only for comedy . . . from the Renaissance through Romanticism to the present day it has become the major mode of poetic allusion. . . . The prevalence of transumptive allusion is the largest single factor in fostering a tone of conscious rhetoricity in Romantic and Post-Romantic poetry. To transume means "to take

across," and as a transfer of terms we can define transumption as a taking across to the poem's farther shore. Quintilian uneasily saw this as a change-of-meaning trope. "It is the nature of *metalepsis* to form a kind of intermediate step between the term transferred and the thing to which it is transferred, having no meaning in itself, but merely providing a transition."[43]

And yet what is effected by the metalepsis seen in the translation of "The Raven" is not the fantasy of totalization that Bloom reads metalepsis as being, but an irony that suspends the text forever in the middle of this 'carrying over', an endless repetition of transumption, translation. If metalepsis, as we see it here, represents the *ne plus ultra* of metaphor (and I agree with Bloom that it does), it is no less the *ne plus ultra* of irony. The sign is virtually dissolved in the tension that constitutes it. It is precisely the epistemological violence of overdetermination that defines literariness, which, however, a given text may exploit more or less effectively.[44]

It should be apparent by now that the unsymmetrical Other, the final, mediating term of the dialectic is nothing but an *a posteriori* metalepsis; it is what the dialectic of textuality omits and yet is necessary to understanding. The literariness of the

43. Bloom, *A Map of Misreading*, 102.

44. See Riffaterre, *Semiotics of Poetry*: "It is a fact that no matter how strange a departure from usage a poem may seem to be, its deviant phraseology keeps its hold on the reader and appears not gratuitous but in fact strongly motivated; discourse seems to have its own imperative truth; the arbitrariness of language conventions seems to diminish as the text becomes more deviant and ungrammatical, rather than the other way around. This overdetermination is the other face of the text's derivation from one matrix: the relationship between generator and transforms adds its own powerful connection to the normal links between words—grammar and lexical distribution. The functions of overdetermination are three: to make mimesis possible; to make literary discourse exemplary by lending it the authority of multiple motivations for each word used; and to compensate for catachresis. The first two functions are observable in literature in general, the last only in poetic discourse" (21). I would suggest that the "one matrix" which, according to Riffaterre, determines overdetermination, is the heterogenous Otherness that arbitrarily imposes closure on the text, or tries to; the matrix has to be supplied, reinvented and reinscribed, by each successive reader. It is nowhere in the text itself.

text depends on this mediation, transumption after the fact, occurring in an unforeseen way, a way that threatens to subvert
signification without really having to, for to actually subvert
signification would be to cross the fine line between the literary
and the nonsensical. Metalepsis, because it is constituted precisely as allusion, as a *missing* connection, must always be a
matter of surmise, of reconstruction, of interpretation. Whether
the same metalepsis was at work in the act of writing the text,
we cannot know, and in fact it could not matter less. Metalepsis
by definition is what the text excludes. The writer's use of this
or that unsymmetrical Otherness to mediate the tension that is
his text, to set up that tension as a text, does not preclude the
possibility that the same text might have been written, mediated, by other allusions, other metalepses—indeed, that it might
have been *better* constituted by other mediative terms. So the
act of reading, as it casts about for its own unsymmetrical term,
as it translates the text, might actually improve upon the author's intentions. We might even say that a text that lends itself
to such new transumption, or mediation, a text whose tension
suggests ever more astonishing and unforeseen othernesses, is
more readable, and thus more literary, than one whose solutions
are more restricted, whose intentions seem incontrovertible.

The French text and English text of Poe realize such a tension,
productive of new readings, to an even greater degree in collusion than the English text alone. French, because it is more
morphologically overdetermined than English, might be said to
be more readable, in the sense just described, than English. Poe's
English text succeeds in enacting a severe tension, one so severe
as to generate widely discrepant judgments and quite contradictory readings; Poe's French text might be said to modulate that
tension, increase the possibilities of reading it, transuming it,
mediating it, while not reducing it below the level of the extraordinary, the grotesquely incongruent, the intensely literary.
Here indeed we might be witnessing an exemplary instance of a
writer's intentions having been improved upon by reading that
happened to coincide with literal translation. Together, the English and French make a truly extraordinary case of a text pro-

ductive of readings. That is why Poe's text is a privileged point
of entry into this dialectical model. It marks a point at which
southern literature and French literature are as evidently involved in as fruitful a dialectic as they will ever be. That dialectic is much easier to see because of the literal coincidence of
translation with the generation of meaning. Each tradition will,
from this point, work its way back into its own more or less
independent idiom of symbolic language, to be revitalized from
time to time by similar tranfusions of tension from the other
tradition, reenactments of the primal scene. We can, then, look
for the model to burst, from time to time, back into operation on
the level of literal translation between the two languages and
cultures, points at which an English text needs its French other
to achieve its literariness, and vice versa. Less striking examples
will be encountered in which a suitable *semblable* can be found
closer to hand, but operating within the very same ethos of loss,
plunder, bereavement, dispossession, death, defeat. There will
also be instances in which each tradition finds a suitable other
in some third tradition that they share in common, in which an
effect of overlapping occurs between them.

Always to be kept in mind is that the history of literary relations between France and the South, and perhaps, as Valéry says
in his essay on Poe's "Eureka," the history of the mind, have
been absurdly glorious and gloriously absurd. The suggestion is
that the significance of these relations is reducible to two things,
which are really one: defeat and the grotesque, or rhetorical
violence. The grotesque defeats verisimilitude, but without itself
being victorious. That is what Flannery O'Connor pointed to
when she said that southern writers had had their "Fall." Valéry,
reading Poe, arguably the first southern writer of the grotesque,
reached the same conclusion without any reference to the historical event of the Civil War but rather to a mythical, sublimely
misconstrued Edgar Poe, bogus southern aristocrat. No one illus-
trates better the principle that Valéry derived from "Eureka": he
is a mythic origin, a primal catastrophe that continues to generate fallout on both sides of the Atlantic, and from one side to the
other.

The relation between France and the South, based on the grotesque, is finally grotesque, a failure of understanding, a mistake. Nowhere is this more apparent than in the case of Poe. And yet both sides continue to be nourished by the error. What this suggests is what Walker Percy has observed in his famous essay on metaphor: that metaphor, indeed all figurative language, is a 'mistake', necessarily grotesque.[45] This thesis bears the unmistakable (*sic*) imprimatur of French philosophical influence. As O'Connor wrote, "Not every lost war would have had this effect on every society, but we were doubly blessed, not only in our Fall, but in having the means to interpret it. Behind our own history, deepening it at every point, has been another history."[46] The evidence is everywhere in these pages that that other history has often been, not the religious one to which she refers here, but the French literary tradition. If the connection is one of misconstrual, accident, error, if it is grotesque, that is precisely what makes it an archetype of literary connections in general.

In provisional conclusion, *raven* is a name for the point at which signification breaks down and literariness, if it is to occur, will occur. It is the locus of the purely other, death, or whatever cipher one chooses to paste over its absence. It must be articulated in terms combining a tension of resemblance and difference, short of nothingness but sufficiently *different* so that the dialectic, or circuit, of signification is engaged, while it remains extraordinary, incongruous—in the extreme, grotesque.

45. Walker Percy, *The Message in the Bottle* (New York, 1975), 64–82.
46. O'Connor, *Mystery and Manners*, 59.

III. THE RAVEN'S FURTHER ADVENTURES IN SYMBOLISM

Allusions to and derivations from the primal instance of translation are many in subsequent symbolist works. I mean not to
catalog them here but to give some sense of their nature and
direction by examining specific examples. The first of these
comprises two poems, both by Paul Verlaine and both entitled
"Nevermore." The first poem repeats Poe's naming of loss in the
idiom of time, by the use of the imperfect and perfect tenses, as
analepsis. The second translates the temporal figure into a spatial one within which the chiasmus of temporal and spatial loss,
the tautological separation and equation of diachrony and synchrony (language as referential act and language as aseity), is
enacted. The second poem's gesture to Poe is mediated through
a previous gesture, making it especially easy to see what the
later of the two poems accomplishes that the earlier does not,
and also what has been assumed about Poe's poem in the first
that makes the second possible. It also suggests the failure of
closure implicit in any such nod at a precursor. Here is the text
of the first poem:

> Souvenir, souvenir, que me veux-tu? L'Automne
> Faisait voler la grive à travers l'air atone,
> Et le soleil dardait un rayon monotone
> Sur le bois jaunissant où la bise détone.
>
> Nous étions seul à seule et marchions en rêvant,
> Elle et moi, les cheveux et la pensée au vent.
> Soudain, tournant vers moi son regard émouvant:
> "Quel fut ton plus beau jour?" fit sa voix d'or vivant,
>
> Sa voix douce et sonore, au frais timbre angélique.
> Un sourire discret lui donna la réplique,
> Et je baisai sa main blanche, dévotement.
>
> —Ah! les premières fleurs, qu'elles sont parfumées!

Et qu'il bruit avec un murmure charmant
Le premier *oui* qui sort de lèvres bien-aimées![1]

Memory, memory, what do you want of me? Autumn / Made the
thrush fly through the atonal air, / And the sun darted a monotonous ray / On the yellowing wood on which the north wind
played out of tune. // We were alone and walked as we dreamed /
She and I, hair and thoughts to the wind. / Suddenly, turning to
me her affecting look: / "What was your most beautiful day?" said
her voice of living gold, // Her gentle and sonorous voice, with the
cool angelic tone. / A discreet smile gave her the answer, / And I
kissed her white hand, devotedly. // —Ah! the first flowers, how
sweet they are! / And how it soughs with an enduring murmur /
The first *yes* that comes from beloved lips!

The poem is an analepsis that looks back to another analepsis.
It enacts the covert plot to which John Porter Houston referred
in his discussion of Verlaine and Poe. The poem looks back at a
moment that appears now to have been the narrator's *plus beau
jour*. Part of it, however, was an unspoken response to the question, "Quel fut ton plus beau jour?" that alludes to an even more
ambiguous, covert past, which exceeds not only the text but also
language and can be signified only by "un sourire discret." The
plus beau jour, the fabulous origin to which the poem looks, is
strictly a phenomenon of the past, of loss, which entirely defies
representation, or naming. The text fuses perfectly the ethos
of mourning in "The Raven" and the narrative strategy of "The
Purloined Letter." The *plus beau jour*, the moment of possession and totalization, is, like the purloined letter, like the raven,
like the grotesque in general, a pure signifier, "to the extent that
it 'is destined . . . to signify the annulment of what it signifies'—
the necessity of its own *repression*, of the repression of its message." The purloined letter in Poe's story is never read, never
reveals any message or refers to anything; it signifies by having
certain effects in the story, by being twice purloined. Shoshana
Felman, writing on Lacan's discussion of the Poe story, goes on:

1. Paul Verlaine, *Oeuvres complètes*, eds. Y.-G. Le Dantec and Jacques Borel
(Paris, 1962), 61.

"It is not only the meaning but the text of the message which it would be dangerous to place in circulation." But in much the same way as the repressed *returns* in the *symptom*, which is its repetitive symbolic substitute, the purloined letter ceaselessly returns in the tale—as a signifier of the repressed—through its repetitive displacements and replacements. "This is indeed what happens in the repetition compulsion," says Lacan. Unconscious desire, once repressed, survives in displaced symbolic media which govern the subject's life and actions without his ever being aware of their meaning or of the repetitive pattern they structure.[2]

The double theft of the letter in Poe's story is repeated by the double displacement of possession in Verlaine's poem. The pure signifier is the reference (*sourire discret*) to the moment of possession, which itself is never inscribed in the text. The pure signifier is loss itself, the anteriority of the moment; the *plus beau jour* continues to have effects because it is virtual rather than actual.

Each analepsis of the poem mourns a previous one, by turns repressing and losing the fabulous origin to which it looks. Poe himself, the *glaive nu*, dead French Poe, is of course the pure signifier, the 'purloined letter', generating the effects of the poem. The poem's desire for the virtual, hypothetical totality implied by that origin fuels the poem's movement, taking it farther and farther away from the first 'name', the first 'loss' of that postulated totality. The poem's title suggests the paradox, as well as the poet from whom it was purloined. It contains two English words, each of which negates the other, *never* and *more*. *Never* is a negative name of eternity, pointing to past and future. *More* is similarly limitless, but acts as a positive and temporally specific limitation, a contradiction, of this negative infinity (never). The tension between the words establishes a difference between the past (a hypothetically pure anteriority) and the present, and it is this dialectical difference that the poem's analepses enact. The *plus beau jour*, pure anteriority, has replaced the purloined letter, and analepsis, diachrony, has translated the purely spatial relay of intersubjectivity in Poe's story.

2. Felman, "On Reading Poetry," in Smith (ed.), *The Literary Freud*, 137–38.

Felman provides schematic depictions of the relay as described by Lacan.

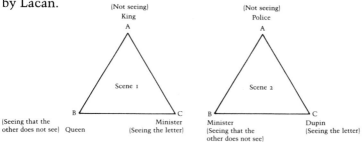

She goes on to 'translate' them into the following more general schema.[3]

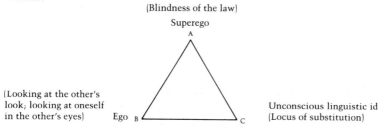

C is the point at which purloinment (loss, misplacement) occurs. Translated into the temporal language of analepsis, it is the *moment* of the look back at a previous moment. The two analepses of Verlaine's poem might be represented thus:

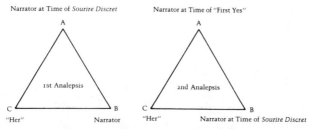

In the first analepsis, the narrator sees himself unaware of his own happiness and "her" seeing him unaware of it. At the time that he was with her, he was looking back at a previous moment that we may assume he had also taken for granted and that she had seen him taking for granted. Each analepsis names or re-

3. *Ibid.*, 136–37.

enacts a loss that it cannot specify but can only characterize in terms of a previous loss, an anteriority that is always situated by reference to another anteriority. And in fact, the act of reading imposes another analepsis on these two.

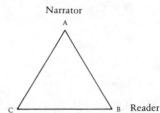

The reader 'looks back' at the narrator who is unable to see himself enacting the loss he looks back to, though his recollection mirrors his present narration and the loss enacted by it. Reading must always postulate an anterior moment of writing, of 'meaning to say', on the part of the author. It must, in other words, postulate a primal act of composition, an anterior subjectivity that is the author himself. Reading repeats the loss enacted by the text, so that it loses the text by enacting it: analepsis within analepsis within analepsis, all tending toward some fabulous origin that they cannot specify. If they could specify it, it would be neither fabulous nor original. For Verlaine's poem, given its title and subject, Poe is the voice of that origin. Schematically represented, the narrator and the poem enact the following dialectics:

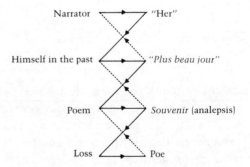

The second "Nevermore" transposes the temporal figuration into the language of space. Here is the text of it:

> Allons, mon pauvre coeur, allons, *mon vieux complice,*
> Redresse et peins à neuf tous tes arcs triomphaux;
> Brule un encens ranci sur tes autels d'or faux;
> Sème de fleurs les bords béants du précipice;
> Allons, mon pauvre coeur, allons, *mon vieux complice!*
>
> Pousse à Dieu ton cantique, ô chantre rajeuni;
> Entonne, orgue enroué, des *Te Deum* splendides;
> Vieillard prématuré, mets du fard sur tes rides;
> Couvre-toi de tapis mordorés, mur jauni;
> Pousse à Dieu ton cantique, ô chantre rajeuni.
>
> Sonnez, grelots; sonnez, clochettes; sonnez, cloches!
> Car mon rêve impossible a pris corps, et je l'ai
> Entre mes bras pressé: le Bonheur, cet ailé
> Voyageur qui de l'Homme évite les approches,
> —Sonnez, grelots; sonnez, clochettes, sonnez, cloches!
>
> Le Bonheur a marché côte à côte avec moi;
> Mais la FATALITE ne connaît point de trêve:
> Le ver est dans le fruit, le réveil dans le rêve,
> Et le remords est dans l'amour: telle est la loi.
> —Le Bonheur a marché côte à côte avec moi.[4]

Let us go, my poor heart, let us go, *my old accomplice,* / Raise up and paint anew all your triumphal arches; / Burn a rancid incense on your altars of false gold; / Strew with flowers the gaping edges of the precipice; / Let us go, my poor heart, let us go, *my old accomplice!* // Impel your canticle to God, o rejuvenated chorister; / Strike up, hoarse organ, some splendid *Te Deums*; / Prematurely old man, put some make-up on your wrinkles; / Cover yourself with russet tapestries, yellowed wall; / Impel your canticle to God, o rejuvenated chorister. // Ring, little bells; ring, handbells; ring, great bells! / For my impossible dream has taken flesh, and I have / Pressed it between my arms: Happiness, that winged / Voyager which avoids the approach of Man, / —Ring, little bells; ring,

---

4. Verlaine, *Oeuvres complètes*, 81–82.

handbells; ring, great bells! // Happiness walked side by side with me; / But FATALITY knows no respite: / The worm is in the fruit, awakening in the dream, / And remorse is in love: such is the law. / —Happiness walked side by side with me.

The vocabulary of the poem begins with a series of metonymies in which the narrator addresses himself in the present tense. He addresses some of these metonymies to himself, to his other self, and is apparently addressed by the rest of them. The metonymic language refers to a church or cathedral, a spatial totality that is never specified. These synchronic metonymies address each other through a series of different, diachronic acts: raising up, painting, burning, strewing, making music, covering, ringing. An identity of act with sound is suggested, as in "The Raven," by the substitution of verbs such as "ringing" for "raising up."

At the beginning of the third stanza, the present tense is replaced by the past, and metonymical naming by metaphorical. Loss is named as the worm in the fruit, as the inevitable waking from sleep and dream, and as the remorse inseparable from love, rather than as a ruined church inhabited by a "prematurely old man" (priest? organ player? chorister? congregation of one?). These figures all mock the totality to which metaphor is often thought to pretend. They neither restore, transume, or transcend but only represent, in condensed rather than dispersive images, the failure of totalization and possession.

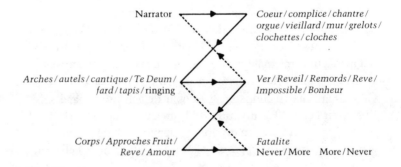

Again, the dialectic of naming is tautological: on the right, we see *rêve impossible*, on the left, *rêve*; on the right *bonheur*, on the left, *amour*. The sentence that marks the shift from metonymy to metaphor and present to past is "Mon rêve impossible a pris corps" ("My impossible dream has taken flesh"). The impossible dream of totality has taken shape, named itself, as pure anteriority, or progressive loss, in the synchronic description of a cathedral or church. What the first poem used analepsis to depict, this one describes by ecphrasis, a spatial allegory of description. Giving shape to time describes the present as becoming the past, as loss (analepsis), and it situates the poem at the place and time of crossing over, of losing, of translating time into space and space into time. The present can only contemplate itself by translating itself into past, which in the symbolic language of losing is translation; metonymy can only contemplate itself as metaphor. The poem is an endless repetition of such reversals, in which totality and meaning, its objects, are endlessly named and lost. Thus the poem is an allegory of its own inadequacy: 'nevermoreness'. The relay of the poem might be represented thus:

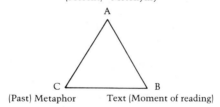

Metaphor and metonymy translate the diachronic and synchronic representations of the first "Nevermore" poem, so that there is also a relay from the second poem to the first, or the first to the second, depending on which is read first.

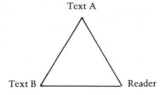

Text A is overdetermined by Text B; Text B is made through overdetermination to seem cognizant of Text A's dependence on it; the real agent of that overdetermination is the reader. Reading is the perpetual locus of substitution that makes texts realize their poeticity. Writing, the composition of the text, would be in this sense a 'first reading'.

In 1870 France suffered one of its most humiliating national defeats at the hands of the emerging German nation under Bismarck. At the same time, the American South was being subjected to occupation under the guise of Reconstruction, which would teach it an unquiet, resentful stoicism and firmly entrench the poetics of loss and defeat, articulated by Poe, as the literary ethos of the region. Out of the Franco-Prussian War came the end of Napoleon III's empire and the beginning of the Third Republic, the longest lived of all France's republican governments. Elections to empower a National Assembly, held at German insistence, revealed a split between Paris and the rural masses that had existed since the Revolution of 1789: of more than six hundred deputies only two hundred were republican and the rest monarchist. Civil war broke out between the assembly and Parisian republicans, who had suffered siege by the Germans for four months, refusing to give up long after Napoleon III had. The Paris Commune was set up as a rival republican government, lasting from March to May, 1871. With defeat imminent, the *communards* engaged in an orgy of destruction, setting fire to public buildings and murdering the archbishop of Paris. The National Assembly's recriminatory measures made the *communards* seem demure and retiring by comparison: 330,000 people denounced, 38,000 arrested, 20,000 executed, 7,500 deported.[5]

The preceding events coincided with the emerging poetic consciousness of Rimbaud. In August, 1870, he fled his home for the first time, only to be arrested on August 31 at the Gare du Nord.

5. These figures are taken from R. R. Palmer and Joel Colton, *A History of the Modern World* (New York, 1971), 627–28.

A second flight ended in a return to his mother under police escort. In December, 1870, the community of Mezières, a suburb of Charleville, where the Rimbaud family lived, was heavily bombed. In late February, 1871, Rimbaud fled Charleville for the third time and stayed in Paris for two weeks during the time when the Commune was formed. Thus war, and not only with the Germans, but civil war, was well known to Rimbaud before his seventeenth birthday. He knew it as defeat, devastation, the triumph of the peasant mentality he had come to despise so vehemently in Charleville. He wrote in a letter to Georges Izambard, his teacher, "On est exilé dans sa patrie!" ("We are exiled in our own country!").[6]

In Rimbaud's poem "Les Corbeaux," Poe's raven has become the muse of war and devastation. In "Chant de Guerre Parisien" Rimbaud had already established the destructiveness of war as a metaphor for the derangement of poetry.

> Thiers et Picard sont des Eros,
> Des enleveurs d'héliotropes;
> Au pétrole ils font des Corots:
> Voici hannetonner leurs tropes
>
> Thiers and Picard are Cupids, / Thieves of heliotropes; / They
> paint Corots with gasoline: / Here their tropes are buzzing about

The warriors lay waste to the landscape, 'painting' it with fires, bombs, and gasoline, turning flowers into lucent figures, transforming heliotropes into *helio*, 'towards the sun', and *trope*, 'turning'. Fire translates the referential object into a real enactment of its name (a misconstrual, a pun) for the name refers to the way in which the stems bend so that the plant receives a maximum of light, not its potential for combustion; the name is overdetermined). So Thiers and Picard are poets after all: "Ils

---

6. Wallace Fowlie (ed. and trans.), *Rimbaud: Complete Works, Selected Letters* (Chicago, 1966), 298–99. In citing Rimbaud, I have used Fowlie's dual language edition. For biographical information, see Fowlie, *Rimbaud: A Critical Study* (Chicago, 1965), especially pp. 10–20. See also Arthur Rimbaud, *Oeuvres complètes*, eds. Rolland de Renéville and Jules Mouquet (Paris, 1954).

sont familiers du Grand Truc!" ("They are familiar with the Big Trick!"). In the letter in which this poem was included, he wrote that "je m'encrapule le plus possible. . . . Il s'agit d'arriver à l'inconnu par le dérèglement de *tous les sens*" ("I am degrading myself as much as possible. . . . It is a question of reaching the unknown by the derangement of *all the senses*"). What many readers of Rimbaud have missed entirely is that he is talking about reaching the unknown as ignorance, as misconstrual, not as transcendence, not as any positive sense of an *inconnu* that could be assimilated to Catholicism or any wish to totalize. "Il arrive à l'inconnu, et quand, affolé, il finirait par *perdre l'intelligence de ses visions*, il les a vues!" ("He reaches the unknown, and when, bewildered, he ends by *losing the intelligence of his visions*, he has seen them!" [emphasis mine]).[7] Poetry involves the exhaustion of knowledge as such, the repudiation of signification and of the pure signifier, which, like fire, destroys the referent. And poetic vision must reach beyond language. It must apply the more apparent fluidity of words to the immolation of the 'real'. Literature is no more or less than an exaggeration of perception. The comforting illusion that the indeterminacy, the grotesqueness, of poetry can be confined to purely linguistic phenomena is just that—an illusion.

The *corbeaux* are synecdoches of the bleak, charred, ruinous defeat of knowledge, the loss of the totality of the sign. But the narrator of the poem pleads with the *corbeaux*, his muses, "saints du ciel," to leave "les fauvettes de mai" for those who are shackled by "la défaite sans avenir"—whether to give the dead soldiers hope, nostalgia for spring in this winter of the spirit, or to be destroyed by them, rather than by the *corbeaux*, we are not told. The *fauvettes* (warblers), unseen in the forest, emblematic of past and future springs, are the other of the *corbeaux*—the pure signifier, purloined letter, nameless lost Lenore, ideal Beauty—by reference to which the *corbeaux* take on their own power as pure signifiers, tropes of tropes. Instead of analepsis

7. Fowlie, *Rimbaud: Complete Works, Selected Letters*, 68–71, 70–71, 306–307.

within analepsis or an opposition of metaphor and metonymy, here we see the raven engaged in a purely ornithological dialectic, but one which achieves the same effect as the Verlaine poems.

> Seigneur, quand froide est la prairie,
> Quand, dans les hameaux abattus,
> Les long angélus se sont tus . . .
> Sur la nature défleurie
> Faites s'abattre des grands cieux
> Les chers corbeaux délicieux.
>
> Armée étrange aux cris sévères,
> Les vents froids attaquent nos nids!
> Vous le long des fleuves jaunis,
> Sur les routes aux vieux calvaires,
> Sur les fosses et sur les trous
> Dispersez-vous, ralliez-vous!
>
> Par milliers, sur les champs de France,
> Où dorment les morts d'avant-hier,
> Tournoyez, n'est-ce pas, l'hiver,
> Pour que chaque passant repense!
> Sois donc le crieur du devoir,
> O notre funèbre oiseau noir!
>
> Mais, saint du ciel, en haut du chêne,
> Mât perdu dans le soir charmé,
> Laissez les fauvettes de mai
> Pour ceux qu'au fond du bois enchaîne,
> Dans l'herbe d'où l'on ne peut fuir,
> La défaite sans avenir.[8]

Lord, when the meadow is cold, / When, in the discouraged hamlets, / The long Angeluses are silenced . . . / Over nature stripped of flowers / Have the dear delightful crows / Swoop down from the great skies. // Strange army with solemn cries, / The cold winds assail your nests! / You—along yellowed

8. *Ibid.*, 120–123.

rivers, / Over roads with old cavalries / Over ditches and holes—
/ Disperse and rally! // By thousands, over the fields of
France, / Where sleep the dead of yesterday, / Turn about in
winter, won't you, / So that each passer-by may remember! / Be
then the crier of duty, / O our funereal black bird! // But, saints of
the sky, at the top of the oak, / A mast lost in the enchanted
evening, / Leave alone the May warblers / For those who, in the
depths of the wood, / In the grass from which there is no escape, / Are enslaved by a defeat without a future.

Of course, there is no question that those "Dans l'herbe d'où
l'on ne peut fuir" are the dead casualties of war. That the
fauvettes should be left for them, who cannot hear or see, makes
the narrator's plea for clemency on the part of the *corbeaux*
ironic indeed. But the irony makes more sense when read with
the last line. Who is "enslaved" by "a defeat without a future"?
The dead can hardly be thought of as enslaved any more than
they can be thought to hear or see the warblers. And in fact the
narrator does not imply that the warblers ought to be spared so
that the dead might hear them or see them. The warblers and
the idea of death as enslavement are *leitmotifs* of the living. The
verb *enchaîner* means many things besides 'enslave'—'to connect', for instance, 'to string together'. *Défaite* is 'undoing' (*dé
faire*) as well as 'defeat'. The language of the sentence is severely
paradoxical: an 'undoing' without a future (life-as-dying, a grad-
ual exhaustion of itself, a reduction by increments of Eros until
it is identical with Thanatos) 'connects' the moments of living
together in the narrative of any human existence. It is death as
absolute other, the idea of it, the threat of it, that both orders
and undoes the lives of the living. The *fauvettes*, unseen and
unheard in the forest, in the past and the future, are emblems of
this other, as the *corbeaux* are. The *fauvettes* are the pure anteriority and absence that the *corbeaux* name. In memory, the
fauvettes are the voice of death-as-undoing, Eros as the tension
in Thanatos. They give hope and nostalgia for the past and the
future, and they also, as pure signifiers of the purest signifier,
death, are objects of poetic violence. They arouse the narrator to

enact on them the undoing that they emblematize. "Sois donc le crieur du devoir, / O notre funèbre oiseau noir!" ("Be then the crier of duty, / O our funereal black bird!"). The ravens, devouring and resembling the dead, throw a lugubrious light on the warblers, performing on them the alchemy of poetic derangement and translating them into the idiom of death. That derangement is of course tautological, a kind of self-destruction. The object of Eros is its own reduction. The poet's carrion is his own flesh. The *fauvettes* are emblems of his memory and nostalgia. We might render the poem's dialectic thus:

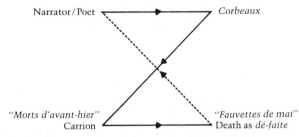

Narrator/Poet   Corbeaux

"Morts d'avant-hier"
Carrion   "Fauvettes de mai"
Death as *dé-faite*

Following Poe's example, the poem's object is its own undoing.

IV. THE CEMETERIES
OF TATE AND VALÉRY
The Ghosts of Aeneas and Narcissus

We might look for instances in which the two literatures, French and southern, would illuminate one another through the mediation of an other foreign to them both, in which the primal instance of Poe, however, would be inscribed. Seeking where to begin, one is immediately confronted by two facts: that the American South produced much great literature after the beginning of the twentieth century and that it had produced little (arguably none besides Poe) before.[1] Many critics have attempted explanations for this bizarrely abrupt outburst of poetic genius that continues, somewhat abated, to the present day. Most of the explanations find their way to the historical trauma of the Civil War,[2] posing a new problem: why should it have taken the South so long (fifty or sixty years, the better part of a century) to translate the experience of defeat into literature, if indeed that defeat does nourish the roots of southern writing in the twentieth century? Irving Howe offers an explanation that defines the possibility of great literature as the embracement of "urban industrialism," a kind of pragmatic identification with the northern victor and his "liberal," "progressive" capitalism. "Only at the point where the South began to abandon its fantasies of a glorious homeland defeated by commercial invaders, to examine slightly its appalling heritage of slavery and to enter, kicking, into the modern world of urban industrialism—only then, as a reward for the pain of self-examination, did we get the alloyed genius of Faulkner, the craft of Katherine Anne Porter, the wild humor of the early Erskine Caldwell."[3] That explanation seems

1. See Allen Tate, *Essays of Four Decades* (Chicago, 1968), 517–46.
2. See, for instance, O'Connor, *Mystery and Manners*, 51–59; Donald Davidson, *Still Rebels, Still Yankees and Other Essays* (Baton Rouge, 1972), 159–79; Lewis P. Simpson, *The Brazen Face of History: Studies in Literary Consciousness in America* (Baton Rouge, 1980), 115–24.
3. Irving Howe, "Southern Agrarians and American Culture," in *Celebrations*

simplistic for more than the obvious reason: that Howe wishes, for polemical reasons of his own, to deny the southernness of anything admirable to come from the South and, in case that fails, to qualify its admirableness as "alloyed." Even if we take Howe seriously, there remains the fact that in the 1920s the South was not much more basically industrial than it had been in 1865. A more credible explanation is offered by Allen Tate. "With the war of 1914–1918, the South reentered the world— but gave a backward glance as it stepped over the border: that backward glance gave us the Southern renascence, a literature conscious of the past in the present."[4] That theory makes the achievement of southern writers synonymous with a look back at loss and with a loss of innocence shared with the nation as a whole. According to Tate's view, the only thing setting the South apart would be its possession of a myth, a symbol of loss and of decadence (in the etymological sense of *decadere*, 'to fall away from'), which made it possible for Tate and others to translate their sense of modern apocalypse into the symbolic language of poetry. The symbol, that is, the myth of the Civil War, could scarcely be more apocalyptic, more one of holocaust, doom, defeat, loss. Could that fact account for its power and for its continuing vitality in the work of such writers as Shelby Foote?

Such a thesis appears plausible when one considers the resemblance, so apparent and so fascinating to Tate himself, between the southern myth of defeat and the classical myth of the fall of Troy.[5] The European Renaissance had looked to the same myth the same way, to the strikingly similar end of opening "a po-

---

and Attacks (New York, 1979), 161–62. Tate paraphrases this view quite accurately: "The provincial ideas of the critics of the North and East . . . followed a direction somewhat as follows: The South, backward and illiberal, and controlled by white men who cherish a unique moral perversity, does not offer in itself a worthy subject to the novelist or the poet; it follows that the only acceptable literature that the South can produce must be a literature of social agitation, through which the need for reform may be publicized." Tate, *Essays of Four Decades*, 543.

4. Tate, *Essays of Four Decades*, 545.

5. See Thomas M. Greene, *The Light in Troy* (New Haven, 1982), 66–67. Greene writes that "the Aeneid is the classic statement of the Roman task because Virgil made it an epic of what I should like to call *transitivity*, that is to say of historical mediation of threatened but preserved continuities" (161).

lemic against what it called the Dark Ages." Like Petrarch,
du Bellay, and Ronsard before the monolith of medieval civiliza-
tion, Tate invoked the ghost of Aeneas along with that of Jefferson Davis before the gorgon of northern industrial capitalism
and progressivism. Thomas M. Greene has elaborated the role of
the myth in the Renaissance.

> This ubiquitous imagery of disinterment, resurrection, and renas-
> cence needed a death and a burial to justify itself; without the
> myth of medieval entombment, its imagery, which is to say its
> self-understanding, had no force. The creation of this myth was
> not a superficial occurrence. It expressed a belief in change and
> loss, change from the immediate past and loss of a remote, pres-
> tigious past that might nonetheless be resuscitated. "The men of
> the Renaissance," wrote Franco Simone, "saw a rupture where
> earlier there had been a belief in a smooth development, and from
> this rupture they took the origins of their enthusiasm and the
> certitude of their originality." A civilization discovered its cultural
> paths by the light behind it of a vast holocaust, and it used this
> mythical light as the principle of its own energy. It made its way
> through ruins by the effulgence cast in their destruction, finding
> in privation the secret of renewal, just as Aeneas, sailing west-
> ward from the ashes of his city, carried with him the flame that
> had consumed it burning before the Penates.[6]

So Tate found symbols of loss and renewal and of the South's
defeat in the myth of Aeneas.[7] His discovery would offer a
reason for the sixty-year hiatus between the end of the war and
the beginning of the southern renascence: the loss needed time
to become a story, a myth, rather than a lived experience. Just as
du Bellay and Ronsard identified themselves with classical antiquity, Tate identified himself with the European culture from
which he believed the Old South to have sprung, and through
the mediation of Europe, he reached back to Aeneas.[8] The Old

6. Greene, *The Light in Troy*, 3.
7. See Tate, *Collected Poems: 1919–1976* (New York, 1977), 68–71.
8. See Lewis P. Simpson, "The Southern Republic of Letters and *I'll Take My Stand*," in William C. Havard and Walter Sullivan (eds.), *A Band of Prophets: The*

South had burned like Troy and like Europe in 1914, and Tate and his fellow Fugitives wrote by the light of the South's mythical combustion as though it repeated, with perfect symmetry, the other two.

His identification with the European and the classical was to find expression in Tate's affinity with another poet as severely classical in temperament as himself, the French writer Paul Valéry. Two of Tate's earliest and strongest influences were Poe, arguably the only important proto-southern writer, and Valéry, who was only slightly Tate's senior. By an accident, he failed to actually meet Valéry in 1932, five years after the composition of "Ode to the Confederate Dead" and five years before its final revision, but he wrote that prior to 1932 he had read all of Valéry's important poems. One of these was "Le Cimetière Marin," a poem that Tate seems to have viewed as a precursor to his "Ode."[9]

Valéry's poetic temperament could scarcely have been more like Tate's own, given obvious differences of culture, language, and circumstance. Tate himself was exhilarated as a young poet by that kinship.[10] Valéry too had found in classical mythology a narrative figure for his poetic self: the story of Narcissus. Valéry, as well as Tate, admired Poe extravagantly. Valéry's affinity with Poe, in which he followed Mallarmé and Baudelaire, adds an uncanny reflectiveness to the relation: a French writer who identifies with the first southern poet of loss and decadence (who, before the actual event of the war, set a morbid tone for southern letters that the war confirmed and deepened as the typically southern tone) is identified with by another "postlapsarian"

Vanderbilt Agrarians After Fifty Years (Baton Rouge, 1982), 65–91. Tate wrote to Donald Davidson that "we must be the last Europeans—there being no Europeans left in Europe at present." Quoted in Lewis P. Simpson, "The Sorrows of John Peale Bishop," *Sewanee Review*, XC (Summer, 1982), 480–84.

9. Allen Tate, *Memoirs and Opinions 1926–1974* (Chicago, 1975), 128–39.

10. *Ibid.*: "Here, in 'Pages Inédites,' was a man educated in the French classical tradition and fired imaginatively by his early entretiens with Mallarmé: whose apparently casual utterances gave me something more than the shock of recognition. It was rather the sense of my own identity, of a sameness within vast, elusive differences" (129).

southern writer who found a precursor in Poe. So what we see in the texts of these two poets is unmistakably inscribed in a dialectical exchange between French and southern men of letters that had begun with Baudelaire and Poe and would continue with Sartre and Faulkner. In classicism and in Poe, Valéry, and the "Southern legend of defeat and frustration," Tate found the symbolic language he needed to make great poetry.[11]

What is strikingly familiar about Tate's "Ode" and Valéry's "Cimetière" is what they share with the literature of the Renaissance: a "ubiquitous imagery of disinterment, resurrection, and renascence" which "needed a death and burial to justify itself." What the two poems have topographically in common is water. In Valéry's poem, the sea is juxtaposed in the narrator's vision with a cemetery as the intense light of noon blurs the horizon between them. The sea is, as it had been for Poe, 'that which drinks'—a metaphor for the stasis of death ("le calme des dieux") in which and against which the tension of life is enacted.[12] So the light plays on the water, between the tombstones.

> Quel pur travail de fins éclairs consume
> Maint diamant d'imperceptible écume
> Et quelle paix semble se concevoir!

> What pure work of fine lightnings consumes / Many a diamond of imperceptible foam / And what peace seems to be conceived!

The dazzling turmoil of light, water, and earth becomes a figure for the alchemy of living, the perpetual flux of perception.

> Tout est brûlé, défait, reçu dans l'air
> A je ne sais quelle sévère essence . . .
> La vie est vaste étant ivre d'absence . . .

> All is burned, undone, received into the air / In I don't know what severe essence . . . / Life is vast, being drunk with absence . . .

11. Twelve Southerners, *I'll Take My Stand, the South and the Agrarian Tradition* (Baton Rouge, 1977), 397. For their respective affinities with Poe, see Tate, *Essays of Four Decades*, 385–400, and Valéry, *Leonardo Poe Mallarmé*.

12. For the symbology of water in Poe (as 'that which drinks'), see Bachelard, *L'Eau et les rêves*, and Chapter 2 herein.

The dead are not distinct from this movement of translation, disfiguration, and flux.

> Ils ont fondu dans une absence épaisse,
> L'argile rouge a bu la blanche espèce,
> Le don de vivre a passé dans les fleurs.
> . . . .
> La larve file où se formaient des pleurs.

> They have melted in a thick absence, / The red clay has drunk up the white specie, / The gift of living has passed into the flowers. / . . . . / The maggot creeps where tears used to form.[13]

'That which drinks' is not simply water, but all that partakes of life, the stasis and immobility in which life is confined and to which it tends. One of its avatars is verse and another is the worm who devours the flesh of the dead—in French, the same word, ver(s).

> Le vrai rongeur, le ver irréfutable
> N'est point pour vous qui dormez sous la table
> Il vit de vie, il ne me quitte pas!

> Amour, peut-être, ou de moi-même haine?
> *Sa dent secrète est de moi si prochaine*
> *Que tous les noms lui peuvent convenir!*
> Qu'importe! Il voit, il veut, il songe, il touche!
> Ma chair lui plaît; et jusque sur ma couche,
> A ce vivant je vis d'appartenir.

> The true gnawer, irrefutable worm / Is not at all for you who sleep beneath the slab / He lives on life, he does not leave me! // Love, perhaps, or hatred of me? / *His secret tooth is so close to me / That all names can suit him!* / What matter! He sees, he wants, he dreams, he touches! / He likes my flesh; and even on my bed, / I live to belong to this living thing! (emphasis mine)

Language, poetry, perception, imagination—all of the senses— live by partaking of decay, flux, *dé-faite*, of which love and hate,

13. Paul Valéry, *Oeuvres*, ed. Jean Hytier (2 vols.; Paris, 1957), I, 147–51.

Eros and Thanatos, are part. The narrator resolves not to be reduced or immobilized by the stasis latent in the desire of death. It is death to which desire tends without daring to embrace, yet inevitably embraces, by turning back on itself.

> Zénon, cruel Zénon! Zénon d'Elée!
> M'as-tu percé de cette flèche ailée
> Qui vibre, vole, et qui ne vole pas!
> Le son m'enfante et la flèche me tue!

> Zeno, cruel Zeno! Zeno of Elea! / Have you pierced me with that winged arrow / Which quivers, flies, and does not fly! / The sound gives birth to me and the arrow kills me!

Instead, he will embrace the shattering and rend(er)ing, the translation of death-in-life and life as dying, and live by it. "Courons à l'onde en rejaillir vivant!" ("Let us run to the wave to spring out of it living!"). The poem, at its close, has turned the doves that appeared in its first stanza into sails, its metaphor into catachresis.

> La vague en poudre ose jaillir des rocs!
> Envolez-vous, pages tout éblouies!
> Rompez, vagues! Rompez d'eaux réjouies
> Ce toit tranquille où picoraient des focs!

> The wave dares to spurt in powder from the rocks! / Fly away, dazzled pages! / Break, waves! Break with joyous waters / The tranquil roof where sails used to peck!

The first line of the poem had been "Ce toit tranquille, où marchent des colombes" ("The tranquil roof, where doves walk").

The poem reduces the distinction of fire and water ("Tant de sommeil sous une voile de flamme!" ["So much sleep under a veil of flame!"]), life and death, vision and language, into the dialectic of loss, pouring everything into the sea, 'that which drinks', death.[14]

---

14. *Ibid.*

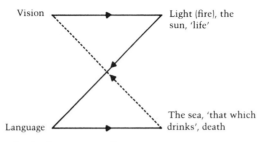

Through the symbolic language of water, perception knows itself, knows the loss of itself, its self-immolation in the fire of words and light (vision).

The play of differences is evident also in Valéry's use of the Narcissus story and indeed in the story itself. Narcissus was the child of a nymph and a river god, making him a mythic synecdoche of water. The nymph Echo fell victim to an unrequited love for Narcissus which consumed everything of her but her voice. To avenge the suicide of another spurned lover, this one a man, Artemis caused Narcissus to fall into a love that was coincident with loss, a desire indistinguishable from mourning. Seeing himself reflected in the water (from which he had sprung), "How could he endure both to possess and yet not to possess? Grief was destroying him, yet he rejoiced in his torments; knowing that at least his other self would remain true to him." His final words were repeated by Echo, who "although she had not forgiven Narcissus, grieved with him."[15] In his "Petite Lettre sur les Mythes," Valéry wrote: "What would we be then without the help of that which does not exist? Very little, and our minds, quite unoccupied, would languish if fables, *misunderstandings*, abstractions, beliefs, and monsters, hypotheses and alleged metaphysical problems did not populate our depths and our natural shadows with beings and images without objects [emphasis mine]. Myths are the souls of our actions and our loves. We cannot act except by moving toward a phantom. We can only love what we create." At the same time, he believed that "the idea of death is the mainspring of laws, the mother of religions,

15. Robert Graves, *The Greek Myths* (2 vols.; New York, 1955), I, 286–88. See also Hollander, *The Figure of Echo*, especially pp. 6–22.

the agent, either secret or terribly manifest, of politics, the essential stimulant of glory and of great loves,—the origin of a quantity of researches and meditations. Among the strangest products of the human spirit's irritation by this idea (or rather by this need of the idea which is imposed on us by the verification of the death of others), figures the antiquated belief that the dead are not dead, or are not exactly dead."[16] The theme of the dead not entirely dead, the *cor(ps) beau parlant* (beautiful speaking corpse/raven), is incarnated in Valéry's poetry as Narcissus, dead but also alive in Echo, whose voice alone survives to repeat, like Poe's raven, "forevermore."

In Valéry's "Narcisse parle," Echo has become a figure of the act of reading, a repetition, an imitation compelled by desire that is coincident with loss. Reader and author are each other's Echo, or image (Narcissus' reflection), doomed to unquenchable desire, the lust to know, to read, to possess the poem. Not even the author can requite the impulse by saying the poem means this or that. We can only repeat its words in our own voices, which is all it and we are as we read it, not visual images but merely voices, words, *figuras* or *imagos* in the rhetorical sense, like Echo, dissolved in the water of desire: "Je ne sais plus aimer que l'eau magicienne" ("I no longer know how to love anything but the magical water").[17] The dialectic of vision and language, water and light, is perfectly encapsulated here in the spatial allegory of the Narcissus myth.

16. Valéry, *Oeuvres:* "Que serions nous donc sans le secours de ce qui n'existe pas? Peu de chose, et nos esprits bien inoccupés languiraient si les fables, les méprises, les abstractions, les croyances et les monstres, les hypothèses et les prétendus problèmes de la metaphysique ne peuplaient d'êtres et d'images sans objets nos profondeurs et nos ténèbres naturelles. Les mythes sont les âmes de nos actions et de nos amours. Nous ne pouvons agir qu'en nous mouvant vers un fantôme. Nous ne pouvons aimer que ce que nous créons" (966–67). "L'idée de la mort est le ressort des lois, la mère des religions, l'agent secret ou terriblement manifeste de la politique, l'excitant essentiel de la gloire et des grandes amours,—l'origine d'une grande quantité de recherches et de méditations. Parmi les produits les plus étranges de l'irritation de l'esprit humain par cette idée (ou plutôt par ce besoin d'idée que nous impose la constatation de la mort des autres), figure l'antique croyance que les morts ne sont pas morts, ou ne sont pas tout à fait morts" (958–59).

17. *Ibid.*, 82–83.

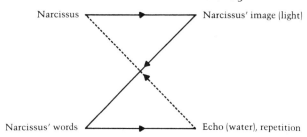

If we compare this spatial allegory of perception with the more temporal, historical one that Tate found in the story of Aeneas, we can see just how the two poets' visions overlap: in the symbolic discourse of water, the sea that Aeneas crossed to reach Rome and the liquid reflection of Narcissus that was to be his Echo.

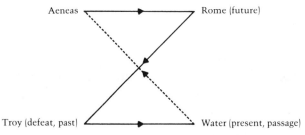

We might expect to find the same transposition from a spatial to a temporal allegory in "Ode to the Confederate Dead." What we find is rather more complex than that: a spatial metaphor for Aeneas' temporal allegory of the South's burden of flight from the past and defeat. Narcissus, Aeneas, the cemetery—space, time, back to space again—create an opposition as fallacious as any. Space and time are only allegories of each other.

In the landscape of the "Ode" we find all of the thematic elements of Valéry's "Cimetière" except the sea: tombstones, the "inexhaustible bodies that are not / Dead, but feed the grass row after rich row," trees and sky and all the trappings of nature, and Zeno's gloss on it all, with the addendum of Parmenides, whose philosophy described nature as Valéry had, as an immense, depthless immobility against which tensions exhaust themselves, a depthless space no arrow's flight can plumb. And finally, there is the worm, the ver(s) of Valéry's cimetière,

here incarnated as the serpent of Valéry's poem "Le Serpent."
And if the sea has been omitted, repressed, it oozes from every
fissure, from every line etched in the stones.

> The brute curiosity of an angel's stare
> Turns you, like them, to stone,
> Transforms the heaving air
> Till plunged to a heavier world below
> You shift your sea-space blindly
> Heaving, turning like the blind crab.

Here the 'flood' of Zeno and Parmenides, the devouring, dis-
solving depthlessness of sea, is scattered, squelched, and occulted in synecdoches: slabs, "the cold pool left by the mounting
flood."[18]

The tombstones are smooth, reflective, catching the light like
petrified water but not reflecting images, only words: names,
dates, epitaphs, angels. The words, like the sculpted angels, are
ossifications of death, turning "you, like them, to stone," raising
the 'ocean' around us. The sea has coagulated here like blood
and assumed the viscosity of solid matter.

> Now the salt of their blood
> Stiffens the saltier oblivion of the sea,
> Seals the malignant purity of the flood,
> What shall we who count our days and bow
> Our heads with a commemorial woe
> In the ribboned coats of grim felicity,
> What shall we say of the bones, unclean,
> Whose verdurous anonymity will grow?
> The ragged arms, the ragged heads and eyes
> Lost in these acres of the insane green?

Such is the Narcissus landscape after the death of Narcissus and
his reenfleshment as Aeneas, lover turned warrior, striver after
self become simply striver. Narcissus and Aeneas have *defeat* in
common. The narrator of the poem is visiting the ruined scene
of that defeat—the scene of Narcissus' demise, Aeneas' rout

18. Tate, *Collected Poems*, 20–23.

and flight, Narcissus' allegorization at death in Echo's words,
Aeneas' flight. The mimesis of the poem, in its allegorical uncertainty, reflects both. The "twilight uncertainty of an animal, / Those midnight restitutions of the blood . . . the sudden
call, the rage," could be the lovers or the warrior's lust. "The
cold pool left by the mounting flood" could be semen or blood.

> You know who have waited by the wall
> The twilight certainty of an animal,
> Those midnight restitutions of the blood
> You know—the immitigable pines, the smoky frieze
> Of the sky, the sudden call: you know the rage,
> The cold pool left by the mounting flood,
> Of muted Zeno and Parmenides.
> You who have waited for the angry resolution
> Of those desires that should be yours tomorrow,
> You know the unimportant shrift of death
> And praise the vision
> And praise the arrogant circumstance
> Of those who fall
> Rank upon rank, hurried beyond decision—
> Here by the sagging gate, stopped by the wall.[19]

It is surely, revisited, the primal scene of the dialogue between
France and the South, Tate and Valéry, Valéry and Poe, Poe and
Tate. It is a landscape in which Poe would have found himself
perfectly at home. The thematic topography, as well as the
verse—the scoring, soughing, pounding alliteration of the r's and
s's and d's, breaking like an acid surf on the lips—and the maca-
bre vocabulary are Poe's.

> You hear the shout, the crazy hemlocks point
> With troubled fingers to the silence which
> Smothers you, a mummy, in time.
>   The hound bitch
> Toothless and dying, in a musty cellar
> Hears the wind only.[20]

19. Ibid.
20. Ibid.

But unlike in "The Raven," they are tempered by a restraint that
Tate had learned in large part from the French, from Valéry's
control and economy of form.[21]

The vocabulary of the poem is calculatedly ironic, displacing
time into space, narrative into symbol, diachrony into synchrony. Autumn is a "plot" (a piece of ground, a place, as well as
a narration) that grows recollected time from dead matter.

> Autumn is desolation in the plot
> Of a thousand acres where these memories grow
> From the inexhaustible bodies that are not
> Dead, but feed on the grass row after rich row.

And the narrative stance of the poem doubts any distinction
between narcissism and heroism, between "the patient
curse / That stones the eyes," the soldier's curse on defeat,
and Narcissus' self-execution.

> Stonewall, Stonewall, and the sunken fields of hemp,
> Shiloh, Antietam, Malvern Hill, Bull Run.
> Lost in that orient of the thick-and-fast
> You will curse the setting sun.
> . . . .
> And in between the ends of distraction
> Waits mute speculation, the patient curse
> That stones the eyes, or like the jaguar leaps
> For his own image in a jungle pool, his victim.

The end of both courses is defeat, death, whether in love or war.
Can knowing that leave any advantage to one or the other?
Can it even sustain the distinction between them?

> What shall we say who have knowledge
> Carried to the heart? Shall we take the act
> To the grave? Shall we, more hopeful, set up the grave
> In the house? The ravenous grave?

Shall the defeated South make an idol of its own defeat and
live by that morbid gospel, or embrace it yet more fervently? For

21. Tate, *Memoirs and Opinions*, 123–39, especially 131–32.

the moment, the poem's echo answers, it shall wallow in the drunkenness of its despairing conundrum, loss.

> The gentle serpent, green in the mulberry bush,
> Riots with his tongue through the hush—
> Sentinel of the grave who counts us all![22]

The serpent, here stripped of the pretense to philosophy or method that Valéry had given it in "Le Serpent," is a simile of the worm, itself a metonym of death, the deep water on which life's light plays out, and so another avatar of Echo: all gone but the riot of voice, inarticulate hissing, repeating the hush of death, the tautology of loss that knows itself to be loss and cannot help it.[23] This becomes more apparent in the French translation.

> Le doux serpent, *vert* dans le buisson de mûres,
> S'ébaudit avec sa langue à travers le silence,
> Sentinelle de la tombe qui fait notre compte à tous! [emphasis
>   mine][24]

Green in French establishes a phonemic equivocation with *ver(s)*, 'worm' and 'verse'. And *langue*, more readily than the English *tongue* it translates, means 'language' as well. So that if we had the French read to us and had to translate it back into English, we might very well get: "The gentle serpent, verse in the mulberry bush, / Frolics with his language through the silence." Tate's poem is an allegory of a culture compelled to an obsession with the past, suspended in the negativity of the present between the two nights of past and future, and this is an allegory of perception (Heideggerian perception), of reading, and of Tate's 'translation' of Valéry's allegory of these.[25]

That we are dealing with allegory, not mimesis, is more apparent in the French translation of the poem, "Ode aux Morts Con-

22. Tate, *Collected Poems*, 20–23.

23. Tate, *Memoirs and Opinions*, 137–38.

24. Tate, *Collected Poems*, 211–14. The translation, by Jacques and Raïssa Maritain, first appeared in *Le Figaro*, May 24, 1952.

25. Martin Heidegger, *Being and Time*, trans. John Macquarrie and Edward Robinson (New York, 1962).

fédérés." For a Frenchman, not likely to assume a historical referent, the title announces an allegorical tone: ode to the confederated dead, to the notion of death. To the French reader, what are Shiloh, Antietam, Malvern Hill, Bull Run? Who is Stonewall? They are only names yielded by the headstones, names given to the unimportant shrift of death. Death's characteristic figure is sure to be catachresis, as that of Valéry's poem was too—anonymous bones, the screech owl's lyric seeding the mind, the furious murmur of chivalry, the whispering of leaves, the rioting serpent, seasonal eternity, casual sacrament, leaves soughing rumours, headstones staring (reminiscent of Valéry's palpitating pines, noon the just, the scintillation which sows disdain and the devouring gulf, the sails which peck, in "Le Cimetière Marin"). Catachresis is an exaggerated metalepsis, more violently equivocal and at once integrative and dispersive. The poem is lost, scattered, in its language, its reading, its Echo(es). Here is a schematic rendering of the poem:

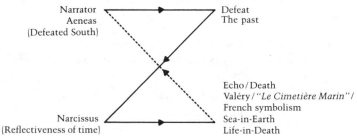

Tate chose to include only six translations in his *Collected Poems*, and though none of these was of Valéry, two were of Baudelaire. The use of catachresis in "Une Charogne" and "Correspondances" must have been part of what drew him to them. "Correspondances" does not, as many have read it, assert a totality of man and nature realized by the senses and expressed by the symbol. Its figural structure (catachresis) describes a loss of man and nature in the senses, the 'defeat' of knowledge and totalization occasioned by the play of sensual codes that is perception: nature is a temple, pillars are alive, and forests are symbols that look back at man with familiarity, emitting *confused* words. The much vaunted 'unity' here is founded on confusion, and a specifically linguistic confusion. It is through association—projection, a sensual rhetoric of hyperbolic simile (soft oboes, singing incense, smells fresh like a baby's flesh to the touch), entropic displacement from one sensual code to the next—that the 'mind and the senses' make sense. The unity is in the tautology of perception, the senses perceiving each other and the mind articulating nature to itself in terms of its own perceptual codes.

"Une Charogne" is built around the central allegorical catachresis of a living corpse.

> Les mouches bourdonnaient sur ce ventre putride,
>> D'où sortaient de noirs bataillons
> De larves, qui coulaient comme un épais liquide
>> Le long de ces vivants haillons.
>
> Tout cela descendait, montait comme une vague,
>> Ou s'élancait en pétillant;
> On eût dit que le corps, enflé d'un souffle vague,
>> Vivait en se multipliant,
>
> Et ce monde rendait une étrange musique,
>> Comme l'eau courante et le vent,
> Ou le grain qu'un vanneur d'un mouvement rythmique
>> Agite et tourne dans son van.[26]

Tate's version of these stanzas gives a sense of his paradoxical achievement in translating the two poems by Baudelaire.

> The flies swarmed on the putrid vulva, then
>> A black tumbling rout would seethe
> Of maggots, thick like a torrent in a glen,
>> Over those rags that lived and seemed to breathe.
>
> They darted down and rose up like a wave
>> Or buzzed impetuously as before;
> One would have thought the corpse was held a slave
>> To living by the life it bore!

---

26. Baudelaire, *Oeuvres complètes*, 58.

> This world had music, its own swift emotion
> Like water and the wind running,
> Or corn that a winnower in rhythmic motion
> Fans with fiery cunning.

And finally: "all forms receded . . . / Into a perfect art!"[27] Life
is not death and death is not life, but neither is entirely itself
either. Time works on the body a rhetoric of the most violent
catachresis, making beauty into carrion and carrion into a kind
of beauty: "Et le ciel regardait la carcasse superbe / Comme une
fleur s'épanouir" ("And the sky watched the superb car-
cass / Bloom like a flower"). The overcharged senses swoon before filth as before beauty: "La puanteur était si forte, que sur
l'herbe / Vous crûtes vous evanouir" ("The stench was so powerful that on the grass / You thought you would faint").[28]

Tate's translations not only retain most of the figural language
of the originals, a feat in itself, but succeed as poems on their
own. They are unmistakably poems by Allen Tate, however. To
imbibe the French precursor and distill him more or less whole
into Tate's own idiom was prerequisite, undoubtedly, to Tate's
emergence as a strong poet from under the "Covering Cherub"
of French symbolism.[29] Succeeding because they hew closely to
the figural language of the originals, the translations are not acts
of misprision themselves, but they are rehearsals for the misprision of Tate's mature poetry.

He discovered in Baudelaire, as in Valéry, the poetics of loss
and its practice as catachresis, but he also alchemized from
them an English voice capable of executing that poetic. In his
version of "Correspondances," for instance, composed in 1925,
there are suggestions of the powerful alliterative rhythms of the
later "Ode": "a unity umbrageous and infinite, / Vast as the
night stupendously moonlit, / All smells and colors and sounds

27. Tate, *Collected Poems*, 165–66.
28. Baudelaire, *Oeuvres complètes*, 58.
29. William Blake's "Covering Cherub" has entered critical discourse through
the mediation of Harold Bloom. See Bloom, *The Anxiety of Influence* (New York,
1973), 24, and Tate, *Memoirs and Opinions*, 195–207.

correspond," and "transports of the spirit and the sense!" By comparison the French translates: "une ténébreuse et profonde unité, / Vaste comme la nuit et comme la clarté, / Les parfums, les couleurs et les sons se répondent," and "les transports de l'esprit et des sens!"[30] The English has a dirgelike majesty that depends on the rhythm of stress. Even when, as in the last line, the alliteration of the French (the s's, d's, and r's) is reproduced, it has an entirely different character on account of the percussiveness, absent in the French. Baudelaire's language susurrates, as a slithering whisper in the ear, as hypnotic, drug-induced percolation, while Tate's intones, perorates percussively. To hear the full effect of the latter, we have to skip three years to "A Carrion," or two to the "Ode."

> The sun bore down upon this rottenness
>> As if to roast it with gold fire,
> And render back to nature her own largeness
>> A hundredfold of her desire

Where else would one look for the source of "The hound bitch / Toothless and dying" in the "Ode" but in Baudelaire.

> Behind the rocks a restless bitch looked on
>> Regarding us with jealous eyes,
> Waiting to tear from the livid skeleton
>> Her loosed morsel quick with flies.

In the Baudelaire poem, the hound devours death; in the "Ode," the consequence of that act is articulated, the consequence of having known "the twilight certainty of an animal," of having tasted knowledge. The consequence is defeat, to hear the wind only. "Dazed by the wind, only the wind / The leaves flying, plunge." That sinuous rustle, slithering *chuchotement*, riot of the serpent/verse's *langue*, is French, for Tate the *lingua franca* of pure alterity, Death.

Perhaps now is the time to state an implication first touched

---

30. Baudelaire, *Oeuvres complètes*, 46.

upon in our encounter with Mallarmé's translation of his own "Tombeau d'Edgar Poe" into English. To make a distinction between an author's translation and someone else's translation of him is to assume, emanating from the mythic origin of the text called 'author', a power of subjectivity, a continuity of intention, enunciation, and interpretation in which language is nothing but a transparent medium, a tool that neither limits, nor defines, nor much affects its use. Our readings do not support such a view. They imply rather that subjectivity, the agent of intent and fabulous origin of the text, is nothing but a myth that is conditioned by and dependent on language, not the other way around. Whether a writer is translated or is translating, the same dialectic of words is at work. The translator is as subordinate to the dialectic, as lost in it, as what he translates. Subjectivity, the 'author' or the 'reader', is nothing but another sort of text. In any instance of translation—whether from one language to another, or from one sort of text, as a written, printed one, into the text that is a reader's or a writer's 'subjectivity'—signification occurs as an overdetermination of each text by the other text(s), in which no text can properly be said to take precedence or to set the terms by which it 'means'. It can only mean by being dependent on other texts. That is as true of author as of reader, of reader as of text. Such a theory by no means implies that what someone writes is not conditioned by its author. Every text, whether a reader, writer, or literal printed page, is different. Otherwise, signification could not occur at all. It is the ratio of resemblance and difference between both kinds of text and among authors, texts, and readers that determines any particular instance of overdetermination and signification. Given the vast possibilities for discrepancy, the variety of permutations is endless.

V. FAULKNER AND
SYMBOLISM

There is no single work in Faulkner's opus that could permit an
approach such as that to Tate's "Ode," Verlaine's "Nevermore"
poems, Rimbaud's "Chant de Guerre Parisien," or Poe's "Raven."
My aim here is to point out the ways in which the dialectic with
French, the phenomenon of translatedness, may illuminate
Faulkner's opus. Because of the size of that opus, even the size of
those parts of it that might be taken as representative, my discussion must appear less than definitive. What cannot be over-
looked here is that my subject is not the body of work called
'Faulkner', but the phenomenon of translatedness in which that
body of work is submerged. Nowhere else herein will the necessary discrepancy between the two seem so glaring, or even dis-
turbing; but it is a crucial point to be considered, not in spite of
its necessary shortcomings, but on account of them. Faulkner,
no less than other writers invoked, is only contingent to my
study, as a symptom of the phenomenon under discussion, and
not *the* "thing-in-itself," or even *a* "thing-in-itself."[1]

My premise here is that just as Poe himself had been for symbolism, so symbolism became the heterogenous Other for subsequent southern writing. Many readers of Faulkner who know of
the success of his prose works in France do not know that some
of his earliest efforts were in poetry and that he, too, suckled at
the bosom of French. His translations of Verlaine and his emula-
tions of Mallarmé (and even Villon, as much a practitioner of
the poetics of loss as any) are not, however, nearly so strong as
Tate's. It is clear that Faulkner had absorbed the rhetoric of
those poets. He understood as well as anyone Verlaine's use of

1. Two very valuable studies applying recent continental (especially Lacanian)
theory to Faulkner are John T. Irwin, *Doubling and Incest/Repetition and
Revenge: A Speculative Reading of Faulkner* (Baltimore, 1975) and André
Bleikasten, *The Most Splendid Failure: Faulkner's "The Sound and the Fury"*
(Bloomington, 1976). I refer the reader who wishes more direct, comprehensive
treatment to these works.

painting as an object for poetry in order to subvert the reader's recourse to mimesis, and he understood Mallarmé's autistic allegories of form. He could understand these things in English, but he could not use them to make a poetic voice for himself. Even when not a translation but merely an allusion to the precursor poem, Faulkner's poetry presents a weak comparison with his prose. What he learned from the French poets is in his prose, however, and bears closer examination.

What Faulkner found in Verlaine and Mallarmé was the tautological relation of form and referent, subject and object, language and vision, the verbal and the plastic arts, the past and the present, the real and the representation of the real. Verlaine's poetic enterprise in *Fêtes Galantes* was to make poems out of the phantasmagorical whimsy of late eighteenth-century boudoir embellishments. Of those works Diderot, ferocious (but ironic) realist in the tradition of Vitruvius, could say only, "Always small paintings, small ideas, frivolous compositions, fit for the boudoir of a little mistress . . . or other personages without manners and of a petty taste." Diderot meant that the paintings were grotesque. Of one such artist Diderot could write only that "he has not for an instant seen nature . . . he is without taste."[2] The plastic arts aimed at no appearance of continuity—through rep-

2. Denis Diderot, *Oeuvres esthétiques*, ed. P. Vernière (Paris, 1968): "Toujours petits tableaux, petites idées, compositions frivoles, propres au boudoir d'une petite maitresse . . . ou autres personnages sans moeurs et d'un petit goût" (468). The painter in question is Boucher, who inspired Diderot to frenzies of moral indignation. "Je ne sais que dire de cet homme-ci. La dégradation du goût, de la couleur, de la composition, des caractères, de l'expression, du dessin, a suivi pas à pas la dépravation des moeurs. Que voulez-vous que l'artiste jette sur la toile? Ce qu'il a dans l'imagination, et que peut avoir dans l'imagination un homme qui passe sa vie avec les prostituées du plus bas étage?" (453–54). Of Baudouin's "Le Coucher de la Meriée," he wrote: "Monsieur Baudouin, faites-moi le plaisir de me dire en quel lieu du monde cette scène s'est passée? Certes, ce n'est pas en France" (470). Such grotesquerie was to Diderot "un mélange inexplicable de corruption et de barbarie" (472). "Tout ce qui prêche aux hommes la dépravation est fait pour être détruit; et d'autant plus sûrement détruit, que l'ouvrage sera plus parfait" (471).
A perfection of form unanchored in reality is an incitement to transgression against the conventions which constitute that reality. An art that does not assume a totalized and incontrovertible reality will lead to behavioral catachresis. Loss in art, the defeat of the real, will beget loss, the defeat of the real, in more

resentation, subjectivity, or well-mannered phenomenology—of artifice with nature, subject with object. Instead, the aesthetic of naughty, bedroom frivolity fuses representation and perception with, as Valéry put it, "that which does not exist"—myth, imagination, daydream. Art can be neither assimilated to nature nor divorced from it. If artistic images are self-referential, refer only to other artistic or imaginary images, what sort of images might not be? What about the ones cast on our retinas?

Baudelaire, before the *Fêtes Galantes* appeared in print, had written in "L'Oeuvre et la Vie d'Eugène Delacroix" of art as translation, not only within the verbal arts or the plastic arts but between them. The idea of translation between the two arts is implicit in his homage to Delacroix and his repetitive use of the word *traduire*. "It is, for the rest," he wrote, "a diagnosis of the mental state of our century that the arts aspire, if not to supplement each other, at least to lend themselves, reciprocally, new forces."[3] Great art, said Baudelaire, is a machine, and the greatest art is the machine that is made in the way most likely to "leave an eternal trace in the human memory" ("faites de la manière la plus propre à laisser une trace éternelle dans la mémoire humaine"). Thus he speaks of Delacroix's as an art of *mnémotechnie*. He says further that it translates "l'invisible . . . l'impalpable . . . c'est le rêve, c'est les nerfs, c'est l'*âme*" ["it's the dream, it's the nerves, it's the soul"].[4] So that great art is a *machine à traduire*, a *machine mnémotechnique*—an engine

---

immediate and palpable ways. "Je ne puis me dissimuler qu'un mauvais livre, une estampe malhonnête que le hasard offrirait à ma fille, suffirait pour la faire rêver et la perdre" (472). The grotesque art is criticized, on supposedly aesthetic grounds, for not respecting the only reality there is; yet it is dangerous precisely because it threatens the very notion of such a reality. If it were as awful as Diderot says, in a purely aesthetic sense, it would not be dangerous. It can only be threatening if it is aesthetically effective. Of course Diderot admits this, while he also contradicts it.

3. Baudelaire, *Oeuvres complètes*: "C'est du reste, un des diagnostics de l'état spirituel de notre siècle que les arts aspirent, sinon à se suppléer l'un l'autre, du moins à se prêter réciproquement des forces nouvelles" (531). I am indebted to my former colleague Timothy Raser for insights into Baudelaire's concept of translation applied to the visual arts. See Raser, ""Baudelaire's Art Criticism" (Ph.D. dissertation, Yale University, 1982.)

4. Baudelaire, *Oeuvres complètes*, 530–31.

that, connected to a suitable power source (a reader), translates impalpable nothingness, the sensual and temporal nullity of the soul (*l'âme*), into a temporal and sensual trace. This *machine à traduction* must not partake of such shoddy mechanics as realism. "Never will Eugene Delacroix, despite his admiration for the ardent phenomena of life, be confused with that tomb of artists and vulgar literary hacks whose myopic intelligence takes shelter behind the vague and obscure word *realism*."[5]

Realism is aesthetic hypocrisy, a meaningless truism; it ascribes a primacy to nature, to a reality from which it excludes itself. Why bother with art if it is no more than an imitation of something superior to which there is direct access? The significance of referential realism is its 'bankruptcy'. Nature is nothing more than art before it is art. It is a phone book, a catalog, a dictionary—an ecphrasis of itself from which art may be extracted by an act of vehement, fervent, translation.[6]

> Nature is no more than a dictionary, he [Delacroix] repeated frequently. To fully understand the extent of meaning implied in this sentence, it is necessary to imagine the numerous and ordinary uses of the dictionary. One looks there for the meanings of words, the generation of words, the etymology of words, finally one extracts from it all of the elements which compose a sentence or a story; but no one has ever considered the dictionary as a composition, in the poetic sense of the word. The painters who obey the imagination look in their dictionary for those elements which accommodate their conception; still, adjusting them with a certain art, they give them an entirely new physiognomy. Those who have no imagination copy the dictionary. From this results a very great vice, the vice of banality, which is more particularly suited to those among the painters whom their specialty brings closer to so-called inanimate nature, for example, landscape painters, who generally consider it a triumph not to show their personality. By dint of contemplating and copying, they forget to feel and to think.

5. *Ibid.*: "Jamais Eugène Delacroix, malgré son admiration pour les phénomènes ardents de la vie, ne sera confondu parmi cette tourbe d'artistes et de littérateurs vulgaires dont l'intelligence myope s'abrite derrière le mot vague et obscur de réalisme" (532).

6. *Ibid.*, 531.

> For this great painter [Delacroix], all the parts of art, of which
> one takes this, the other that as the principal part, were, are, I
> mean to say, no more than the very humble servants of a unique
> and superior faculty. If a very clear execution is necessary, it is in
> order that the dream be very clearly translated; if it is very rapid,
> it is so that nothing is lost of the extraordinary impression which
> accompanied the conception; that the artist's attention should
> bear even on the material cleanliness of his tools is conceivable
> without any trouble, given the necessity that every precaution be
> taken to render execution agile and decisive.[7]

There is no such thing as artistic realism, since realism not
only segregates art from reality but consigns it to a status of
dependence and inferiority. It conceives an impossible and ludicrous task for itself: to 'copy' an endless dictionary. That is not
art. Nor is it more faithful to the real than to art. Art may
resemble nature more or less as it chooses, may translate very
loosely or with great fidelity to details of resemblance, but in
either case it cannot duplicate nature—first, because of the un-
boundedness and flux of nature; second, because what we call

7. *Ibid.*: "La nature n'est qu'un dictionnaire, répétait-il fréquemment. Pour
bien comprendre l'étendue du sens impliqué dans cette phrase, il faut se figurer
les usages ordinaires et nombreux du dictionnaire. On y cherche le sens des
mots, la génération des mots, l'étymologie des mots, enfin on en extrait tous les
éléments qui composent une phrase ou un récit; mais personne n'a jamais con-
sidéré le dictionnaire comme une *composition*, dans le sens poétique du mot.
Les peintres qui obéissent à l'imagination cherchent dans leur dictionnaire les
éléments qui s'accommodent à leur conception; encore, en les ajustant avec un
certain art, leur donnent-ils une physionomie toute nouvelle. Ceux qui n'ont pas
d'imagination copient le dictionnaire. Il en résulte un très-grand vice, le vice de
la banalité, qui est plus particulièrement propre à ceux d'entre les peintres que
leur spécialité rapproche davantage de la nature dite inanimée, par exemple
les paysagistes, qui considèrent généralement comme un triomphe de ne pas
montrer leur personnalité. A force de contempler et de copier, ils oublient de
sentir et de penser.

"Pour ce grand peintre, toutes les parties de l'art, dont l'un prend celle-ci,
l'autre celle-la pour la principale, n'étaient, ne sont, veux-je dire, que les très-
humbles servantes d'une faculté unique et supérieure. Si une exécution très-
nette est nécessaire, c'est pour que le rêve soit très nettement traduit; qu'elle soit
très-rapide, c'est pour que rien ne se perde de l'impression extraordinaire qui
accompagnait la conception; que l'attention de l'artiste se porte même sur la
propreté matérielle des outils, cela se conçoit sans peine, toutes les précautions
devant être prises pour rendre l'exécution agile et décisive" (532).

nature is already a copy of itself, a sensual ecphrasis. In the sense in which realism conceives it, nature is a lost original of which only simulacra remain, duplicates whose fidelity we are in no position to determine.[8] Art is not a thing, but a machine, and what it does is translate and incite to translation. "A well drawn figure penetrates you with a pleasure entirely foreign to the subject. Voluptuous or terrible, this figure owes its charm solely to the arabesque which it cuts in space. The limbs of a martyr being flayed, the body of a swooned nymph, if they are knowledgeably drawn, involve a kind of pleasure in the elements of which the subject counts for nothing; if it is otherwise for you I will be forced to think that you are either an executioner or a libertine."[9]

Every artist, in every medium, demands to be translated. Of course, translating entails misconstrual. It is misprision—the suscitation of a fervent, vehement, disfiguring imagination, which is derangement. We are not interested in a machine for itself, but for what it does. A work of art, like a machine ("destiné à transformer l'énergie et à utiliser cette énergie" ["destined to transform energy and to use that energy"]), but to what end? The transformation of more energy? Perhaps rather like a trope, from the Greek *trepein*, 'to turn': "système de corps transformant un travail en un autre" ["a system of bodies transforming one work into another"]), like an alchemical retort, an ongoing trace of substitution, translation, misprision, disfiguration, refiguration. Art is necessarily its own loss.[10] In ecphrasis, the translation of plastic art into verbal art, Baudelaire, as well as Verlaine, found another symbolic expression of that principle.[11]

8. *Ibid.*, 532–33, 538.
9. *Ibid.*: "Une figure bien dessinée vous pénètre d'un plaisir tout à fait étranger au sujet. Voluptueuse ou terrible, cette figure ne doit son charme qu'à l'arabesque qu'elle découpe dans l'espace. Les membres d'un martyr qu'on écorche, le corps d'une nymphe pâmée, s'ils sont savamment dessinés, comportent un genre de plaisir dans les éléments duquel le sujet n'entre pour rien; si pour vous il en est autrement, je serai forcé de croire que vous êtes un bourreau ou un libertin" (534). This is the very sort of 'perfection' which Diderot thought so offensive and yet so dangerous because of its seductiveness.
10. *Petit Robert* (Paris, 1976), 1018.
11. *Ekphrasis* is the term used by classical Greek rhetoricians to describe this sort of descriptive language. See Michel Beaujour, "Some Paradoxes of Descrip-

Verlaine's poems, taking as their object a group of eighteenth-century paintings, no more 'signify' those paintings than the eighteenth century 'explains' the nineteenth. Verlaine's texts use the symbolic language of plastic art (ecphrasis) to articulate a nineteenth-century (symbolic) poeticity.

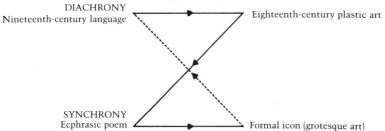

The need of the visual arts to be translated into words suggests Lacan's insistence on the primacy of the symbolic over the imaginary, imagistic, specular order. The symbolic is the only order, according to Lacan, in which overdetermination can occur. And yet Baudelaire speaks of engravers as effective translators. Indeed, could not images behave like language, like signs, as easily as words? Are not words images as well as sounds? Baudelaire's discussion of Delacroix seems to question the absoluteness of Lacan's distinction, insofar as it is grounded in a difference between word and image. Language and image are not distinct from one another at all, as the poetic use of ecphrasis suggests. Nor is perception, the 'real', as Lacan calls it, distinct from the imaginary or the symbolic. What is represented by Lacan's dialectical model of subjectivity is an arbitrary differentiation of the self from its conception of itself (the 'imaginary') and its conception of the other, and this differentiation can only occur on the model of language, of the sign, with its three parts (signifier, signified, and referent) inextricably involved.[12] So the imaginary and the symbolic are involved in a mutual contamination. All perception is structured like language, differentially. The symbolic is simply the level on which

tion," in *Towards a Theory of Description*, Yale French Studies No. 61 (1981), 27–59. See also Michael Riffaterre, "Descriptive Imagery," in *Towards a Theory of Description*, Yale French Studies No. 61 (1981), 107–25.

12. See Lacan, *Ecrits*, I, 249–89.

this self-consciousness of perception-as-language occurs. It is the axis of translation on which the self knows itself through an arbitrary and mistaken transposition into an other language. It is thus the only level on which perception can address itself. Perception can only know itself as language, and it can only know itself as language through a violence of arbitrary translation, self-alienation, splitting away from itself, which brings about an overdetermined area, an intersection of real, imaginary, and symbolic, in which subjectivity can seem to occur through, and as, a *machine à traduire*. As we have seen, either history, another language, or now visual art can with equal efficacity be the medium of the splitting by which understanding occurs.

Verlaine's is a poetry of static representation, a mimesis of stillness, not of action. What is described by the understated descriptiveness (ecphrasis) of the language, which the reader must apprehend as narration in the diachronic act of reading, is the stasis of a picture, the frozen past in the flux of the present. "Fantoches" and "Clair de Lune," both exemplary of such descriptiveness, were 'imitated' by Faulkner, to use Robert Lowell's euphemism for self-exemption from fidelity to an original. And yet, allowing himself those liberties did not advance the budding novelist's poetic idiom in the least. His versions of Verlaine reflect an appreciation for the reflexive referentiality of the poems, the way in which the restrained music of the language suggests the pastel shades alluded to, the same way in which Baudelaire's oboes 'sound' soft. Faulkner opted to respect the form of these verses, their rhyme scheme and even, to the extent possible, the number of syllables in each line. That, of course, was a doomed enterprise; English words, encompassing a greater scale of sounds, do not lend themselves to rhyme as French ones will, and they depend on specific accentuation of syllables within words, unlike French, which falls freely into syllabic, but not into accentual, schemes. What Faulkner discovered was that if French is taken away from Verlaine, all that is left are some vapidly platitudinous descriptions in rhyme which might have been written by any slightly precocious university sophomore coed in maudlin transports of first love. That Faulkner knew this is more or less clear in his fidelity to the form of the poems, and his regression, at the end of "Fantoches," to French—"la lune ne garde aucune rancune."[13] The line does not appear in the French namesake, underscoring the futility of Faulkner's undertaking. The figure is a nonsensical catachresis, determined by nothing so much as the musicality of the /y/ sound, which does not exist in English. The same gesture of frustration and futility appears at the end of "Une Ballade des Femmes Perdues," not a translation of Villon but a variation on a theme of his. What is just as clear as his appreciation of the poems' untranslatability is the inability of Faulkner, unlike Tate, to translate his insightful reading of the French into a voice of his own.

One of the first pieces to appear in a journal of national prominence, Faulkner's "L'Après-midi d'un Faune" suggests a similar, shrewd gleaning of Mallarmé, and though one of Faulkner's better poems, it shows no obvious sign of what was to come from him in prose. It is another attempt to write French, syllabic, rhymed verse patterns in English and is perhaps as successful as the form can be in such an inhospitable language. The problem Faulkner's poem poses is purloined from Poe via Mallarmé—the chiasmus of subjectivity. More immediately, how and where do we locate subject and object of a poem? Mallarmé's "L'Après-midi d'un Faune," through a series of metaphors, metonymies, and synecdoches—beginning with the allegorical catachresis of a faun, to which could be attached a virtually infinite variety of referents—moves toward a reversal of the structure of subjectivity by which the poem is the 'object' of the poet's 'subjectivity', a chiasmus in which each overdetermines the other. In its narrative progress the poem generates all sorts of figures, each a different allegory of the central chiasmus which is poeticity itself, each as defiant of mimetic interpretation and as grotesque as the first.

The poem's first figures, a faun and nymphs, were also subjects of Verlaine's *Fêtes Galantes* and make of the Mallarmé poem just the kind of self-subverting mimesis, imitation of allegory, that can be found in Verlaine.

13. William Faulkner, *Early Prose and Poetry*, ed. Carvel Collins (Boston, 1962), 54, 57–58. See Verlaine, *Oeuvres complètes*, 107, 114, for the original poems "Clair de Lune" and "Fantoches."

Faun	Nymphs

"Ces nymphs, je veux les perpétuer" ["These nymphs, I wish to perpetuate them"].

Dream	Landscape (trees, water)

"Aimai-je un rêve? / Mon doute, amas de nuit an-cienne, s'achève / En maint rameau subtil, qui, demeuré les vrais / Bois mêmes, prouve, hélas! que bien seul je m'offrais / Pour triomphe la faute idéale de roses" ["Did I love a dream? / My doubt, heap of old night, ends / In many a subtle branch, which remaining the true / Woods themselves, prove, alas! that quite alone I was offering myself / As triumph the false ideal of roses"]. Wouldn't the 'ideal mistake of roses' be the 'error' of poeticity, to which Mallarmé alluded in the famous invocation: "Je dis: une fleur! et . . . musicalement se lève . . . l'absente de tous bouquets" ["I say: a flower! and . . . musically arises . . . that one absent from every bouquet"]. [14]

Narrator	Narrative

"Réflechissons . . . / ou si les femmes dont tu gloses / Figurent un souhait de tes sens fabu-leux! / Faune, l'illusion s'échappe des yeux bleus / Et froids, comme une source en pleurs . . . O bords siciliens d'un calme marecage / Qu'à l'envi de soleils ma vanité saccage, / Tacite sous les fleurs d'étincelles, CONTEZ" ["Let us reflect . . . / or if the women you are glossing / Are figures of a wish of your fabulous senses! / Faun, illu-sion escapes from the eyes blue / And cold, like a foun-tain in tears . . . O sicilian edges of a calm swamp / Which at the behest of suns my vanity pil-lages, / Tacit under flowers of sparks, TELL"] Here the faute idéale of the famous fleur is again alluded to, along with the Narcissus myth: the Faun's vanity 'plundering the pool', in contest with the sun, also reflected and mul-tiplied there. "Moi, de ma rumeur fier, je vais parler long-temps / Des déesses; et par d'idolatres peintures, / A leur ombre enlever encore des ceintures" ["I, proud of my clamor, I shall speak lengthily / Of goddesses; and by some idolatrous paintings / Remove from their shadows yet more belts (emphasis mine)]. Is his vanity 'plunder-ing' his images of the 'goddesses' in the same way it plunders the pool? Surely, just as he, the Faun, figures in his 'clamor', his 'painting', along with those goddesses.

Flute	Music

"Ne murmure point d'eau que ne verse ma flûte / Au bosquet arrosé d'accords . . . Tâche donc, instrument des fuites, o maligne / Syrinx, de refleurir aux lacs ou tu m'attends!" ["Murmurs no water which my flute does not pour / On the wood wet with harmonies . . . Try, then, instrument of flights, o malignant / Syrinx, to bloom again in the lakes where you await me!"] Note the equation of water with sound, sound with flight, flute with flower.

Drinking/Eating	Wine/Fermented grapes

"Ainsi, quand des raisins j'ai sucé la clarté, / Pour ban-nir un regret par ma feinte écarté, / Rieur, j'élève au ciel d'été la grappe vide / Et soufflant dans ses peaux lumi-neuses, avide / D'ivresse, jusqu'au soir je regarde au tra-vers / / O nymphs, regonflons des SOUVENIRS divers" ["Thus, when from the grapes I have sucked the clari-ty, / To banish a regret pushed aside by my feint, / Laughing, I raise to the summer sky the empty bunch / And blowing into its luminous skins, avid / with inebria-tion, until night I look through / / O nymphs, let us re-inflate various MEMORIES"].

Pomegranate	Bursting/Murmuring

"Chaque grenade éclate et d'abeilles murmure" ["Every pomegranate bursts and murmurs with bees"].

Blood	Desire

"Et notre sang, épris de qui le va saisir / Coule pour tout l'essaim éternel du désir" ["And our blood, infatu-ated with whoever is going to seize it, / Flows for all the eternal swarm of desire"].

Vision (light, poem)	Shadow (dark, poet, reader)

"Couple, adieu; je vais voir l'ombre que tu devins" ["Couple, goodbye; I am going to see the shadow you became"]. The couple is addressed in the singular (tu), which is reasonable when we consider that we have been dealing in synecdoche all along. Poet and reader place themselves in this sequence of synecdochical substitu-tions, whether by choice or not. The Faun echoes them and they him.

14. Mallarmé, Oeuvres complètes, 50–53.

The poem is Echo, repeating the poet's final words, but in grief over the loss of him—a grief sympathetic with the poet's own (reflexive) loss but removed from it by the tautological chiasmus to which the poem reduces subject and object, writer and written. Desire desiring desire, narrator narrating himself, dream dreaming dream, music playing music, memory remembering the present, vision seeking sight of shadow, grapes being drunk, pomegranates bee-ing burst and murmured, landscape being dreamt by a part of itself—this is all part of the *ordonnance du livre* and the *disparition élocutoire du poète* to which Mallarmé had cryptically alluded.

> The pure work implies the elocutionary disappearance of the poet, who cedes initiative to the words, by the collision of their mobilized inequality; they light up one another with reciprocal reflections like a virtual track of fire on precious stones, replacing perceptible respiration with the ancient lyric breath or the enthusiastic personal direction of the sentence.
>
> An ordonance of the book is breaking through innately or everywhere, eliminating chance; yet it is necessary, in order to omit the author: now, a subject, fatal, implies among the pieces together such an agreement as to placement in the volume as corresponds. Susceptibility by reason that the cry possesses an echo—motifs of the same play will balance for themselves, poised, at a distance, neither the incoherent sublimeness of the romantic mounting of the page nor that artificial unity, previously measured in the book as a whole. All becomes suspension, fragmentary arrangement with alternation and relativity, concurrent with the total rhythm, which would be the silent poem, in blanks; only *translated*, in a manner, by each pedentive.[15]

15. *Ibid.*: "L'oeuvre pure implique la disparition élocutoire du poète, qui cède l'initiative aux mots, par le heurt de leur inégalité mobilisés; ils s'allument de reflets réciproques comme une virtuelle trainée de feux sur des pierreries, remplaçant la respiration perceptible en l'ancien souffle lyrique ou la direction personnelle enthousiaste de la phrase.

"Une ordonnance du livre de vers poind innée ou partout, élimine le hasard; encore la faut-il, pour omettre l'auteur: or un sujet, fatal, implique, parmi les morceaux ensemble, tel accord quant à la place, dans le volume, qui correspond. Susceptibilité en raison que le cri possède un écho—des motifs de même jeu

Faulkner's "L'Après-midi d'un Faune" preserves the sense of a dissolved subjectivity and is violently figural enough to frustrate recourse to mimetic reading. He has, however, done something that Mallarmé did not do. He wrote his poem in the first person, without placing any sure distance between himself and the *I* of the poem (by making it a faun, for instance). Faulkner's technique tempts us to identify poem and poet, something that Mallarmé's text strictly refuses, though every reader, the most subtle with the least, will do it anyway at some point in his reading.

> I follow through the singing trees
> Her streaming clouded hair and face
> And lascivious dreaming knees.
> Like gleaming water from some place
> Of sleeping streams, or autumn leaves
> ....
> . . . and ere she sleep
> The dusk will take her by some stream
> In silent meadows, dim and deep—
> In dreams of stars and *dreaming dream*.[16] (emphasis mine)

The *she* is another allegorical figure, vague enough and yet concrete enough to generate untold significations, none of them satisfactory. The poem then moves into a nostalgia for some equally vague, oneiric totality: "I have a nameless wish to go / To some far silent midnight noon." The insistence on silence and namelessness would certainly appear to place language outside the bounds of the midnight noon, the place and time of no-time and no-place, in which the hypothetical totality of man and nature was destroyed—"a sound like some great deep bell stroke," the heart of the earth "that broke / For springs before

s'équilibreront, balancés, à distance, ni le sublime incohérent de la mise en page romantique ni cette unité artificielle, jadis, mesurée en bloc au livre. Tout devient suspens, disposition fragmentaire avec alternance et vis-à-vis, concourant au rythme total, lequel serait le poème tu, aux blancs; seulement traduit, en une manière, par chaque pedentif" (366–67).

16. Faulkner, *Early Prose and Poetry*, 39–40.

the world grew old." The last pair of lines is very perplexing. We have a catachresis ascribing a heart to the earth, which breaks. Having a broken heart is a maudlin metaphor for having suffered a loss in love. We cannot doubt that there is some sort of loss and fragmentation (breaking) implied here; it is evident in the way "she" is described, as synecdochical catachresis: lascivious knees, clouded hair and face.

But what sort of springs are they for which this occurred: temporal springs, spatial ones, springs of water? The indeterminacy suggests that the fragmentation and loss being described is identical with a breach between time and space, a gap, however, in which neither is distinct from the other and in which each is contaminated by the other. Once we have posited diachrony and synchrony, paradigm and syntagm, narrative progression and semiotic simultaneity, we cannot grasp either except by way of the other. Water, that which drinks, consumes, dissolves, undoes, is time. Both of them are death—slow death, death as flux, process, death-as-life. Death is only accessible to language as incongruence, catachresis, a violence of figuration and an impasse of communication, an insoluble dilemma. Tate's query remains:

> What shall we say who have knowledge / Carried to the heart?
> Shall we take the act / To the grave? Shall we, more hopeful, set
> up the grave / In the house? The ravenous grave?

The central myth of Faulkner's fiction is the South as Aeneas and Narcissus, lost in contemplation of its own rotting corpse, having carried the act to the grave and somehow survived to set up its grave in the house. Such narratives as *As I Lay Dying* and "A Rose for Emily" delineate the myth with brutal yet ironic indirectness. The latter story is an allegory of this *topos*, ironically equating nuptial and renewal with death.

> A thin, acrid pall as of the tomb seemed to lie everywhere upon
> this room decked and furnished as for a bridal: upon the valance
> curtains of faded rose color, upon the rose-shaded lights, upon the
> dressing table, upon the delicate array of crystal and the man's

toilet things backed with tarnishing silver, silver so tarnished that the monogram was obscured. Among them lay a collar and a tie, as if they had just been removed, which, lifted, left upon the surface a pale crescent in the dust. Upon a chair hung the suit, carefully folded; beneath it the two mute shoes and the discarded socks.

The man himself lay in the bed.

For a long while we just stood there, looking down at the profound and fleshless grin. The body had apparently once lain in the attitude of an embrace, but now the long sleep that outlasts love, that conquers even the grimace of love, had cuckolded him. What was left of him, rotted beneath what was left of the nightshirt, had become inextricable from the bed in which he lay; and upon him and upon the pillow beside him lay that even coating of the patient and biding dust.

Then we noticed that in the second pillow was the indentation of a head. One of us lifted something from it, and leaning forward, that faint and invisible dust dry and acrid in the nostrils, we saw a long strand of iron-gray hair.[17]

It is the ravenous grave, set up in the boudoir. Other works, such as *Sartoris*, are more subtle. Poe's depiction of the hypersensitive, morbid dandy, Roderick Usher, in "The Fall of the House of Usher," is the prototype for such characters as Miss Emily Grierson and Bayard Sartoris.

What to do with the dead self, the defunct subjectivity, to which one clings so ferociously and which is all one has to cling to? How to live with death? How to live in the present, smothered by the burden of the past?

The signboard comes in sight. It is looking out at the road now, because it can wait. New Hope. 3 mi. it will say. New Hope. 3 mi. New Hope. 3 mi. And then the road will begin, curving away into the trees, empty with waiting, saying New Hope three miles.

I heard that my mother is dead. I wish I had time to let her die.

17. William Faulkner, *Selected Short Stories of William Faulkner* (New York, n.d.), 60–61.

I wish I had time to wish I had. It is because in the wild and outraged earth too soon too soon too soon. It's not that I wouldn't and will not it's that it is too soon too soon too soon.

Now it begins to say it. New Hope three miles. New Hope three miles. That's what they mean by the womb of time: the agony and the despair of spreading bones, the hard girdle in which lie the outraged entrails of events.[18]

This narration is characterized by the most radial parabasis coupled with the narrative representation of a character performing ecphrasis of a sign in her own head. The location of the sign, whether by the road or in Dewey Dell's head, whether we are dealing with the sign itself or Dewey Dell's ecphrasis of it, is the object of the narration's ecphrasis—New Hope. 3 mi. or New Hope, three miles. The beginning and ending of the parabasis cannot be specified. It is, then, permanent parabasis, Schlegelian irony.[19]

What is suggested in the preceding passage is the chiasmus of time and space and of inner and outer reality or image (sign); but beyond that, we can expect to stabilize the irony of such a narration only by imposing the most arbitrary sort of interpretive closure, which would not read so much as repress and decapitate. Faulkner's characters are not subjects; they are agglomerations of parabasis, irony, and temporal chiasmus, patchworks of lies. Nor is this falseness reducible to intentionality, a wish to mislead, what Wayne Booth wishfully describes as stable irony.[20] To read a sign saying no more than "New Hope. 3 mi." is to engage in the most vehement misprision, arbitrary association, and overdetermination. There is nothing to heal the aporia of this sign and Dewey Dell's reading of it ("New Hope three miles"), or the reader's reading of the narration's reading of Dewey Dell's reading of it, a sign unlikely to have ever had an actual referent anyway.

18. William Faulkner, *As I Lay Dying* (New York, 1964), 114–15.
19. See Paul de Man, "The Rhetoric of Temporality," in *On Interpretation*, ed. Charles S. Singleton (Baltimore, 1969), 200–201.
20. Wayne Booth, *The Rhetoric of Irony* (Chicago, 1974).

Quentin, who kills himself in *The Sound and the Fury* only after narrating his last living day in the past tense (experiencing the present of it as though past, the moment of the present from the vantage point of closure and otherness), represents, as a figure, an exploration of the act of knowledge carried to the grave. Perception for him is a perpetual parabasis of time and desire, dread and love, and finally lust for closure, embracement of death: "QUENTIN III . . . who loved death above all, who loved only death, loved and lived in a deliberate and almost perverted anticipation of death as a lover loves and deliberately refrains from the waiting willing friendly tender incredible body of his beloved, until he can no longer bear not the refraining but the restraint and so flings, hurls himself, relinquishing, drowning."[21] It would, not surprisingly, take a French critic to understand what Faulkner was about. The roots of interior monologue were, after all, French, pioneered by Mallarmé's friend Edouard Dujardin in *Les lauriers sont coupés* and implicit in the free indirect discourse of Flaubert. Sartre reciphered the old dialectic of loss, in its newest southern avatar, into an expository French in which Faulkner 'became himself' for the world. "*Tel qu'en lui-même enfin.*" The historical, metaphysical terminology of that discourse is surely familiar to us by now.

> The Sartorises bear the heavy burden of two wars, two series of (hi)stories: the war of Secession in which the grandsire Bayard died, the war of 1914 in which John Sartoris died. The (hi)stories appear and disappear, pass from mouth to mouth, and are dragged along in the daily gestures. They are not exactly of the past; rather a super-present. . . . It is with (hi)stories that the heroes in Faulkner forge their destiny: through these careful, beautiful tales, sometimes embellished by several generations, an unnameable Act, buried for years, signals to other Acts, charms them, draws them, as a rod draws lighting. Cunning power of words, of (hi)stories; yet Faulkner does not believe in these incantations: ". . . what had been a hare-brained prank of two heedless and reckless boys had become a gallant and finely tragic focal point to

21. William Faulkner, *The Sound and the Fury* (New York, 1954), 411.

which the history of the race had been raised . . . by two angels
valiantly fallen and strayed, altering the course of human events."

. . . : . . . .

So, here is the man he presents to us and whom he wants us to
adopt: he's Undiscoverable; he can't be seized though his gestures, which are a facade, nor by his (hi)stories, which are false,
nor by his acts, indescribable flashes. And yet, beyond the con-
duct and the words, beyond the empty consciousness, the man
exists, we sense a real drama, a sort of intelligible character which
explains everything. What is this exactly? Defect of race or of
family, Adlerian inferiority complex, repressed libido? Sometimes
this, sometimes that: according to the (hi)stories and the characters; often Faulkner does not tell us. And besides he is not concerned with it: what matters to him is rather the *nature* of this
new being; a nature above all *poetic* and magic, whose contradictions are numerous but veiled. Seized through its psychic manifestations, this "nature" (what other word to give it?) participates
in psychic existence, it is not even precisely the unconscious, for
it seems often that the men it leads can turn around and look at
it. But on the other hand, it is immutable and fixed as an evil
destiny, Faulkner's heroes carry it in them from birth, it is as
obstinate as stone and rock, it is *thing*. A thing-spirit, a solidified
spirit, opaque, behind the consciousness, of shadows whose essence is however, clarity: this is the magical object *par excellence*; Faulkner's creatures are hexed, a stifling atmosphere of
sorcery surrounds them. And this is what I was calling disloyalty:
these hexes are not possible. Not even conceivable. And Faulkner
holds back from making us conceive them: all of his efforts aim
to suggest them.[22]

22. Jean-Paul Sartre, *Critiques littéraires (Situations I)* (Paris, 1947): "Les Sartoris portent le pesant fardeau de deux guerres, de deux séries d'histoires: la
guerre de Secession où mourut l'aieul Bayard, la guerre de 1914 où mourut John
Sartoris. Les histoires paraissent et disparaissent, passent d'une bouche à l'autre,
se traînent avec les gestes quotidiens. Elles ne sont pas tout à fait du passé;
plutôt un sur-présent. . . . C'est avec les histoires que les héros de Faulkner se
forgent leur destin: à travers ces beaux récits soignés, embellis parfois par plusieurs générations, un Acte innommable, enseveli depuis des années, fait signe à
d'autres Actes, les charme, les attire, comme une pointe attire la foudre. Sour-

The characters without coherent selves—living in a present that is remembered and a mythical, fabulous, originary past that is more immediate to the characters than the present—are all fauns become men. In the present they must, as readers of each other, struggle with the conundrum of an impossible yet imperative totality hovering just beyond their faces and words and gestures. "The men whom Faulkner likes, the Negro of *Light in August*, Bayard Sartoris, the father of *Absalom, Absalom*, have secrets; they are silent. The humanism of Faulkner is undoubtedly the only acceptable one: he despises our well-adjusted consciousness, our loquacious consciousnesses of an engineer. . . . He dreams of a total obscurity in the very heart of consciousness, a total obscurity which would make us ourselves, in our-

---

noise puissance des mots, des histoires; pourant Faulkner ne croit pas à ces incantations: ' . . . ce qui n'avait été qu'une folle equipée de deux gamins écervelés et casse-cou, grisés de leur propre jeunesse, était devenu le sommet de bravoure et de tragique beauté jusqu'où deux anges vaillamment égarés et déchus avaient, en modifiant le cours des évènements, . . . haussé l'histoire de la race.'

. . . .

Donc, voilà l'homme qu'il nous présente et qu'il veut nous faire adopter: c'est un Introuvable; on ne peut le saisir ni par ses gestes, qui sont une façade, ni par ses histoires, qui sont fausses, ni par ses actes, fulgurations indescriptibles. Et pourtant, par-delà les conduites et les mots, par-delà la conscience vide, l'homme existe, nous pressentons un drame véritable, une sorte de caractère intelligible qui explique tout. Qu'est-ce au juste? Tare de race ou de famille, complexe adlérien d'infériorité, libido refoulée? Tantôt ceci, tantôt cela: c'est selon les histoires et les personnages; souvent Faulkner ne nous le dit pas. Et d'ailleurs il ne s'en soucie pas beaucoup: ce qui lui importe, c'est plutôt la *nature* de cet être nouveau: nature avant tout *poétique* et magique, dont les contradictions sont nombreuses mais voilées. Saisie à travers des manifestations psychiques, cette 'nature' (quel autre nom lui donner?) participe de l'existence psychique, ce n'est même pas tout à fait de l'inconscient, car il semble souvent que les hommes qu'elle mème peuvent se retourner vers elle et la contempler. Mais d'autre part, elle est immuable et fixe comme un mauvais sort, les héros de Faulkner la portent en eux dès la naissance, elle a l'entêtement de la pierre et du roc, elle est *chose*. Une chose-esprit, un esprit solidifié, opaque, derrière la conscience, des ténèbres dont l'essence est pourtant clarté: voilà l'objet magique par excellence; les créatures de Faulkner sont envoûtées, une étouffante atmosphère de sorcellerie les entoure. Et c'est ce que j'appelais déloyauté: ces envoûtements ne sont pas possibles. Ni même concevables. Aussi Faulkner se garde bien de nous les faire concevoir: tous ses procédés visent à les suggérer" (13–17). The translation of Sartre is my own; the passage cited in the translation is from Faulkner, *Sartoris* (New York, 1979), 9.

selves. Silence. Silence outside of us, silence within us, this is the impossible dream of a puritanical ultra-stoicism."[23]

It took Sartre to point out that Faulkner and Proust were practicing the same aesthetic of being as mourning, present as past, time as loss. Faulkner was able to pursue that aesthetic to a more radical violence of narrative temporality because he did not bear Proust's burden of French classicism. And this is true, as it had been since Poe: the grotesque, be it temporal or spatial, narrative or descriptive, loses much of its excessiveness in French, its character of transgression, the rude specificity that is prerequisite to the achievement of incongruence. The aesthetic violence is more visible in English, but it is easier to bear, easier for the canon to absorb, in French. "Only Faulkner is a lost man and it is because he feels lost that he takes risks, that he goes all the way to the end of his thought. Proust is a classicist and a Frenchman: Frenchmen get lost in the short run and always wind up finding themselves again. Eloquence, the taste for clear ideas, intellectualism, forced Proust to keep at least the appearance of chronology."[24]

At the same time that Sartre glibly translated Faulkner's aes-

23. Sartre, *Critiques littéraires*: "Les hommes qu'aime Faulkner, le nègre de *Lumière d'Août*, Bayard Sartoris, le père dans *Absalon*, ont des secrets; ils se taisent. L'humanisme de Faulkner est sans doute le seul acceptable: il hait nos consciences bien ajustées, nos consciences bavardes d'ingénieurs. Mais ne sait-il pas que ses grandes figures sombres ne sont que des dehors? Est-il dupe de son l'inconscient: il rêve d'une obscurité totale au coeur même de la conscience, d'une obscurité totale que nous ferions nous-mêmes, en nous-mêmes. Le silence. Le silence hors de nous, le silence en nous, c'est le rêve impossible d'un ultra-stoicisme puritain" (16–17).

24. Ibid.: "Seulement Faulkner est un homme perdu et c'est parce qu'il se sent perdu qu'il risque, qu'il va jusqu'au bout de sa pensée. Proust est un classique et un Français: les Français se perdent à la petite semaine et ils finissent toujours par se retrouver. L'éloquence, le goût des idées claires, l'intellectualisme ont imposé à Proust de garder au moins les apparences de la chronologie" (93). Sartre appears to have grossly misunderstood Proust, as so many do, for instance when he says: "je sais, par exemple, que le salut, pour Proust, est dans le temps même, *dans la réapparition intégrale du passé*" [emphasis mine] (91). Nothing could be more foreign to the Proustian metaphysic of time than an "integral reappearance of the past." Such a thing could not possibly occur in Proust's work and certainly does not. André Bleikasten offers a useful critique of Sartre's reading of Faulknerian temporality, in *The Most Splendid Failure*, 121–43.

thetic practice for the French reader—by pointing out to those French readers, of which Sartre was one, the limitations of their smug, classical self-sufficiency, by making them look at themselves from the vantage point of an otherness—he confirmed, as he wished to deny, Faulkner's view of men as crazy quilts of mendacity. Faulkner's model of time exposes the problem of history as one of language. The distinction of past, present, and future is not much help in reading his fiction. Cognition is memory, but memory does not know the truth; it cannot deliver the fabulous origin. Memory does not know how to totalize. All it knows is how to crank out stories, duplicates, translations, ecphrases, of a lost original, with myriads of subplots subject to conscious and unconscious omission, deletion, and revision. The future is nothing but a projected version of the past, a speculation on its outcome as if it had already occurred, ecphrases of the finished picture as it might look. The present and the future are nothing but translations, tropes, turnings, inflections of the past, itself nothing but a catalog of translations perpetually subject to fresh revision and interpretive violence. Temporality is diachronic ecphrasis. There are only two possible ways out of this labyrinth. One is death, temporal totalization. Death most assuredly puts an end to the discrepancies of past and future, the present in which the past and its other reflect one another. The other way is idiocy, Benjy's way, a forgetting of time that only morons and animals can achieve, which criminals, pariahs, and fugitives may sometimes approximate by virtue of their constant flight and virtual rootlessness. It is this possibility of forgetting time that appeals to Sartre and that he interprets as the possibility of freedom. "It is because he has forgotten time that the hunted Negro in *Light in August* suddenly wins his strange and atrocious happiness."[25] Sartre is not, strictly speaking, wrong to see it as such. The question that needs to be asked is, Can freedom in any real sense be coincident with idiocy and persecutedness? Sartre addresses this question in his own way, by asserting that only through the transgression of criminal behav-

25. *Ibid.*: "C'est parce qu'il a oublié le temps que le nègre traqué de *Lumière d'août* gagne tout à coup son étrange et atroce bonheur" (92).

ior and a transgression of the label *criminel*, with the onus implied by it, is freedom achieved. But how much sense does this make, especially when freedom has no positive outcome and does not effectively transgress against the temporality within which it must remain, but rather simply forgets it? What Sartre proposes is a kind of accursed and nihilistic stoicism whose most celebrated exponent in southern literature might be Flannery O'Connor's Misfit. But the Misfit knows that all his transgressions are to no end, not even that of pleasure.[26] We are left with two alternatives, self-execution or lobotomy, neither of which appears to offer much hope of liberation from anything except the wish to be liberated.

The dialectic of Faulknerian subjectivity might look like this:

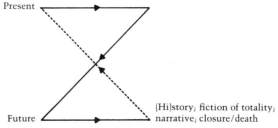

Sartre must finally insist, for his own existential purposes, on a distinction between memory, cognition as memory, present as future past, being as language, and being as action. He must insist on history as history (event, act, deed) and not as story (fiction). He can certainly do this within the bounds of Faulkner's subjective model, but only by suppressing the contamination, the aporia, within the word *histoire*, the synonymity and disjuncture of literary chronology and real chronology.

Faulkner has cast the synchronic dialectic he learned from symbolism, which symbolism had learned from Poe, into the narrative language of diachrony, history. What Faulkner (and Proust, in his more classical fashion) attempted must finally appear as an ecphrasis of time, itself an ecphrasis of diachronic

26. Flannery O'Connor, "A Good Man Is Hard to Find," in *Three by Flannery O'Connor* (New York, 1962), 129–43.

cognition. It is an ecphrasis then of human experience considered as an ongoing series of synchronic ecphrases, a gallery notebook describing all the pictures which, in the past, have been the present: the translation of what we see into what we think, what we think into what we remember, what we remember into what we saw. Ecphrasis is always unfinished because it is reflexive, tautological. "Stability itself," as Montaigne said, "is nothing but a more languid motion."[27] It would be the most simple-minded literalism to treat ecphrasis as referential, as though it did succeed in immobilizing or even meant to, though this is what sooner or later every reader, the Benjys with the Derridas, must do in order to read at all. At least the Derridas know that they are doing it.

27. Michel de Montaigne, "Du repentir," in Albert Thibaudet and Maurice Rat (eds.), *Oeuvres complètes* (Paris, 1962): "La constance mesme n'est autre chose qu'un branle plus languissant" (782). Montaigne continues instructively: "Je ne puis asseurer mon object. Il va trouble et chancelant, d'une yvresse naturelle. Je le prens en ce point, comme il est, en l'instant que je m'amuse à luy. Je ne peins pas l'estre. Je peints le passage." There, in so many words, is a large part of the theory behind the new novel of Robbe-Grillet, Sarraute, Butor, and Simon—not so new, after all.

VI. THE RAVEN RE-VERSED
Surrealism and Beyond, or Time, Bird, and Word Turned Inside Out

Beginning with surrealism, French writers were taking another direction in working out the implications of dialectical symbolism. Its engagement with Poe implied that the generation of literariness depended on accident as much as anything. Was the orderly sequence of past, present, and future (the logic of temporality) the most literary (grotesque) instance of such a dialectic? Probably not. Proust and Valéry, as well as Faulkner and Tate, had found time—as loss. How to lose it—as loss? The automatic writing experiments of Breton and Soupault demonstrate that we are indeed caught in the web of words, imprisoned in poeticity whether we like it or not.[1] We can write words down at utmost random and catch some pernicious, obdurate sense straining through them. We can achieve a poetic derangement as richly formal and calculated in its impudent *hasard* as Verlaine's or Mallarmé's tortured perfections of music and form, purchased at the price of so much *main d'oeuvre*. The bird talks, though he does not know what he is saying. No one can shut him up. The *corps* is *beau* though rotten, and death nourishes life in spite of itself, just as Merlin's living soul languishes in his deceased form in Apollinaire's *L'Enchanteur Pourrissant*. Death keeps feeding life (life as dying), and the black bird keeps babbling, and as long as he babbles, he makes some kind of sense. His vocabulary has come a great ways from *nevermore*. Now he can say:

> L'une est vive, l'autre est mort. Mon bec ne peut percer la pierre, mais tout de même je sens une bonne odeur de cadavre. Tant pis, *tout sera pour les vers patients*. Ils sont bien méchants ceux qui fabriquent des tombes. Il nous privent de notre nourriture et les cadavres leur sont inutiles. Attendrai-je que celle-ci meure? Non, j'aurais le temps de mourir moi-même de faim et ma couvée at-

1. André Breton and Philippe Soupault, *Les Champs magnétiques* (Paris, 1971).

METAMORPHOSES OF THE RAVEN / 116

tend la becquée. Je sais où est Merlin, mais je n'en veux plus. Aux portes des villes meurent des enchanteurs que personne n'enterre. Leurs yeux sont bons, et je cherche aussi les cadavres des bons animaux; mais le métier est difficile, car les vautours sont plus forts, les horribles qui ne rient jamais et qui sont si sots que je n'en ai jamais entendu un seul prononcer une parole. Tandis que nous, les bons vivants, que l'on nous capture, pourvu que l'on nous nourrisse bien, et nous apprenons volontiers à parler, même en latin.[2] [emphasis mine]

Il s'envola en croassant.

The one is alive; the other is dead. My beak cannot pierce stone, but just the same I smell a good aroma of cadaver. Too bad, *all will be for the patient worms/verses.* They are very unkind, those who make tombs. They deprive us of our nourishment, and cadavers are useless to them. Shall I wait for that one [the lady of the lake, keeping watch over Merlin's tomb] to die? No, I would have time enough to die of hunger myself and my brood awaits feeding. I know where Merlin is, but I don't want any more of him. At the gates of the city some enchanters die whom no one buries. Their eyes are good, and I am also looking for the cadavers of good animals; but the business is difficult, for the vultures are stronger, the horrible ones which never laugh and which are so stupid that I never heard one say a word. While we, high livers, if we are captured, provided we are well nourished, we willingly learn to speak, even in Latin.

He flew off cawing.

It is impossible to know with certainty whether *l'une* of the first sentence is *La Dame au Lac,* who has imprisoned Merlin in the tomb, or Merlin's soul, *âme,* which survives in his dead body like Sartre's thing-spirit in Faulkner's characters; whether *l'autre* is Merlin, in which case the *corbeau* misreads Merlin's death as total rather than merely corporeal, or Merlin's body. Merlin's voice survives his flesh, like the voice of Narcissus, through the good offices of Echo and like the absent name-lessness of Lenore, which survives in the repetition of *never-*

2. Guillaume Apollinaire, *Oeuvres en prose,* ed. Michel Decaudin (Paris, 1977), 14.

more. The *corbeau* figures in *L'Enchanteur Pourrissant* as a chiasmus of the magician, not a self-conscious voice (a soul, or thing-spirit) in a dead body, but a purely iterative voice in the living body of an animal that has no soul and does not understand the words it speaks (notwithstanding the apparent precocity of the specimen). The raven can only repeat, by its own admission, and yet it makes as much sense as the *enchanteur*. In this chiasmus of bird and dead sorcerer, repetition and signification overdetermine one another in a most subtle fashion. The bird, through its name (*corps/beau*) translated in the phrase "je sens une bonne odeur de cadavre," becomes a kind of olfactory, ornithological Narcissus, an overdetermination of itself. In French, *sentir le cadavre* can mean 'to smell the cadaver' or 'to smell *like* the cadaver'. The chiasmus of dead man and living bird is enacted in the equivocation of language.

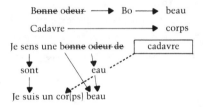

Chiasmus generates the entire phrase from *corbeau*—from singular (*suis*) to plural (*sont→sens*), from masculine (*un cor(ps)/beau*) to feminine (*une odeur*), from *beau corps* to *cor(ps) beau*. It is in the tension of these reversals that subjectivity appears to occur, that the imagistic signifier (the enchanter's dead body or the bird) and the phonic signifier (the voice of the *enchanteur* or the iterative voice of the bird) the imaginary and the symbolic, overlap to achieve overdetermination. What ought to be mute and inanimate—a corpse, a body of language, a text—talks to us in the only idiom we can understand, that of life. The fiction that the bird talks just as people do, that he possesses a subjectivity and means to say what he says, is the very fiction of literariness. The conventions of literature and reading demand that we treat the text, the dead body, the dumb bird, as though it were alive and knew what it meant to say—project a thing-spirit behind it, a fabulous origin. The corpse is quite dead, the bird is quite dumb, and the text is quite null, until it is read, rewritten.

In *Calligrammes*, Apollinaire makes a more explicit use of the dual nature of language to achieve the splitting necessary to set a *machine à traduire* in motion. It is the image, the shape formed by the characters of words, that allows us to read them at all, by limiting the permutations our decoding works on them. The sign is overdetermined automatically, if it signifies, by an intersection of shape and sound, what the eye sees and the (inner) ear hears. Each letter has its own shape and sound. Each word, each sentence can contradict, confirm, or elaborate the shape and sound of each character it contains. The form of a sentence becomes a figurative rhetoric of its own, a turning, a translation of the words within it. Thus language translates both vision and hearing into signs and transposes them onto the symbolic axis—no longer real images or sounds, too distinctly other to admit of reading, and no longer simply specular images partaking of the imaginary, but an involvement and contamination of all these things. There is no better example of language swallowing its own tail, erasing as it circles itself, than Apollinaire's *miroir*.[3]

```
                    DANS

              FLETS    CE

                 RE        MI

            LES              ROIR

          SONT                  JE

         ME                     SUIS

      COM                          EN

   NON          Guillaume          CLOS

    ET          Apollinaire        VI

   GES                            VANT

        AN                      ET

       LES                    VRAI

         NE                COM

          GI      ME

           MA    ON

                 I
```

3. Guillaume Apollinaire, *Calligrammes* (Paris, 1966), 58. This sort of poem was by no means invented by Apollinaire. It has a long lineage reaching back to

IN

TIONS   THIS

REFLEC   MI

THE   RROR

ARE   I

AS   AM

JUST   EN

NOT   Guillaume   CLOSED

AND   Apollinaire   A

GELS   LIVE

AN   AND

THE   TRUE

NES   JUST

GI   AS

MA   ONE

I

---

classical Greece. See John Hollander, "The Poem in the Eye," in *Vision and Resonance* (New York, 1975), 245–87, in which several Greek examples are reproduced; *The Greek Bucolic Poets*, trans. J. M. Edmonds (Rev. ed.; Cambridge, 1977); *The Greek Anthology*, trans. W. R. Paton (London, 1916); a number of such poems, including some Greek *technopaignia*, are reproduced in Charles Boltenhouse, "Poems in the Shapes of Things," *Art News Annual*, XXVIII (1959) 64–83. Berjouhi Bowler, *The Word as Image* (London, 1970), contains many examples of oriental figure poems. According to Hollander, "The first English figured or shaped poems were possibly influenced by French texts, themselves modeled on the *technopaignia* (Rabelais's bottle ode in the fifth book of Pantagruel may be remembered; there are also some wings by Mellin de Saint-Gelais)" (259). See François Rabelais, *Oeuvres complètes*, ed. Jacques Boulenger and Lucien Scheler (Paris, 1955), 881. According to the editors, only since the 1565 edition of the *Cinquiesme livre* have the verses beginning "O/Bouteille/ Pleine toute/De mistères" been arranged in the shape of a bottle. That means that Rabelais himself, who is thought to have died in 1553, and whose authorship of the entire *Cinquiesme Livre* is doubtful, was probably not responsible for the 'figuring' of the text. In any case, whatever the ancestry of Apollinaire's *Calligrammes*, their significance for this study is only in the postsymbolist, AP (after Poe) context. The English tradition has tended to look askance at such poetry as excessively and grotesquely contrived—that is, offensive to mimetic canon in a way of which those offended were only partly aware. Here is Hollander, quoting Joseph Addison: "From the late seventeenth century in England on, shaped, patterned, or 'figured' poems have been considered the essence of the trivial or tricky. 'The first species of false wit which I have met with is venerable for its antiquity,' writes Addison in the *Spectator* in 1711, 'and has produced several pieces which have lived near us as long as the Iliad itself: I mean these short poems, printed among the minor Greek poets, which resemble

The sense of the poem is its exploitation of chiasmus achieved through its shape. "Dans ce miroir je suis enclos vivant et vrai comme on imagine les anges et non comme les reflets Dans ce miroir . . ." We cannot know whether it is 'correct' to stop reading at *reflets*. If we do, we are still faced with a reversal, a mirror that is not a mirror, one that does not reflect, which lies against its own lie. The only thing that is unproblematic is the poet's name. But even that is not his real name, which was Polish— Wilhelm Apollinaris de Kostrowitski. The discrepancy between the one name and the other, between the name and the named, reflects, as chiasmus, the aporia written in the mirror's 'frame'. What is implied is a tautology of writer and written, of subjectivity and text. The poem projects, beyond life and death, the impossible possibility of an angelic world of totalization and origin, otherness, in which the solution to this tautology would lie. The mirror-text at once admits its inadequacy, a function of its specular nature, and holds out the possibility of an immanence, an enclosure belied by that reflectiveness. In a real mirror, immanence is always a mirage, an image of what is outside. The mirror's dependence on alterity is prerequisite to the conception of any immanence at all, illusory or angelic. Totalization is grounded in its own failure.

A tautology, as a mathematical construction, admits of no solution—x equals x—unless we arbitrarily replace one of the variables with a fixed quantity. If we try to solve the equation by analogy, as, for example, we would do by saying, x is to x as 5 is to 3, $5x = 3x$, we obtain a numerical non sequitur: $x = 3/5(x) \rightarrow x/x = 3/5 \rightarrow 1 = 3/5$. The trouble is that x is not entirely itself. When we insist that a poem or a novel means this or that, ascribing primacy to one symbolic code or another, such as history, biography, linguistics, anthropology, or psychology, we enact the same sort of non sequitur—not that there is any real choice. It is in those misprisions, those defiances of logic, that the pleasure of the text lies.[4]

---

the figure of an egg, a pair of wings, an axe, a shepherd's pipe and an altar'" (253). See also Hollander, *Rhyme's Reason* (New Haven, 1981), 30–32.

4. For a discussion of how Chomsky and Suzanne Langer fall into just this trap

Michel Leiris' "Glossaire j'y serre mes gloses" (Glossary I keep my glosses in it) is one of the most explicit and fecund exploitations of poetry as tautological misprision—the generation of meaning through mistranslation, overdetermination of language by itself, through repetition and rearrangement. A good example is "Le plongeoir de Narcisse."[5]

```
            L
            E
          H   I
          C   R
        MI      IS
          C   R
          H   I
            E
            L
```

The title is already felicitously interesting (overdetermined): "Narcissus' Diving Board" points to the way in which desire, in the myth, impels Narcissus to translate his stasis, or contemplation, into movement, pursuit—drowning, death. What exactly would a diving board represent? An invitation to death by drowning? The line of demarcation between stasis and movement? The apparatus required to move between them and towards water, that which drinks, death?

Sound, as well as shape, achieves the same sort of poetic overdeterminedness, though a bit less flamboyantly.

ô (étOnnée, la bOuche mOlle s'arrOndit, gObe l'ObOle de l'hOstie . . .)
o (astOnished, the sOft mOuth rOunds itself, swallOws dOwn the ObOlus of the hOst . . .)

PHENOMENES—leur faix nous mène (faux noumène).

VIE—un Dé la sépare du viDe.

LIFE—a throw of the Die separates it from the voiD.

---

apparently without knowing it, see Percy, *The Message in the Bottle*, 295–96, 304.

5. Michel Leiris, *Mots sans mémoire* (Paris, 1969), 115.

METAMORPHOSES—maladie metaphysique des morts.
(Formation métallique? Mal morose.)[6]
METAMORPHOSES—metaphysical illness of dead people.
(Metallic formation? Morose disease).

The first example is perfectly self-referential: if we read it aloud, we make with our lips the shape we see on the page. The others exploit homonymities of sound, but ô makes a point that applies to all: the word is an image, whether the image refers to anything other than a sound or not. Literariness is simply an exploitation of the splitting and doubling of language, a celebration of the defeat of determination, of the misplacement of sense. To arrest the *machine à traduire* is to destroy it.

Trancher le noeud gordien
ou mettre l'oeuf debout
en arasant sa pointe
c'est prouver qu'on ne connaît rien
à notre jeu de qui-perd-gagne.

To cut through the gordian knot / or stand the egg up / by shaving off its end, / This proves that you know nothing / About our game of who-wins-loses.

Purely iterative language, language used as ecphrasis of itself, can explode into fabulous playthings if its generative overdeterminedness is respected.

Hominien du cheveu à la plante
il a suffi (enfin patient) de les énumérer
pour que les choses bonnes ou nocives
éclatent en fabuleux joujoux
aux pages d'un catalogue d'an neuf.[7]

Hominid from hair to sole / it has sufficed (finally patient) to enumerate them / in order that all things good or harmful / burst into fabulous toys / in the pages of a catalog of the new year.

6. *Ibid.*, 100, 104, 113, 98.
7. *Ibid.*, 150, 151.

René Char enacts willful indeterminacy in the symbolic language of war and history. One of the most fruitful ways of reading his poetry, however, is as an allegory of the entropy of genre, as a gloss on literary history. His work infuses the dialectic of poetic defeat with the historical blood of World War II and prepares the way for a new kind of poetry and fiction that is overdetermined generically and temporally, that achieves poeticity through a subversion of generic and temporal distinctions. What Char achieves is to turn Faulkner and Proust inside out. The last paragraph of Robert Desnos' "J'ai tant rêvé de toi" describes the progress of the reversal by which mourner becomes mourning, and Echo becomes Hypnos—sleep, oblivion, bringer of dreams.

> J'ai tant rêvé de toi, tant marché, parlé, couché avec ton fantôme
> qu'il ne me reste plus peut-être, et pourtant, qu' à être fantôme
> parmi les fantômes et plus ombre cent fois que l'ombre qui se
> promène et se promènera allègrement sur le cadran solaire de ta
> vie.[8]

8. Robert Desnos, "J'ai tant rêvé de toi," *Domaine Public* (Paris, 1953), 95. See also his very interesting "L'Ode à Coco," from which here is my translation of some excerpted lines:

> Coco! gouty concierge's green parrot,
> Perched on a stomach, his bitter monologues
> Exciting to extremities the mastiff's anger,
> Making surge a gallop of zebras and wild asses.

> Nightmare, his black beak will plunge into a skull
> And two grains of sun under the eyelid peel
> Will bleed in the night on white eider-down.

> The love of a bigot has perverted your heart;
> Long ago puffing up your collar like a turtle dove,
> Coco! you warbled to the sky of the equator
> Sonorous outcries that charmed the parakeets.
> Came the sailor whistling the out-of-date polka
> Came the obscene bigot and her beehive cap,
> Then the wooden perch in the golden cage:
> The tropical refrains deserted your throat.

> Shady adventurer-nobleman adorned with loud colors
> O general of empire, o splendid foreigner,
> You simulate for me, grotesque voyager,
> The eagle effigy of a lectern, perched on a sextant.
> . . . .
> The poison of my dream is voluptuous and sure

I have dreamed so much of you, walked, talked, slept so much with your ghost that there is no longer anything left to me, perhaps, and yet, nothing but to be a ghost among the ghosts and more a shadow by a hundred times than the shadow which walks and will walk lightly on the sundial of your life.

This poem (by the sort of accident of misprision that apotheosized Poe in France, making him a myth of origin) mythologized the death of Desnos. When Desnos died of typhoid fever immediately after his release from a concentration camp, the first notice of his death appeared in the Czech journal *Svobodné noviny*. The obituary ended by citing the last paragraph of "J'ai tant rêvé de toi" in Czech translation. The same notice was then published in French, with the poem translated *from the Czech*. This translation of a translation became known as "Le Dernier poème," alleged by the Swiss literary review *Labyrinthe* to have been the last verses of Desnos, written in the concentration camp.[9] Thus was Desnos poignantly and erroneously inscribed in the imaginary and symbolic language of history as a poetic,

---

And the heavy phantasms of the perfidious drug
Will never produce in a lucid mind
The horror of too much love and too much horizon
That for voyager me songs give birth to.

Desnos' "Apparition" mentions *corbeaux* in the context of the topos of war (239–40).

9. Here is the text of the so-called "Le Dernier poème":

J'ai rêvé tellement fort de toi,
J'ai tellement marché, tellement parlé,
Tellement aimé ton ombre,
Qu'il ne me reste plus rien de toi.

Il me reste d'être ombre parmi les ombres
D'être cent fois plus ombre que l'ombre
D'être l'ombre qui viendra et reviendra
            dans ta vie ensoleillée.

Ibid., 408. See Adolph Kroupa, "La Légende du Dernier Poème de Desnos," *Les Lettres françaises*, June 9, 1960, pp. 1,5. It is astonishing that such a widely used anthology as *The Penguin Book of French Verse* (Harmondsworth, 1975) would present "Le Dernier poème" as one of Desnos' most significant works, repeating the long discredited but (apparently) still popular myth that Desnos wrote it in the concentration camp to his wife, Youki.

almost a metaphysical, victim of war, an embodiment of loss and of the loss of loss. What could be more appropriate than that the instrument of such a myth should turn out to be a translation of a translation, mistaken for an original?

Instead of seeing the present as a figure for the past, Char, like Desnos in "J'ai tant rêvé de toi," takes the past (memory, cognition) as a figure of the present's nullity. The past is the directory of names we give to the present. Being in the present is a matter of artful composition in the sense in which Delacroix and Baudelaire conceived the latter, if we turn their dictionary of nature, the present, into a catalog of the past. The post-Proustian subject, defined as memory, takes the present as object and realizes its textual ego as a series of fragments, discontinuous names of the present. This subjectivity is constituted as a constant emission of fragmentary texts. These fragments are inevitably sequential and therefore narrate something, if it is no more than the order in which they were written. But because the texts themselves are emitted and constituted by the past, they cannot describe the past but only infer it as their fabulous origin (invisible source, inaudible voice) and strain toward it as their destination.

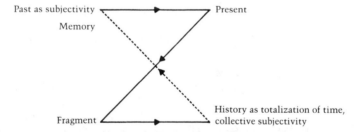

This poeticity affirms that subjectivity can only know itself as a text, in the endlessly repeated instant of reading, deciphering, and translating, and that the subject, as fragmentary, can only articulate its being in a suite of instantaneous repetitions, stringing moments like beads on the string of history. The fragmentary text makes the act of reading a perfect iteration of the act of writing. The reader names the fragments of text before him, breaking them into more pieces, or sequences and permutations

of pieces—*histoires*, (hi)stories—in which he articulates his own
being to himself. This concept of a text rules out any credible
illusion of a definitive edition. The only way in which the text
can be treated responsibly is by respecting its mobility. Between
reading and writing there is a perfect tautology of dialectical
cognition (so-called subjectivity) in which the fragment is erased
and recomposed as it is read, "tout lendemain fertile étant fonction de la réussite du projet" ("every fertile tomorrow being a
function of the success of the project"). Texts are shed like excrement by writers only to 'pass through' readers who 'excrete'
them in their turn.

> Le poète ne peut pas longtemps demeurer dans la stratosphère du
> Verbe. Il doit se lover dans de nouvelles larmes et pousser plus
> avant dans son ordre.

> The poet cannot for long remain in the stratosphere of the Word.
> He must coil himself up in new tears and push further ahead in
> his order.

> Il existe une sorte d'homme toujours en avance sur ses
> excréments.

> There exists a kind of man always ahead of his excrements.

> L'effort du poète vise à transformer *vieux ennemis* en *loyaux
> adversaires*, tout lendemain fertile étant fonction du projet, sur-
> tout là où s'élance, s'enlace, décline, est décimée toute la gamme
> des voiles où le vent des continents rend son coeur au vent des
> abîmes.[10]

> The effort of the poet aims to transform *old enemies* into *loyal
> adversaries*, every fertile tomorrow being a function of the success
> of the project, especially there where is thrown, intertwined,
> where declines, is decimated the whole scale of sails where the
> wind of continents renders up its heart to the wind of abysses.

Perception is a perpetual interpretive violence, a fragmentation, for which war is a vivid historical metaphor.

10. René Char, *Fureur et mystère* (Paris, 1967), 87, 91, 93.

Cette guerre se prolongera au delà des armistices platoniques. L'implantation des concepts politiques se poursuivra contradictoirement, dans les convulsions et sous le couvert d'une hypocrisie sûre de ses droits. Ne souriez pas. Ecartez le scepticisme et la résignation, et préparez votre âme mortelle en vue d'affronter intra-muros des démons glacés analogues aux génies microbiens.

This war will be prolonged beyond any platonic armistices. The implantation of political concepts will be pursued contradictorily, in the convulsions and under the cover of a hypocrisy sure of its rights. Do not smile. Put aside skepticism and resignation, and prepare your mental soul for an intramural confrontation with frozen demons analogous to microbial spirits.

Time is shattered and shattering:

Midi séparé du jour. Minuit retranché des hommes. Minuit au glas pourri, qu'une, deux, trois, quatre heures ne parviennent pas à baillonner.

Noon separated from day. Midnight cut away from men. Midnight with the rotten knell, that one, two, three, four o'clock do not succeed in gagging.

Le combat de la persévérance.
La symphonie qui nous portait s'est tue. Il faut croire à l'alternance. Tant de mystères n'ont pas été pénétrés ni détruits.

The combat of perseverance. / The symphony which carried us is silent. We must believe in alternation. So many mysteries have been neither penetrated nor destroyed.

L'acte est vierge, même répété.

The act is virgin, even repeated.

La ligne de vol du poème. Elle devrait être *sensible* à chacun.[11]

The line of flight/theft of the poem. It ought to be *palpable* to each.

---

11. *Ibid.*, 87, 93, 110, 98, 111.

Meaning flight as well and theft, the word *vol*, describing a line, is precisely what the poem is and does. No longer a whole narrative or part of one, no longer making any pretense to totalize or to inscribe itself in an illusion of harmonious order and closure (a symphony), the sequence, the narrative, the *ligne* of the poem is in the repeated plagiary by each reader; each repetitious reading is a virgin enactment of the *sur-présent*, which, in Sartre's eyes, the Faulknerian past barely held back from becoming. It is no longer holding back. The history of a poem's reading is ecphrasis of the site of a repeated theft, the agent of which, the thief, is never visible and yet ever absent from the scene of the crime. That thief would not be the reader precisely, but perhaps his readerly self, or his act of reading, ever persevering, believing in alternation, repetition, and iteration—a virtually silent percussion, no drumbeat but rather footsteps or bird wings that we might have heard or not, or might have made up. Each successive reading/theft/flight is tautological with respect to all the others, yet discontinuous, non sequitur, virginal paradox. "Le poème est ascension furieuse; la poésie, le jeu des berges arides" (The poem is furious ascent; poetry, the play of dry river banks/barges), and "La source est roc et la langue est tranchée" (The spring is rock and the tongue/language is cut/said).[12] The French *trancher* signifies decapitation, truncation, *and* enunciation, as in the expression used above in Leiris' poem, *trancher le noeud gordien*, to resolve, determine, clinch the matter, to totalize and immobilize it. The source/*source*/ spring is not a source at all; nothing plays between the dry river banks but air, the furiously ascending wind, the reader's breath, psyche—desire of desire, dialectically tautological desire. The word *psyche* derives from the Indo-European root *bles*, 'breath'; *influence* from Latin *influere*, 'to flow in', closely related to *inflare*, 'to blow in', 'to play on wind instruments' (like the raven's *cor*); and the myth of Psyche is that of a girl in love with love itself.[13] If we read *berge*

12. *Ibid.*, 101.
13. Harold Bloom, *Poetry and Repression* (New Haven, 1976), 1; Harold Bloom and Lionel Trilling (eds.), *Romantic Poetry and Prose* (New York, 1973): "The Hellenistic Psyche (for her story see *The Golden Ass* by Apuleius, Latin author

as barge, or boat, we have poetry as the play of arid barges, vessels run aground, immobilized. The word is an aporia of movement and stasis, and of two different kinds of each—the movement of a boat or the wind countermanded by the absence of water, prerequisite to the boat's motion and whose place the wind has usurped. That which drinks has been drunk up, displaced by the reader's influent breath, or desire.

Ideally, the text consists of no more than a substantive, "l'alcool silencieux des démons" ("the silent alcohol of demons"), or of a subjectless predicate, "agir en primitif et prévoir en stratège" ("to act as a primitive and to foresee as a stratagem"). It demands a reading that either does not read it, that repeats it without any movement to comprehend (inscribe it in some 'symphony', personal or hypothetical)—"Accumule, puis distribue. Sois la partie de l'univers la plus dense, la plus utile et la moins apparente" ("Accumulate, then distribute. Be the densest part of the universe, the most useful and the least apparent")—or, a reading that succeeds in reading it only by the most arbitrary of translations. Either strategy effectively erases the text. Thus, "Nous sommes pareils à ces crapauds qui dans l'austère nuit des marais s'appellent et ne se voient pas, ployant à leur cri d'amour toute la fatalité de l'univers" ("We are like those toads who in the austere night call to and do not see each other, folding up in their cry of love all the fatality of the universe"). Always fatality, fabulous origin, death, now swallowed up and misplaced in the folds made by so many echoes, all psyches, desires desiring desire. Unless a poem is thus erased, and fatality, origin, and author so enfolded, the poem is not a poem. "Pour qu'un héritage soit réellement grand, il faut que la main de défunt ne se voie pas" ("For an inheritance to be truly great, it is necessary that the hand of the deceased not be seen"). Reader and writer have no choice but to evacuate the text, which is diastole to the systole of inflow, or influence; inhalation is premised upon exhalation, respiration (life) upon expiration (death). There can be

---

of the 2nd century, A.D.) was a mortal with whom Cupid or Eros fell in love" (537).

no anxiety of influence, for there is no breath, no presence, but one's own. There is no anxiety save that of directionless, reflexive desire, the psyche in its insufficiency groping after Eros. There is no predecessor, no object of desire, save desire itself and the endless shapes and self-dissolving names we sometimes give it. "Réponds 'absent' toi-même, sinon tu risques de ne pas être compris" ("Reply 'absent' yourself, otherwise you risk not being understood"). The rhetoric of this poetry is ellipsis and catachresis; the breaking up of understatement and omission is fragmented into even smaller bits by metaleptic aporias: "Les yeux seuls sont encore capables de pousser un cri" ("The eyes alone are still capable of crying out"); "Nuit, de toute la vitesse du boomerang taille dans nos os, et qui siffle, siffle" ("Night, with all the speed of a boomerang in our bones, and which whistles, whistles"); "Chante ta soif irisée" ("Sing your iridescent thirst").[14]

In *Les Feuillets d'Hypnos*, written while Char was active in the Resistance in the south of France, the poetry was able to nourish itself on the historical presence and otherness of war and occupation, defeat. The poems achieve a generic ambiguity that, like Faulkner's temporal chiasmi, belies the distinction of history and literature and goes still further. Char's poetic experiment shows us the extent to which distinctions of genre—foremost among which is that between fiction and nonfiction, literature and history—depend upon adherence to a triadic model of subjectivity and temporality: signifier/signified/referent, subject/act/object, past/present/future. All of these leave out the fourth essential term by which subjectivity enjoys the illusion of existing: death, loss, defeat, otherness, totality. Distinctions between lyric and narrative, fiction and nonfiction, depend on the representation in a prescribed manner of these models of being and time through a linear progression of beginning, middle, and end, which is derived from the models themselves, but which is adduced as proof of their veracity. That is the sort of reasonable non sequitur described previously by

14. Char, *Fureur et mystère*, 104, 127, 120, 130, 126, 112, 104, 129.

mathematical analogy. Such tautological proof of the Cartesian model of being is behind the notion of organic form, which considers literary works as "complex integrated wholes which secure their aesthetic effects primarily as a consequence of their being such wholes."[15] Despite some nuances of dissent, this assumption is the basis of I. A. Richard's *Practical Criticism* and indeed of the entire New Criticism. To assume that the New Critics were wrong to make such assumptions would, however, be far more naïve than they themselves were. Interpreting, reading, the organic model itself, *is* the fourth term that the dialectic wishes to hide; thus not only does it belie the textual self-sufficiency it alleges, but it belies it by the breath that alleges it.

Char's self-conscious subversion of temporal subjectivity denies us any refuge in generic categorization. His poetry might be autobiography, novel, aphorism, or simply journal. Yet, he himself says, "These notes borrow nothing from the love of self, from the short story, from the maxim or the novel."[16] These are the fragments and the detritus of tension, illusion, desire, combustion, cognition, loss—texts of event (l'évènement) imitated as if through hallucination texts of history, deed, reality, by which the real is obliterated in the act of its perception, subsumed in the breath of its being as loss and in its own failed struggle to escape that implosion.

> A fire of dry grass might just as well have been their editor. The sight of tortured blood once caused some of them to lose their track, reduced their importance to nothing. They were written in tension, anger, fear, emulation, disgust, ruse, furtive meditation, the illusion of the future, friendship, love. This is to say how much they are affected by event. Afterwards more often passed over in haste [*survolées*] than reread.
>
> This notebook might not have belonged to anyone, inasmuch as the life of a man is subjacent to his peregrinations and difficult of

15. *Princeton Encyclopedia of Poetry and Poetics*, 594.
16. Char, *Fureur et mystère*: "Ces notes n'empruntent rien à l'amour de soi, à la nouvelle, à la maxime ou au roman" (85).

separation from a sometimes hallucinatory mimeticism. Such
tendencies were fought against, nevertheless.[17]

Survolées can mean 'superpurloined', 'overstolen', as well as
'passed over in haste'.

The mythic chiasmus of Aeneas and Narcissus, reflected by
that of Echo and Psyche, sees here a new name: Hypnos, god of
sleep, son of Erebus and night, closely related to Thanatos,
death, to Hermes, bearer of dream messages, and to Lethe, the
river of oblivion, that which drinks memory. It is by the incan-
tatory power of Hypnos that we enter "the House of the Dead,"
the place of otherness and death, origin and afterworld.[18] The
mourning of Echo, her repetition of the past in the present, has
become a projection of the present's virtuality and nullity into
the past, an incantation that mesmerizes memory, reversing
without undoing it. Sleep approximates the only access to freedom that Proust's and Faulkner's temporal rhetoric can admit—
madness, death, forgetting. Freedom is to be achieved only by a
*hypno*tic rhetoric, which is the inverse of the rhetoric of memory and mourning. Hypnotic rhetoric is one of present tense,
which makes of narrative history an infinitely discontinuous
sequence of fragments, turnings, inflections, transmutations—a
Chimera rather than an Echo. As Eluard put it:

> Femme avec laquelle j'ai vécu
> Femme avec laquelle je vis
> Femme avec laquelle je vivrai
> Toujours la même
> Il te faut un manteau rouge

17. *Ibid.*: "Un feu d'herbes sèches eût tout aussi bien été leur éditeur. La vue
du sang supplicié en a fait une fois perdre le fil, a réduit à néant leur importance.
Elles furent écrites dans la tension, la colère, la peur, l'émulation, le dégoût, la
ruse, le recueillement furtif, l'illusion de l'avenir, l'amitié, l'amour. C'est dire
combien elles sont affectées par l'évènement. Ensuite plus souvent survolées que
relues.
    "Ce carnet pourrait n'avoir appartenu à personne tant le sens de la vie d'un
homme est sous-jacent à ses pérégrinations, et difficilement séparable d'un mi-
métisme parfois hallucinant. De telles tendances furent néanmoins combattues."
    18. James Hillman, *The Dream and the Underworld* (New York, 1979), 34.

Des gants rouges un masque rouge
Et des bas noirs
Des raisons des preuves
De te voir toute nue
Nudité pure ô parure parée

. . . .

On ne peut me connaître
Mieux que tu me connais

Tes yeux dans lesquels nous dormons
Tous les deux
Ont fait à mes lumières d'homme
Un sort meilleur qu'aux nuits du monde[19]

Woman with whom I have lived / Woman with whom I
live / Woman with whom I will live / Always the same / You
need a red coat / Some red gloves a red mask / And some black
stockings / Some reasons some proofs / Of seeing you all
naked / Pure nudity o ornament adorned! // . . . . No one knows
me / Better than you know me // Your eyes in which we
sleep / Both / Have given my lights of a man / A better fate than
in the nights of the world

Thus the epigraph to *Les Feuillets d'Hypnos* establishes Hypnos
as the maker of changes, combustor that freely turns season, or
time (winter), into space (granite) and into itself (sleep), time's
inversion, and itself into fire.

The poetry aims at an achievement of presence by an exacer-
bation of absence, of lucidity through derangement, and recuperation through embracing loss. By identifying itself with the
discontinuity and absence that have fueled it, by becoming the
nameless lost Lenore, it intends to reach beyond absence and
mourning into a furious presence of purloinment and flight, beyond disease into a feverish, furious health. "Nous sommes des
malades sidéraux incurables auxquels la vie sataniquement
donne l'illusion de la santé. Pourquoi? Pour dépenser la vie et

19. Paul Eluard, *Oeuvres complètes*, ed. Marcelle Dumas and Lucien Scheler
(2 vols.; Paris, 1968), I, 366.

railler la santé? (Je dois combattre mon penchant pour ce genre de pessimisme atonique, héritage intellectuel)" ["We are sidereal incurable invalids to whom life satanically gives the illusion of health. Why? To spend life and mock health? (I must struggle against my penchant for this kind of atonic pessimism, intellectual heritage)"].[20] No longer content to mourn loss, the poetry means to enact it, to become theft and flight, flight of theft and theft of flight.

Poetry of expatriation, flight, and fragmentation did not begin with Char. Its ancestry traces back to Chamfort and the aphoristic tradition in French. For the purposes of this study, however, the first stirrings of its present avatar were in the ecphrastic poems of symbolism, seeking to imitate the action of immobility—perhaps most notably in Rimbaud's *Illuminations*, the title of which comes from the English, meaning 'colored plates'.[21] In the poems of Saint-John Perse fragmentariness found an early twentieth-century voice, one in whose idiom the raven is translated anew, as *Perroquet*.

Perse makes of the story of Robinson Crusoe a myth of exile, of man living apart from the world of continuity and illusion, struggling to sustain some semblance of it. And this poetry, which turns Poe's poetics of mourning inside out, needed to turn the raven inside out as well. So he becomes, out of necessity and circumstance, a parrot. The past that drinks is replaced by the present that burns, and the beautiful corpse by the otherness of exile, exoticism, transit, embarcation, *le perroquet/pair au quai* (the other on the landing). The bird is third hand in Perse's text, having been captured and given away by a sailor and sold by an old woman. He perches on the landing (arid, indoor *quai*) next to a window, at just the juncture of inside and outside, light and dark.

Le Perroquet

C'est un autre.
Un marin bègue l'avait donné à la vieille femme qui l'a vendu.

20. Char, *Fureur et mystère*, 106.
21. Fowlie, *Rimbaud*, 117.

Il est sur le palier près de la lucarne, là où s'emmêle au noir la
brume sale du jour couleur de venelles.

D'un double cri, la nuit, il te salue, Crusoé, quand, remontant
des fosses de la cour, tu pousses la porte du couloir et élèves
devant toi l'astre précaire de ta lampe. Il tourne sa tête pour tour-
ner son regard. Homme à la lampe! que lui veux-tu? . . . Tu regardes l'oeil rond sous le pollen gâté de la paupière; tu regardes le
deuxième cercle comme un anneau de sève morte. Et la plume
malade trempe dans l'eau de fiente.

O misère! Souffle ta lampe. L'oiseau pousse son cri.[22]

It is an other.

A stuttering sailor had given it to the old woman, who sold it. It
is on the landing next to the window, there where the dirty fog of
alley-colored day mingles with the dark.

With a double cry, at night, it greets you, Crusoe, when, coming
up the grave pits of the courtyard, you push open the hall door and
raise before you the precarious star of your lamp. It turns its head
to turn its gaze. Man with the lamp! What do you want of him?
. . . You look at the round eye beneath the spoiled pollen of the
eyelid; you look at the second circle as a ring of dead sap. And the
sick plumage soaks in the watery dung.

O misery! Blow out your lamp. The bird cries out.

The parrot is an ornithological other, emitting double cries. It
ought to talk but only cries out. The text does the talking and
establishes an ambiguous identity between itself and the bird.
When we see "Homme à la lampe!" we are induced by the ex-
clamation point and apparent change of perspective to assume
an instance of free indirect discourse, to place these words in the
parrot's mind, if not his mouth. The next sentence renders such
a reading problematic: "Que lui veux-tu?" Who is *lui*? The man
with the lamp? In that case the narrator is asking Crusoe what
he wants from the bird or the bird what he wants from Crusoe.
Or could *lui* still be the parrot? If it is, "What do you want of
him?" is addressed to the reader or to the narrator or perhaps to

22. Saint-John Perse, *Eloges, suivi de La Gloire des Rois, Anabase, Exil* (Paris,
1960), 65.

Crusoe—"What do you want of the narrator/reader?" The most likely answer is that all of these readings are valid. What does everyone want from the bird-text? That he talk, surely. On this point he will not or cannot gratify. He only cries out, doubly, otherly, greeting us, men with lamps. In that otherness there seems to lurk a query. What query would we have it be? The question is, what question to put, and where to put it? Is the bird-text asking us or are we asking it? What is the question? The answer is *otherness*, the black, blank, empty eye of death, dung-stanched. It looks back, seeing, crying out, saying nothing. The cry is night, day's double, the other of 'referentiality'. It is still the bird of death, but discontinuous death, shattered and scattered. It is death as life, occulted debility dipping its diseased *plume* (quill) into the ink of excrement and inscribing the noise of night in the dark.

Perse's Crusoe has nothing in common with Defoe's. What had been in the eighteenth century, as Paul Zweig puts it, "a dream of sanity," of familiarity and natural order in a world once thought to be wild and threatening, is seen in Perse's revision to be haunted by a dark, bird-shaped irony. Zweig writes that "when Crusoe peered into the abyss of nature and isolation, he did not discover an essential darkness, as Conrad did 180 years later . . . he discovered a profoundly domestic, ultimately familiar world."[23] Perse's Crusoe finds that even in the homey trappings of domestication there remains undomesticated darkness; the parrot may learn to speak man's language, but he does not know what it means, and he does not forget the language of nature—inarticulate noise. Order is premised on disorder; it depends on and is invested by it. The nightmare lurks just behind the happy dream.

This poeticity, to borrow another analogy from mathematics, calculates plenitude as the asymptote of absence, and closure as an infinite differential.

> Et puis après la fin de tout le règne animal, l'air et le sable en petit grains lentement y pénètrent [à la coquille], cependant que sur le

23. Paul Zweig, *The Adventurer* (Princeton, 1981), 123.

sol il luit encore et s'érode et va brillament se désagréger, ô stér-
ile, immatérielle poussière, ô brillant résidu, quoique sans fin
brassé et trituré entre les laminoirs aériens et marins, ENFIN! *l'on*
n'est plus là et ne peut rien reformer du sable, même pas du verre,
et C'EST FINI![24]

And then after the end of the entire animal reign, the air and
the sand in small grains slowly enter it [the shell] yet on the
surface of the earth it still shines and erodes and will brilliantly
disintegrate, o sterile, immaterial dust, o lustrous residue, though
endlessly churned and ground between the rollers of air and sea,
FINALLY! *one* is no longer there and can make nothing again from
the sand, not even glass, and IT IS FINISHED!

By means of such dazzlement of disaggregation, poetry pretends
to obliterate subjectivity in favor, not of objectivity, but of ob-
ject-ness. It presents a most radical paradox, for the reification of
subjectivity, of the Proustian-Faulknerian temporal intersubjectivity, is to be achieved only by a violence of subjectivity—a
sensibility more excessively acute than even Roderick Usher's,
so acute that its apprehension of the present obliterates its consciousness of the past. By radicalizing absence, by becoming absence, this poetry means to achieve 'recuperation'.

Figure delayée dans l'eau
Dans le silence
Trop de poids sur la gorge
Trop d'eau dans le bocal
Trop d'ombre renversée
Trop de sang sur la rampe
Il n'est jamais fini
Ce rêve de cristal[25]

Figure spun out in the water / In the silence / Too much weight
on the throat / Too much water in the jar / Too much shadow
spilled / Too much blood on the stairs / It is never finished / This
dream of crystal

24. Francis Ponge, *Le Parti pris des choses, suivi de Poèmes* (Paris, n.d.), 77.
25. Pierre Reverdy, *Main d'oeuvre, poèmes 1913–1949* (Paris, 1949), 404.

This is reification without closure: crystal may be solid, but it is not visible in water—not distinct from that which drinks, lately that which is drunk up.

The place of such a poetry is what Yves Bonnefoy calls *le vrai lieu.*

> The true place (*vrai lieu*) is a fragment of duration consumed by the eternal, at the true place time undoes itself in us. And I can just as well write, I know, that it does not exist, that it is only the mirage, on the temporal horizon, of the hours of our death,—but does the word *reality* still mean anything now, and can it disengage us from the engagement contracted with the object of memory, and which is to be forever searching? I maintain that nothing is truer, and more reasonable too, than vagrancy, for—need I say it?—there is no method for coming back to the true place. Perhaps it is infinitely near. It is also infinitely far. Thus being, in our instant, and ironic presence.
>
> The true place is given by randomness, but in the true place randomness loses its character of enigma.
>
> Already, for the one who searches, and even if he knows very well that no path guides him, the world around him will be an abode of signs. The least object, the most fugitive being, will by the good they do awaken the hope of an absolute good. The fire that warms us is not the true fire. Its very substance is proof of this. It is here, it is not here. . . . I say that desire of the true place is the path of poetry.[26]

26. Yves Bonnefoy, *L'Improbable, suivi de Un rêve fait à Mantoue* (Paris, 1980): "Le vrai lieu est un fragment de durée consumé par l'éternel, au vrai lieu le temps se défait en nous. Et je puis écrire aussi bien, je le sais, qu'il n'existe pas, qu'il n'est que le mirage, sur l'horizon temporel, des heures de notre mort,— mais le mot de *réalité* a-t-il un sens maintenant encore, et peut-il nous dégager de l'engagement contracté envers l'objet de mémoire, et qui est de toujours chercher? Je prétends que rien n'est plus vrai, et plus raisonnable ainsi, que l'errance, car—est-il besoin de le dire?—il n'est pas de méthode pour revenir au vrai lieu. Il est peut-être infiniment proche. Il est aussi infiniment éloigné. Ainsi l'être, dans notre instant, et l'ironique présence.

"Le vrai lieu est donné par le hasard, mais au vrai lieu le hasard perdra son caractère d'énigme.

"Déjà, pour celui qui cherche, et même s'il sait bien qu'aucun chemin ne le guide, le monde autour de lui sera une demeure de signes. Le moindre objet,

What Bonnefoy describes is a *sur-realism*, in the literal sense, a realism of realism, an ironic realism, the other of Faulker's and Poe's ironic absence.

> It [poetry] works the transmutation of the result into the possible, of memory into anticipation, of deserted space into procedure, into hope. And I could say that it is an *initiative realism*, if we were to give it, at the final moment, the real. . . . I am thinking of the poet of the most limpid hope and the most intense pain. In the most secret of those who, in the French nineteenth century, formed that sort of quadrangle where every thought loses itself, and also finds itself, in infinite refractions. Purely, as an incarnation of poetry, he unfleshed himself in that love without resource, that of being mortal. But his desire remains his desire, his thrust towards plenitude has held in the honesty of the heart the feeling of the unpossessable.[27]

The poet referred to here is, in Bonnefoy's mind, Mallarmé. I wonder if Mallarmé himself would not have agreed that it ought rightfully to be Poe. In any case, the new poetry no longer mourns; it is mourning, mourning of mourning:

> I call this union of lucidity and hope melancholia. . . . It is that gift, at the least, that a true poet can make. And in his poverty, give his good a place to stay.
>   Poetry has long wished to live in the house of the Idea, but as it

---

l'être le plus fugitif, par le bien qu'ils feront, réveilleront l'espoir d'un bien absolu. Le feu qui nous réchauffe dit qu'il n'est pas le vrai feu. Sa substance même en est la preuve. Il est ici, il n'est pas ici. . . . Et je dis que le désir du vrai lieu est le serment de la poésie" (128).

27. *Ibid.*: "Elle opère la transmutation de l'abouti en possible, du souvenir en attente, de l'espace désert en cheminement, en espoir. Et je pourrais dire qu'elle est un *réalisme initiatique* si elle nous donnait, au dénouement, le réel. . . . Je pense au poète du plus limpide espoir et de la plus vive douleur. Au plus secret de ceux qui, dans le XIXe siècle français, ont formé cette sorte de quadrangle où toute pensée se perd, et aussi bien se retrouve, en des réfractions infinies. Purement, comme une incarnation de la poésie, il s'est décorporé dans cet amour sans ressource, celui de l'être mortel. Mais son désir est demeuré le désir, son élan vers la plénitude a maintenu dans l'honnêteté du coeur le sentiment de l'impossédable" (130).

is said, it has been run out of that house, it has run away *crying in pain*. Modern poetry is far from its possible abode. The great room with the four windows is still refused it. The repose of form in the poem is not honestly acceptable. But the luck of the poetry to come, at least inasmuch as happiness (and I can well consent to this happiness now), is that it is on the verge of knowing, in its durable exile, what *presence* can open up. After so many hours of anguish. Was this so hard then? Wasn't it enough to notice, on the flank of some mountain, a windowpane in the evening sun?[28]

This poetry is, in Bonnefoy's words, "anti-platonic," which is by no means to say that it is Aristotelian. It is the other of Platonic idealism, or form: a realism of formlessness, of fragmentation, which makes an ideal form of discontinuity.

Thus in his own poetry can Bonnefoy say that "here is undone the (k)night of mourning" ("voici défait le chevalier du deuil"). (Bonnefoy, translator of Shakespeare, is perfectly aware of the English overdetermination latent in *chevalier*.) In the *vrai lieu* of this poem, night and mourning are undone, and the subjectivity (knight), the mourner (Aeneas/Narcissus), the warrior who mourned in his desire, is defeated, having turned into defeat. And so the new poetic voice—not defeated but defeat itself, not having lost but loss—awakens into the immediacy of fragmentariness, "songe qui se poursuit," Hypnos. The (k)night is dead, but still lives, for the new poetry needs him: "Son visage est celui que je cherche / Sur toutes sources ou falaises, frère mort" ("His face is the one I search for / In every fountain or cliff, dead

---

28. *Ibid*,: 'J'appelle mélancholie cette union de la lucidité, de l'espoir. . . . C'est là au moins le don qu'un vrai poète peut faire. Et dans sa pauvreté, donner demeure son bien.
    "La poésie a longtemps voulu habiter dans la maison de l'Idée, mais comme il est dit, elle en a été chassée, elle s'en est enfuie *en jetant des cris de douleur*. La poésie moderne est loin de sa demeure possible. La grande salle aux quatre fenêtres lui est toujours refusée. Le repos de la forme dans le poème n'est pas honnêtement acceptable. Mais la chance de la poésie à venir, en tant au moins que bonheur (et je puis bien, maintenant, consentir à ce bonheur), est qu'elle est au point de connaître, dans son durable exil, ce que peut ouvrir la *présence*. Après tant d'heures d'angoisse. Etait-ce donc si difficile? Ne suffisait-il pas d'apercevoir, au flanc de quelque montagne, une vitre au soleil du soir?" (130–31).

brother"). Aeneas/Narcissus has become the demon/muse of the poem, the other in whose symbolic language poeticity translates itself.

> Il me semble, penché sur l'aube difficile
> De ce jour qui m'est dû et que j'ai reconquis,
> Que j'entends sangloter l'éternelle présence
> De mon démon secret jamais enseveli.[29]

> It seems to me, leaning over the difficult dawn / Of this day which is due me and which I reconquered, / That I hear sobbing the eternal presence / Of my secret demon, never buried.

The past in such poetry is spatialized, transposed entirely into objective immediacy. Its absence is described as a presence of name and place, albeit ruined. The present-ness, presence of this absence, is celebrated, not bewailed. Old summers become windowpanes, and shadows give way to bright light reflected in the panes, the brightest of which, the shadows' "arch-daughter," must be none other than the nameless lost Lenore. Here, one does not remember; one merely sees.

> Tu demandes le nom
> De cette maison basse délabrée,
> C'est Jean et Jeanne en un autre pays.

> Quand les larges vents passent
> Le seuil ou rien ne chante ni paraît.

> C'est Jean et Jeanne et de leurs faces grises
> La plâtre du jour tombe et je revois
> La vitre des étés anciens. Te souviens-tu?
> La plus brillante au loin, l'arche fille des ombres[30]

> You ask the name / Of this low ruined house / It is Jean and Jeanne in an other country. // When the wide winds pass / The

---

29. Yves Bonnefoy, *Poèmes* (Paris, 1978), 87–88.
30. *Ibid.*, 189. See also the interesting bird poems of "Le Chant de Sauvegarde," 129–41, one of which is suggestively entitled "Le Ravin," meaning, in French, gully or ravine and not ostensibly ornithologically oriented. Bonnefoy, as noted in the text, is very aware of English homonymities.

threshold where nothing sings or passes. // It is Jean and Jeanne
and from their grey faces / The plaster of day falls and I
see again / The windowpane of old summers. Do you
remember? / The most brilliant in the distance, arch-daughter
of shadows

To honor the dead, the poem's voice builds a fire to combust
their absence, a fire of poetic derangement, now defined as
oubli, 'forgetfulness', 'oblivion'. Yet this violence of discontinuity nourishes the dead and lives for them. It feeds the lost by
being loss, by its perpetual flight and ever greater distance.

Aujourd'hui, ce soir, nous ferons un feu
Dans la grande salle.
Nous nous éloignerons,
Nous le laisserons vivre pour les morts.

Today, this evening, we shall make a fire / In the great room / We
shall withdraw, / We shall leave it to live for the dead.

The *nouveau romans* of Nathalie Sarraute and Alain Robbe-
Grillet transpose this poetic strategy into fragmented narrative,
or antinarrative, which has no distinctly identifiable beginning,
middle, and end; every sentence is an 'entire' fragment in the
present tense. That sort of narration effects a realism based on
the most absolute irony, parabasis, displacement, and distancing
of the language from itself. The extremity of such ironic realism
approaches stasis asymptotically, making Robbe-Grillet's micro-
scopically detailed narratives indistinguishable from the
ecphrasis of art criticism. The narrative achieves a stasis of representation, while the ecphrasis enacts a representation of stasis.
Sarraute's interior monologue does much the same thing from
the shifting perspectives of her characters' differential subjec-
tivities. The effect of Sarraute's expansive, intersubjective (rather
than objective, pretendedly neutral and exterior) magnification
of detail is to present a gallery of nearly frozen images, virtual
ecphrases of the same scene transposed in various styles and
schools of representation. The irony of both writers is to show
us the contradiction implicit in realism, which causes it to dis-

solve into grotesque disproportion when taken seriously on its own terms and pursued to its logical conclusions.[31] As the density and viscosity of this realism increases, its distinction from dream is more and more ironized; Aeneas, the archetype of the narrative hero, and Narcissus, the archetype of the lyrical hero, become more and more indistinct from Hypnos.

The ironic realism allows a practice of poetic immediacy that would not otherwise be possible within the framework of narration. A long narrative, to achieve an effect of fragmentation, must discover strategies for subverting its apparent continuity, the semblance of totality implied by its sequential length. The practice may entail an absurd specificity, an attention to detail, and a realism so relentlessly, ruthlessly thorough that it renders reality incongruous and grotesque. The effect may be achieved through the use of free indirect discourse or interior monologue in which the text appears to be narrated by its characters, by its own objects, or by itself. The reader then finds himself involved in a parabasis as he reads, becoming the authorial, organizing presence. Or the text may carefully observe Aristotelian unities—moderation and decorum—only to subvert them abruptly by chiasmus or parabasis.

Georges Bataille, for instance, achieves a severely ironic ten-

---

31. Robbe-Grillet has published a collaborative novel with René Magritte, in which a page of text by the former accompanies each reproduction of a painting by the latter. The texts describe and embellish the pictures narratively. The paintings were not done expressly for this work. See Robbe-Grillet and Magritte, *La Belle Captive* (Lausanne-Paris, 1975). Robbe-Grillet is also well known for his *ciné-romans*. The new novelists have been interested in cinema because it neatly reverses the mimetic priority of image and word: the script describes, imitates a reality that is to be translated into real images later. The images are just as much a phenomenon of artifice as the words they imitate. Yet, because they are images, it is much easier for the moviegoer to fall victim to the mimetic fallacy than for the reader to; that is, it is easier for him to forget the artifice and imitation. The image is nonetheless a sign and is involved in a mutual, tautological mimesis with the word. See Robbe-Grillet, *L'Immortelle* (Paris, 1963), translated by A. M. Sheridan Smith as *The Immortal* (London, 1971), and *Instantanés* (Paris, 1962), translated by Bruce Morrissette as *Snapshots* (New York, 1968); Nathalie Sarraute, *L'Ere du soupçon, essais sur le roman* (Paris, 1956) and *Tropismes* (Paris, 1957); Michel Butor, *Les Mots dans la peinture* (Paris, 1969); Jean Ricardou, "De natura fictiones," in *Pour une théorie du nouveau roman* (Paris, 1971).

sion in his erotic stories and novels by combining the most classical and elevated syntax of past tense narration, the *passé simple*, with the most obscenely pornographic vocabulary available to him. The text, ostensibly pornographic and literary, subverts both the eroticism of the vocabulary and the elevated realism of the syntax by the immediacy of nonreferential laughter. Literary desire and sexual desire are defeated at the same time, each by the other. Perhaps the most salutary example of that practice is in *Le Mort*, the dead body—no longer *beau* or even ambiguously deceased as the *corps* was. At the bottom of each page is an aphoristic summation of the preceding narrative: "MARIE TOMBE IVRE MORTE" ("MARIE FALLS DRUNK DEAD"), "MARIE S'ARROSE D'URINE" ("MARIE DRENCHES HERSELF WITH URINE"). These poetic fragments are transposed into classical narrative on each page. For example, above "MARIE S'ARROSE D'URINE," we read:

> MARIE pissait toujours.
>
> Sur la table au milieu des bouteilles et des verres, elle s'arrosait d'urine avec les mains.
>
> Elle s'inondait les jambes, le cul et la figure.
>
> —Regarde, dit-elle, je suis belle.
>
> Accroupie, le con au niveau de la tête du monstre, elle en fit ouvrir horriblement les lèvres.[32]

> MARIE was still pissing.
>
> On the table amongst the bottles and glasses, she used her hands to baste herself with urine.
>
> She inundated her legs, her ass and her face.
>
> —Look, she said, I am beautiful.
>
> Crouched over, her cunt at the level of the monster's head, she made it horribly open its lips.

Whose lips? Her nether ones or his, *le monstre-comte*'s, facial ones? It is surely both. In this passage, bottles and glasses are

---

32. Georges Bataille, *Madame Edwarda/Le Mort/Histoire de l'oeil* (Paris, n.d.), 76.

everywhere, but in the exchange of fluids, they are circumnavi-
gated. The liquid 'refreshment' in question is not what one
would expect—or hope—to find in a scene involving bottles and
glasses, but rather the excretion of a prior consumption. Convention and expectation are flung to the winds, but with their
very own bland and classical locution. Bataille's practice here is
especially interesting because it questions most effectively the
assertions of such recent theorists as Deleuze and Guattari, who
advance models of the self as a 'desiring machine' and of the text
as a 'signifying machine'.[33] Bataille's textual subjectivity is
rather a *machine à faire rire*, which translates both signification
and desire into the frustration and release, circumvention and
satiety, of laughter.

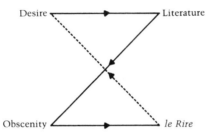

Laughter is after all the absolute other of language, more even
than silence antithetical to signification. Many attempts have
been made to integrate it into a semiotic framework, from
Joubert's *Traité du Ris* to Bergson's *Le Rire* and Freud's *Jokes
and Their Relation to the Unconscious*, none satisfactory except
as instances of the human mind attempting earnestly to transcend incontrovertible limitation, rather like attributing subjective intentions to a raven/parrot's iteration of words and then
verifying one's interpretation by teaching the bird to repeat it.
The situation is convenient, for of course a virtuoso specimen
will repeat virtually anything. And doubtless, in the minuscule
chambers of its own brain, the bird might very well think it
meant something by *nevermore*, might very well intend some
birdish communication. What it might mean and what we might
wish it to mean could not possibly have less in common. Yet,

33. Gilles Deleuze and Felix Guattari, *L'Anti-Oedipe* (Paris, 1972).

like bird-texts, the extent to which laughter incites and nourishes attempts to define it, and simultaneously defies them,
makes it a hyperbole of language, especially suited to the poetics
of immediacy, of subverted desire, of the present in the past.
From a poetics of loss comes a poetics of immediacy and fragmentariness achieved by pursuing incongruence, the innate grotesqueness of time and language, one step further and losing loss
itself.

VII. THE RAVEN RAMIFIED, OR SOUTHERN PROGENY

Hawk, Peacock, Heron, Cockatoo, Peckerwood

The permutations worked on the narrative and poetic paradigms of Tate and Faulkner by southern writers have evolved in ways different from the French but still remarkably akin to them. Each literature can still be read as a commentary on and an overdetermination of the other, even though there has lately been no repetition of the primal scene of translation of the magnitude of Faulkner or Poe. It is not as easy to achieve a semblance of stasis in English as it is in French, or to engage in a hyperbolic realism. The effect of catachresis combined with ellipsis in English is what we found in Poe's language, a grotesque phantasmagoria. In French, the same poem, through a greater ambiguity, be it phonemic or referential, may often attain sublime metaphor as well. The surrealist game of *cadavre exquis*, collective automatic writing, will not work in English as it does in French. Even stretched taut, the semiotic skein that English makes is like that of an insane spider, difficult to synthesize. We already observed that there is an equivocalness and an elasticity, paradoxically rendered possible by the density of the language, that the larger and more widely dispersed lexicon of English, with its greater precision of sound and signification, lacks. This has meant that to turn Faulkner and his tripartite temporality and predominantly analeptic narration into an atemporal ecphrasis has not been possible by the more direct means open to French writers. Contemporary southern writers of fiction and poetry have had recourse to subversions at once more sly and subtle *and* more anticlassical. Within the framework of Faulkner's and Tate's literature of absence, of the loss of presence, it has been possible, somewhat in the manner of Bataille, to set up a tension, sometimes muted, in which the text is forced into a virtual identity with the absence that it takes as object.

William Styron, an extremely successful writer in France, pioneered a reversal of Faulknerian temporality. "Unlike Faulkner," as Richard Pearce has written, "who shows us a present rising out of an ambiguous past, Styron shows us a past that is part of the ambiguous present."[1] The present is a violent accident, perpetually reenacted, and the past is nothing more than a bottomless speculum in which each moment sees itself endlessly repeated, *mis en abîme*. This is often represented by Styron in the symbolic language of history as the experience of war. For instance, in the opening passage of *The Long March*, eight young marines have been slaughtered by the accidental misfiring of two of their own mortar shells. Life, the present, spews itself into the past as death. "It was not so much as if they had departed this life but as if, sprayed from a hose, they were only shreds of bone, gut, and dangling tissue to which it would have been impossible ever to impute the quality of life, far less the capacity to relinquish it. . . . Of course it had been an accident."[2]

More than Styron's novels, Robert Penn Warren's poetry represents what is arguably the most exemplary achievement of the tension between past and present. Warren's poetic idiom, highly elliptical like Char's, also uses catachresis, along with a chiasmus that is at times temporal in nature, in which past and present freely supplant one another, and as often spatial, in which the poem enacts an ecphrasis. It is an ecphrasis not of time, but of its effects, in which time is represented not as a progression, but as a series of transubstantiative reversals, all inscribed in the present tense. Warren's figural language is always spare and often so understated that it is difficult to sort out the figural from the literal. The abrasion of abrupt catachresis and understated, economical description establishes an irony that will not let us decide whether the poem's figural language (catachresis) is in fact representational, referring to some object that it literally describes, or whether the highly elliptical descriptive litotes are intended to collude with the grotesque allegoricalness suggested by the catachresis. Thus, by a hyperbole of ellipsis and

1. Richard Pearce, *William Styron* (Minneapolis, 1971), 11.
2. William Styron, *The Long March* (New York, 1952), 3, 5.

litote, Warren often is able to realize a perfect poetic presence
within an ostensibly mimetic and descriptive poetry of subjectivity and absence. His mimesis of the real is so pared down, so
simultaneously restrained and ironic, that it becomes indistinguishable from allegory. His poetic narratives of experience
become transcriptions of dream, and his poetic voice could be
that of Aeneas, Narcissus, Hypnos, or Hermes. The tension
achieved between mimesis and Platonic formalism, subjectivity
and objectivity, absence and presence, through the use of hyperbolic omission and understatement, ecphrasis and irony, has produced far and away the most powerful poetry being written in
America and ostensibly the English language. In Warren's
poems, the present is an ellipsis of the past, and the past is
nothing more than the simultaneity, superimposition, and surfeit of so much ellipsis and so many understated allegories of
moment. Here is an instance in which his practice of temporal
chiasmus is clearly visible.

> Suddenly. Is. Now not what was *not*,
> But what is. From nothing of *not*
> Now all of *is*. All is. Is light, and suddenly
> Dawn—and the world, in blaze of *is*,
> Burns. Is flame, of time and tense
>
> The bold combustion, and
> The flame of *is*, in fury
> And ungainsayable updraft of that
> Black chimney of what is *not*,
> Roars. Christmas—
>
> Remember, remember!—and into flame
> All those gay wrappings the children fling, then
> In hands of *now*, they hold
> Presents of *is*, and while
> Flame leaps, they, in joy,
> Scream. Oh, children,
>
> Now to me I sing, I see
> Forever on the leaf the light. Snow
> On the pine-leaf, against the bright blue

Forever of my mind, like breath,
Balances. But light,

Is always light, and suddenly,
On any morning, is, and somewhere,
In a garden you will never
See, dew, in fracture of light
And lunacy of gleam-glory, glitters on
A petal red as blood, and

The rose dies, laughing.[3]

The poetic voice, in the present, is taking the present as its own object, realizing its ego as the past, a dialectical friction translated in the symbolic language of fire.

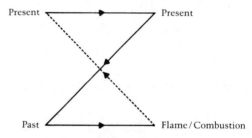

The flame itself is involved in another dialectic.

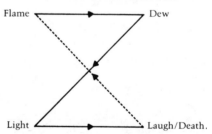

The text, in its own "lunacy of dream-glory," in the glitter of the moment of reading, laughs at itself (in the inner voice of the reader), and so dies, erasing its referential qualities with an irony of the grotesque, with extreme catachresis.

3. Robert Penn Warren, *Selected Poems, 1923–1975* (New York, 1976), 186–87.

In "Evening Hawk," the temporal chiasmus is translated into a more purely spatial language of zoological and luminous allegory, not metaphor but allegory and mimesis. The poem might be simply a poetic reflection on the passage from day to night, or an allegory of time, using hawk, bat, light, and dark as indeterminate symbols. In fact, it is both of these. As trope of trope, figure of figure, emblem of poeticity, the aporial coupling of hawk and bat is Warren's raven, his muse of namelessness.

> From plane of light to plane, wings dipping through
> Geometries and orchids that the sunset builds,
> Out of the peak's black angularity of shadow, riding
> The last tumultuous avalanche of
> Light above pines and the guttural gorge,
> The hawk comes.
>   His wing
> Scythes down another day, his motion
> Is that of the honed steel-edge, we hear
> The crashless fall of stalks of Time.
>
> The head of each stalk is heavy with the gold of our error.
>
> Look! Look! he is climbing the last light
> Who knows neither Time nor error, and under
> Whose eye, unforgiving, the world, unforgiven, swings
> Into shadow.
>   Long now,
> The last thrush is still, the last bat
> Now cruises in his sharp hieroglyphics. His wisdom
> Is ancient, too, and immense. The star
> Is steady, like Plato, over the mountain.
>
> If there were no wind we might, we think, hear
> The earth grind on its axis, or history
> Drip in darkness like a leaking pipe in the cellar.[4]

Poe's temporality is turned inside out, like his bird-muse. It is bird and not bird (aviating mammal), bringer of violence (hawk)

4. *Ibid.*, 4–5.

or evil, or disease (bat, mythic harbinger of ill omen, drainer of blood). It is not speech in either case, but rather motion, spatial flux, at once predatorily smooth (with the powerful suggestion of latent destructiveness, scything cleanly) and sharp, jerky, hacking a vicious, crazy path through the seconds of time. Hieroglyphs are what we are faced with, not a bird that mindlessly repeats human speech aloud, but a couple whose only language is a silence of movement that describes, in the eye of the poem, the progress of the present and, like it, leaves no trace. Against a backdrop of blankly inscrutable form ("The star / Is steady, like Plato"), signs of time swoop, scratch, erase themselves. The catachresis that describes the hawk belies his steadiness; the bat's nervous path is set in a soothing unguent of simile. The distinction between them, like the arcs and scratches they trace, appears only in the virtuality of the reading and instantly disappears. In the light of day the black of the peak stands out; at night the stars upstage the dark. The wind, which is the possibility of their movement, erases all sign of it—no noise, no sign but the wind itself. History, the totality of time, is dissolved in the blind, painless violence of that susurrating erasure. "If there were no wind we might . . . hear / history / Drip in darkness."

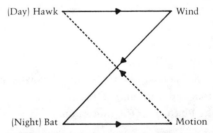

From the perspective of visual space, there is no such thing as error or time, only movement: "the last light / Who knows neither Time nor error." But in the eye and voice of the poem, temporal movement is error, in the French sense of *error*, 'to wander', a blind progress from oblivion and back to it, tracing random shape in the interstice that is lost as it is seen. History

is its own defeat (*dé-faite*, 'undoing'), erased by its own movement, drowned out by the voice of the wind it would echo.

Literariness and history have this in common: they belie
themselves as well as one another, not out of any wish to, but
because they have no choice. They translate languages that they
do not understand (which therefore are not effectively languages
at all); they name what is not nameable. They are "mistakes:
misnamings, misunderstandings, or misrememberings," in a
word, translations, tautological solutions of an equation that admits of no solution.

> But they are mistakes which, in each case, have resulted in an
> authentic poetic experience—what Blackmur calls "that height-
> ened, that excited sense of being"—an experience, moreover,
> which was notably absent before the mistake was made. . . . It
> might be useful to look into the workings of these accidental
> stumblings into poetic meaning because they exhibit in a striking
> fashion that particular feature of metaphor which has most
> troubled philosophers: that it is "wrong"—it asserts of one thing
> that it is something else—and further, that its beauty often seems
> proportionate to its wrongness or outlandishness . . . here some-
> thing very big happens in a very small place.[5]

It is apt indeed that Walker Percy should commit in this passage
so egregiously crude an error himself, describing allegory as an
encoded mimesis and not recognizing it as precisely the condi-
tion of infinite analogy, "density and thingness," which he, with
Allen Tate, wishes to reserve to nature.

> Not that the single linguistic metaphor represents the highest
> moment of the poetic imagination; it probably does not. Dante, as
> Allen Tate reminds us, uses very few linguistic metaphors. The
> "greatest thing by far" which Aristotle had in mind when he
> spoke of the mastery of metaphor as a sign of genius may very
> well have been the sort of prolonged analogy which Dante did use,

5. Percy, *The Message in the Bottle*, 65–66.

in which the action takes place among the common things of experience and yet yields an analogy—by nothing so crude as allegorization wherein one thing is designated as standing for another but by the very density and thingness of the action. As Tate puts it: "Nature offers the symbolic poet clearly denotable objects in depth and in the round, which yield the analogies to the higher syntheses."

Medieval doctrines of representation notwithstanding, allegory is a density of latent error, an equation which only admits solutions that abolish its logic. Percy enacts just such an abolishment here. "And it is wrongest when it is most beautiful."[6]

Percy has focused on this phenomenon as relentlessly as Derrida. Yet he has not gotten as much mileage from it in intellectual circles, probably because he persists in recognizing a mysteriousness, an inexplicableness, a will that invests the ongoing error of knowledge. Derrida denies such a will to err, while confirming it by his denial. Percy confirms it, along with its inexplicableness, by insisting on its intentionality and its identity with spiritual man. In his Catholicism, he prolongs and ramifies the error. And that is why Thomism, and religion in general, has heavily invested the literature of the South and of France—an existential religiosity that is literary because it knows that it is a mistake, worth committing because it is the error of errors, archraven because it would exceed the dialectic of error, or translation, by identifying with it. Derrida's project is exactly the same, except that his religion is the very positivism he pretends to critique, of which he is the most rarefied and subtle avatar, having exempted himself from the tautology of perception in order to expose it.

Neo-Thomism explains the error of knowledge as a tautology of man and God, rendered erroneous by the former's estrangement from the latter. It accounts for error by calling it "inner necessity."

6. *Ibid.*, 66.

Poetic experience brings the poet back to the hidden place, at the single root of the powers of the soul, where the entire subjectivity is, as it were, gathered in a state of expectation and virtual creativity. Into this place he enters, not by any effort of voluntary consciousness, but by a recollection, fleeting as it may be, of all the senses, and a kind of unifying repose which is like a natural grace, a primordial gift, but to which he has to consent, and which he can cultivate, first of all by removing obstacles and silencing concepts. Thus poetic experience is, emerging on the verge of the spiritual preconscious, a state of obscure, unexpressed and sapid knowing—the expression of which, when later on it will come about in a work, will also be sapid. Do we not read, in an old Sanskrit text, that "Poetry is a word whose essence is Savor?" In such *a spiritual contract of the soul with itself*, all the sources are touched together, and the first obligation of the poet is to respect the integrity of this original experience. Any systematic denial of any of the faculties involved would be a sort of self-mutilation.[7] (emphasis mine)

The reductiveness of Jacques Maritain's philosophy of literature and its insistence upon totalization, on the organic unity expressed in the work and on arresting the movement of error, betrays and belies literature—and in doing so contributes to it. "Any systematic denial of any of the faculties involved would be a sort of self-mutilation," Maritain writes. And even as he writes, he commits just such a self-mutilation, in blind perpetration of the metaphor of religion, as though it could be exempted from the indeterminacy, the mysteriousness, it names. The examples of Derrida and Maritain both imply that literary theory needs to exempt itself from its own project, its own translatedness, or rather to believe in its exemption, which is purely illusory.

The religious impulse in novel or poetry, whatever its doctrinal basis, acknowledges this aporia in its practice. A raven or

7. Jacques Maritain, *Creative Intuition in Art and Poetry* (New York, 1974), 176–77.

a parrot or a hawk or a bat, in the natural density of latent error (knowledge), may mean knowledge and error, cognition and memory, original and translation, sound and inscription, and image, all at once. Literature can enact this tension in a small space, dramatize it and radicalize its violence in figures, but it has an advantage over theory in its inability even to pretend to be exempted from that violence. It can suggest mystery or absurdity or nihilism, in the error of reading and knowing, but it cannot exempt itself from that error without addressing the error as error, and that would be to exempt itself from the error. If it did this, it would cross the boundary from literary practice to literary theory.

Percy's own Catholicism is never asserted, never resolved. It is not named and therefore remains viable, literary rather than theoretical. Within the miscalculation of knowing, there are only two possible courses: to exacerbate the error through random violence, epistemological or physical, or to coincide with the error passively. Both courses embrace the ongoing error. There is no difference between the two, and yet there is, an erroneous difference: that between the criminal and the saint, the active nonbeliever and the active believer. They are a chiasmus, but also an aporia. In *Lancelot*, Percy has sketched their dialectical interdependence.

> So you plan to take a little church in Alabama, Father, preach the gospel, turn bread into flesh, forgive the sins of Buick dealers, administer communion to suburban housewives?
>
> At last you're looking straight at me, but how strangely! Ah, all at once I understand you. I read you as instantly as I used to when we were so close. All of a sudden we understand each other perfectly, don't we?
>
> Tell me if I'm right or wrong.
>
> You know something you think I don't know, and you want to tell me but you hesitate.
>
> *Yes.*
>
> You speak! Loud and clear! And looking straight at me!
>
> But I can see in your eyes it doesn't make any difference any

more, as far as what is going to happen next is concerned, that what is going to happen is going to happen whether you or I believe or not and whether your belief is true or not. Right?

Yes.

We are not going to make it this way, are we?

No.

It's all over isn't it? I can see it in your eyes. We agree after all.

Yes.

Yes, but? But what? There must be a new beginning, right?

Yes—

. . . .

So you are going to go to your little church in Alabama and that's it?

Yes.

So where's the new beginning in that? Isn't that just more of the same?

You are silent.

Very well! But you know this! One of us is wrong. It will be your way or it will be my way.

Yes.

All we can agree on is that it will not be their way. Out there.

Yes.

There is no other way than yours or mine, true?

Yes.

. . . .

Very well. I've finished. Is there anything you wish to tell me before I leave?

Yes.[8]

And upon that final ironic affirmation the book ends, and does not end.

Literature, unlike theory, can only approach the spiritual (and

8. Walker Percy, *Lancelot* (New York, 1977), 256–57.

remain distinct from theory) as a tension within its own project. The works of Julian Green achieve such a tension on the thematic level as the conflicting exigencies of body and spirit, of sexual and spiritual desire. The dissonance of these two impulsions, equally irresistible, each an interdiction of the other, defines the dialectic of human being as transgression, or sin. Even in such works as *Leviathan*, written when Green had 'lost his faith,' this dialectic of dissonant desires is at work as a conflict between the biological imperative of sexuality and purely circumstantial impediment. That Green at other times assimilates circumstance with spirit does not much alter the narrative itself. If anything, it softens its violence, for in the Catholic context the spirit holds out latent promise of redemption, of escape from the violence of dialectical desires. In *Leviathan*, we encounter a protagonist whose lust is simply rebuffed by the object it has chosen. The reaction of Guéret to this violence of constraint is violence.

> Et comme elle essayait de se libérer et de crier, il la frappa à la poitrine et au visage, plusieurs fois. Il lui sembla tout à coup que la rivière, les arbres, l'air, tout remuait autour de lui et qu'un rugissement continu emplissait le ciel. Les poings se levaient et retombaient sans qu'il en fût le maître. Sa seule pensée était de fair cesser ces abominables cris qui sortaient de cette bouche, ce son aigu quie pénétrait dans son cerveau comme une arme et le déchirait. Une terreur, la propre terreur de sa victime, le gagnait. Il ne savait plus comment échapper à lui-même, à son crime, comment empêcher ses mains d'agir, comment arrêter ces cris. Les yeux de la jeune fille ne le regardaient plus . . . elle ressemblait déjà à cette vision de l'assassinat qu'il avait eue la nuit dernière.
>
> Brusquement, il saisit la branche qu'il avait jetée de côté et qui était à portée de sa main. Dans l'excès de sa colère il leva son arme et en frappa Angèle au visage, sur les joues, sur le front, jusqu'à ce qu'elle se tût et que le sang derobât aux yeux du vainqueur la vue de ces traits qu'il adorait.

> And as she tried to free herself and cry out, he struck her in the chest and in the face, several times. It seemed to him suddenly

that the river, the trees, the air, everything was moving around
him, and that a continuous roar filled the sky. The fists rose and
fell without him being the master of them. His one thought was
to cease those abominable cries which were coming from that
mouth, that piercing sound which penetrated into his brain like a
weapon and tore it. A terror, the very terror of his victim, over-
came him. He no longer knew how to escape himself, his crime,
how to keep his hands from acting, how to stop the cries. The
girl's eyes no longer looked at him . . . she looked already like the
vision of a murder which he had had last night.

Brusquely, he seized the branch that he had thrown to one side
and that was in reach of his hand. In the excess of his anger he
raised his weapon and struck Angèle with it in the face, on the
cheeks, on the forehead, until she was silent and the blood hid
from the vanquisher's eyes the sight of the features he adored.

He maims Angèle, who has refused him, and still unrequited,
murders the first old man he encounters in the street. Of course,
this does not abate his rage either. Guéret himself is the passive
bystander or *object* in every sentence of the first paragraph here,
except one ("il la frappa"): "Il ne savait plus comment *échapper
à lui-même.*" His arms rise and fall, but he is not the agent of
this action. The memory of the act is like a dream to him, even
as the act, as it occurs, seems like a dream he had the night
before. Yet he remembers it, recognizes its reality.

> . . . ces branches cassées, il les avait vues dans son cauchemar. Se
> pouvait-il que dans sa folie il eût observé tant de petites choses,
> tant de fleurs, d'arbres, de reflets? Quelque chose en lui était
> demeuré éveillé, alors que tout le reste de son être était plongé
> dans une sorte de rêverie effroyable où des actes s'accomplissaient
> qu'il n'avait pas crus possibles, des actes de meurtre et de désir.[9]

> . . . these broken branches, he had seen them in his nightmare.
> Was it possible that in his madness he had observed so many little
> things, so many flowers, trees, reflections? Something in him had
> remained awake, while all the rest of his being was plunged into

9. Julian Green, *Léviathan* (New ed.; Paris, 1973), 153–54, 156.

a sort of horrible daydream in which acts were performed which he would not have thought possible, acts of murder and desire.

Freely projected, dream is memory in reverse. Reality partakes of both memory and dream, their dissonance. The mind, the ego, the wakeful self of Guéret, is passively involved with his dream self, his desire, his id, which disfigures its object without intending to do so, but simply because it is ultimately the nature of desire to try to erase the specificity of the object, to wish to assimilate, totalize, possess, and finalize it as one might a definitive edition. All of these acts are destructive of desire itself, which depends on the object; the effect is to displace desire onto new objects and to subvert the morality of judgment, to reverse cognition and memory, confusing them with dream, and to turn the violence of dream and its rhetoric from the self onto the other. This is an allegory of the text's own projection, representation of Guéret, its splitting of him into cognition and dream, interdiction and desire, active (not knowing) and passive (*his arms* rain blows on Angèle), murderer and victim.

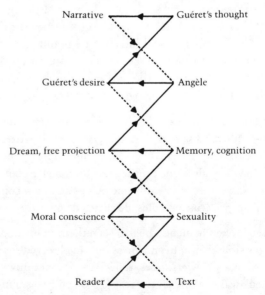

Finally, what is most fascinating about Green—whose name is virtually anagrammatized in Guéret: Greeu(t)—is the literal role of translation in the tension that he uses to intimate the spiritual. Green's family was southern. Five years before his birth, they moved to France. His education and intellectual development were entirely French, and yet he was raised with a sense of being southern, of having blood relations in the South. Biologically he was southern; linguistically and intellectually he was French. Catholicism, to which he converted when he was sixteen, was part of his French intellectual baggage. His sexuality, his bodily, biological being (his 'dream self'), as can be clearly seen in his journal and autobiography, he identified with the South—its tropical heat, its primitive languor, its sweaty, rude, sinewy earthiness, swooningly redolent of sweet magnolia blooms.

> Once again, I rediscovered myself as I had been in years before, a child heaving with confused desires. Why? Was it the heat, the night, the South? I waited for the heavy and panting mass to pass by my door and into the bedroom where I heard it breath and speak in a low voice. To whom? To shadows? Finally the house plunged into an almost supernatural silence. I was naked on my bed. Everyone slept naked these nights of tropical summer. At dawn, one would draw up the light sheet which would protect from the slightly cool breeze off of the Atlantic, but sometimes, before going to sleep, I looked at my body gleaming in the half-dark. There was no sin in looking at one's chest, arms, legs. I asked myself however what good were these agile and robust members, but to this question, what answer? There was no answer. Finally I would go to sleep.

With his cousin Bill Veeder, Green skinny-dipped.

> Horses tied, we took off our clothes and like lightning, I saw Bill throw himself in the water and swim towards the middle of the river. "Come on there!" he cried to me. I hesitated. What he did not know was that I held in the hollow of my hand the medals I always wore around my neck and which I had just taken off with a quick gesture I was ashamed of. I blushed for my medals before

the pretty protestant. Had I some other idea in my head? Did I
fear lest these medals prevent something? But what? What did
I obscurely hope for? The impossible? It was that, without doubt.
I hoped for the impossible, as much, for the rest, as I feared it. My
hand opened slightly, letting the medals slip to my feet, and I
went down into the river.

· ·

There was something so direct and lighthearted in the look of his
black eyes that I almost told him how handsome I found him,
instead of which I waited until he was a little farther away and
climbed quickly up onto the bank to hide my scarcely dry body in
my clothes. When Bill rejoined me, I saw the drops of water
streaming on his chest and arms, and I looked away. His brown
skin gleamed in the last rays of the sun. I had rarely felt so unfor-
tunate. He dressed in his turn and we went home.

We see Green here in the element of the body, the South's great
warm muddy water of drawled English, altogether and thrillingly
unlike the French Seine.

> We had first to cross all of Virginia, which is fairly pleasant, then
> sad North Carolina with its poor vegetation and its little wooden
> houses, finally South Carolina which the Savannah River, wide as
> a branch of the sea, separated from Georgia. Seeing that mud-
> colored stretch over which the express passed, I remembered what
> my mother would say to me about the Seine: "Back home, this
> river would hardly have a name." But in memory, the green Seine
> seemed lovable to me next to this monstrous mass of brown wa-
> ters which moved sinisterly toward the Atlantic.[10]

French is the idiom of Green's mind and Catholic spirit. English,
strange and yet closer to him in a more visceral way, is the
language of his blood, family, body, and ingenuously erotic cous-
ins. In the language of the body, the mind stumbles and is not
sure; it suffers violence. The impossibility of true translation
from one medium, that of mind and spirit, into the other, that of
desire, and back again—a translation that would obliterate the

10. Julian Green, *Oeuvres complètes*, ed. Jacques Petit (Paris, 1977), 1118,
1131, 1109.

difference, the dialectic, the violence of interdiction—is what Green's fiction is all about. The fiction itself represents an attempt to transcribe the very tension in the language of the mind (French), to control and objectify it, to project Green and imprison him in words as Guéret. But the anagram is botched; there is a letter left over, and one turned upside down: together *tu*, the familiar form of second person—"hypocrite lecteur, mon semblable, mon frère!"

In the work of Reynolds Price, we encounter a sense of the mysterious that is frankly Christian, but not Catholic. His books offer proof, if we need any, that the southern writer can deal with matters of spirit without reference to a particular orthodoxy. *Catholicism*, like *raven*, is a name arbitrarily assigned to the namelessness at the heart of the text, its tension. As often as not, Price, in his fiercely deliberate, highly crafted fiction and poetry, is content to achieve a sense of the spiritual within the incidental details of nature and human lives. The high gloss of his self-conscious narrative rhetoric enacts a dissonance that the characters play out thematically. Price places his narrative impulse squarely in the realistic tradition that aims to depict "man in the presence of the natural world." And yet, the mimetic aspect of Price's fiction is doubted by the ecphrasic quality of his highly wrought prose and verse. Some critics, taking the realism rather too seriously, have criticized Price for placing such sophisticated language in the mouths of simple country people. But this is just how Price achieves the fission of unnameableness in his work, the sense of a rheumy spiritual presence in the desert of mimetic realism. His is, not surprisingly, a realism of the grotesque. Its grotesquerie, incongruence with its own realism, is mediated as it is imitated by the intensity of form and the careful attention to language, especially in the description of very small details of act or character, the use of ecphrasis as narrative. *A Generous Man* is one of the best examples of this tension. Price says that

> *A Generous Man* is about a very real world, yes; but it is not a realistic novel. If I must catalogue it, perhaps I'd call it a romance. If *A Generous Man* has literary ancestors, those ancestors are not

really to be found in the novel but in other forms. I was not conscious of this when I began *A Generous Man* nor, in fact, until I had completed the novel; but in all the literature known to me, *A Generous Man* resembles only—in kind, understand—the late plays of Shakespeare (*The Tempest, The Winter's Tale, Cymbeline*), certain operas (say, *The Magic Flute* of Mozart) in that it does negotiate with the "real world" which all human beings perceive, however dull, however bored, however fogged by routine, but a real world which is capable of swelling at moments of intensity to a mysterious, transfigured world, a world in which all manner of "unrealistic" events can and will occur—the return of the dead, outrageous coincidence, great rushes of communication between people, great avowals of love or hate—events of a sort that do not occur in any world which I've experienced with my own eyes and ears, which I suspect, almost *know* to lie only slightly beneath the surface of the world of most men.[11]

The friction between that underworld and ours is expressed in the language Price uses to mediate the latter; as often as catachresis ("safe as houses," "weather screwed down," "fish roared"), and sometimes together with it, Price reverses the order of subject and predicate and modifier, using nouns as verbs and verbs as adjectives, making them bear the chief burden of figuration: "Brown water *ringed*," "panes *broadcasting*," "profoundly *fondued*," "*coated, booted*," "resurrections . . . / Have a habit of *dawning* in the prebreakfast / Deserts," "*Hatted* and *scarfed*, " "I hear his *oaring*."[12]

It is the premise of Price's work that nature confronts us with the same aporia as language, as his language—here one of ecphrasis and mimesis, immobility and movement. Price is not content to confine the fission to language or literature and in this is far bolder than the supposedly boldest literary theorists, Derrida and de Man. He finds a bird to be an emblem of the aporia: heron, symbol of Hermes, bringer of dreams and mes-

11. Carr, ed., *Kite-Flying and Other Irrational Acts*, 94, 87, 78–79.
12. Reynolds Price, *The Annual Heron* (New York, 1980). Also appeared in *Poetry*, December, 1979.

sages, brother of Hypnos. Do the annual visits of a heron mean more than "the obvious— / Migration?" If so, the messages lie beneath the ornithological, natural one and are not visible in it. Is the message that of nature—turn, return, endure—or of super-nature, spirit? Both.

> So left with that—actual phoenix
> At the edge of my yard, possessed of new
> Grace since his nocturnal skirmish with
> The local dingoes; entirely acceptable
> *Minister of silence*—I climb to the otherwise [emphasis mine]
> Empty house and make for myself
> An oracle from his mute persistence
> Through volumes of air, corrosive years—
> *Endurance is fed: here, in time.*
> *Therefore endure. Then make another—*
> *You hope in vain. The heart is fed*
> *Only where I go when I leave you here.*
> *Follow me.*[13]

Price's birds, like Warren's hawk and bat, are characterized as hieroglyphs of motion, whether the heron, stock-still on earth, with folding neck and trailing legs in slow take-off, or the smaller, batlike creatures, "going off against the evening like out of pistols, hard dark bullets that arched dark on the sky and curled and showered to the sturdy trees beneath."[14]

Flannery O'Connor's peafowl are an altogether different story. Color is their salient feature. Colors, like birds, are emblems of the figurative alchemy of language: they cannot be reduced to a specific signified. They are in pure state of allegory, or of gro-tesqueness. We must invent oracles from their muteness, read them by acts of interpretive violence, for there are no fixed val-ues in the equation of their signification. Here is a passage from O'Connor's own experience:

> One of mine stepped from under the shrubbery one day and came

13. *Ibid.*
14. Reynolds Price, *The Names and Faces of Heroes* (New York, 1973), 53.

forward to inspect a carful of people who had driven up to buy a calf. An old man and five or six white-haired bare-footed children were piling out the back of the automobile as the bird approached. Catching sight of him they stopped in their tracks and stared, plainly hacked to find this superior figure blocking their path. There was silence as the bird regarded them, his head drawn back at its most majestic angle, his folded train glittering behind him in the sunlight.

"Whut is thet thang?" one of the small boys asked finally in a sullen voice.

The old man had got out of the car and was gazing at the peacock with an astounded look of recognition. "I ain't seen one of them since my grandaddy's day," he said, respectfully removing his hat. "Folks used to have 'em, but they don't no more."

"Whut is it?" the child asked again in the same tone he had used before.

"Churren," the old man said, "that's the king of the birds!"

The children received this information in silence. After a minute they climbed back into the car and continued from there to stare at the peacock, their expressions annoyed, as if they disliked catching the old man in the truth.[15]

Now, what truth is the old man caught in? Usually we speak of someone being caught in a lie. If the children had in any sense caught or captured the old man, they ought to be pleased. What could this truth have reference to? By antecedent, it refers to nothing more than his saying "that's the king of the birds." But this does not tell us what the peacock is, by any means. Birds have no kings, no government. "King of the birds" is either allegory or grotesque catachresis, or both. We are offered, in effect, two answers to the question "What is it?" The first is, something people used to have and don't any more—something lost or misplaced now suddenly stepping forth in the present as lost-ness, fleshed and feathered. That answer is no more helpful than the second, "the king of the birds." The truth that the old man is caught in here is indeed the lie of these insufficient

15. O'Connor, *Mystery and Manners*, pp. 12–13.

answers. He could do no better. An ornithologist could do no better. We cannot say what "it" is. We can only call it a name: beauty, color, bird. We are caught in that lie of truth.

"The Displaced Person" is all about being caught this way, about the chimerical untrustworthiness of language. It is dominated by the silent, stately emblem of the peacock. "The peacock was following Mrs. Shortley up the road to the hill where she meant to stand. . . . The peacock stopped just behind her, his tail—glittering green-gold and blue in the sunlight—lifted just enough so that it would not touch the ground. It flowed out on either side like a floating train and his head on the long blue reed-like neck was drawn back as if his attention were fixed in the distance on something no one else could see." [16] The peacock is outside language, excessive and scandalous. Might it then be able to see what the rest of us cannot, a truly unmediated vision? *Seeing*, however, is a name, and our visions are colored by our names for them as the peacock's visions would not be, entirely without the bounds of our ken. We must resort to saying "as if."

The story deals with exile, defeat, and loss as historical phenomena—a Polish family fleeing atrocities of war—and linguistic ones. Losing their homeland, the Guizacs have left behind the context in which their language meant something, in which it made sense and could seem natural. In English, they 'see' obscurely if at all.

> The boy was in the center of the group, talking. He was supposed to speak the most English because he had learned some in Poland and so he was to listen to his father's Polish and say it in English and then listen to Mrs. McIntyre's English and say that in Polish. The priest had told Mrs. McIntyre his name was Rudolph and he was twelve and the girl's name was Sledgewig and she was nine. Sledgewig sounded to Mrs. Shortley like something you would name a bug, or vice-versa, as if you named a boy Bollweevil. All of them's last name was something that only they

16. O'Connor, *Three by Flannery O'Connor*, 262.

themselves and the priest could pronounce. All she could make out of it was Gobblehook. She and Mrs. McIntyre had been calling them the Gobblehooks all week while they got ready for them.[17]

The Guizac/Gobblehooks are an otherness, a strangeness that Mrs. McIntyre's waking coma of English-speaking complacency can deal with only as a transgression of linguistic convention, of the 'correct' ways of naming and seeing. "No man of sense," says Socrates in the *Cratylus*, "will like to put himself or the education of his mind in the power of names." Either Mrs. McIntyre does not pass the test of sense, or she has no choice, for she is firmly in the power of names and likes it, for now. Mrs. Shortley, wife of the hired hand, goes so far as to exclude chromatic sensibility from the mental equipment of non-English speakers. "'They can't talk,' Mrs. Shortley said. 'You reckon they'll know what colors even is?'"[18]

Mrs. McIntyre's and Mrs. Shortley's embeddedness in names distinguishes them sharply from the priest, as in their perceptions of the peafowl.

"What a beauti-ful birdrrrd!" the priest murmured.

"Another mouth to feed," Mrs. McIntyre said, glancing in the peafowl's direction.

"And when does he raise his splendid tail?" asked the priest.

"Just when it suits him," she said. "There used to be twenty or thirty of those things on the place but I've let them die off. *I don't like to hear them scream in the middle of the night.*"

"So beauti-ful," the priest said. "A tail full of suns," and he crept forward on tiptoe and looked down on the bird's back where the polished gold and green design began. The peacock stood still as if he had just come down from some sun-drenched height to be a vision for them all. The priest's homely red face hung over him, glowing with pleasure.

Mrs. Shortley's mouth had drawn acidly to one side. "Nothing but a peachicken," she muttered. (emphasis mine)

17. *Ibid.*, 263.
18. Plato, *The Collected Dialogues*, 474; O'Connor, *Three by Flannery O'Connor*, 264.

The Negroes, too, seem more open to the implications of the Polish family's situation, less disposed to view them as necessarily different from everyone else, denatured.

> "They come from over the water," Mrs. Shortley said with a wave of her arm. "They're what is called Displaced Persons."
>
> "Displaced Persons," he said. "Well now. I declare. What do that mean?"
>
> "It means they ain't where they were born at and there's nowhere for them to go—like if you was run out of here and wouldn't have nobody to have you."
>
> "It seem like they here, though," the old man said in a reflective voice. "If they here, they somewhere."
>
> "Sho is," the other agreed. "They here."
>
> The illogic of Negro thinking always irked Mrs. Shortley. "They ain't where they belong to be at," she said. "They belong to be back over yonder where everything is still like they been used to. Over here it's more advanced than where they come from."

Mrs. McIntyre feels no pregnant tension of vision looking at the peacock. She has named him: peachicken. He has, she thinks, nothing to offer, nothing to mean, beyond a name.

> She stood a while longer, her *unseeing* eyes directly in front of the peacock's tail. He had jumped into the tree and his tail hung in front of her, full of fierce planets with eyes that were each ringed in green and set against a sun that was gold in one second's light and salmon-colored in the next. She might have been looking at a map of the universe but she didn't notice it any more than she did the spots of sky that cracked the dull green of the tree.[19] (emphasis mine)

Yet, Mrs. McIntyre, confronted with the linguistic otherness of the Guizac/Gobblehooks, is less sure in her house of names.

> She began to imagine a war of words, to see the Polish words and the English words coming at each other, stalking forward, not sentences, just words, *gabble gabble gabble* [bird noises], flung

19. *Ibid.*, pp. 265–66, 267.

out high and shrill and stalking forward and then grappling with
each other. She saw the Polish words, dirty and all-knowing and
unreformed, flinging mud on the clean English words until everything was equally dirty. She saw them all piled up in a room, all
the dead dirty words, theirs and hers too, piled up like the naked
bodies in the newsreel. God save me! she cried silently, from the
stinking power of Satan![20] (emphasis mine)

The ultimate transgression of the Guizac/Gobblehooks is to
not respect the distinctions of name and color, color and name,
tenuously, uncertainly embedded in a code that attaches specific
significances to each, and establishes taboos. Mr. Guizac, a
"white" man, arranges to have his cousin, still in Poland, marry
a "nigger" so that she can come to the United States.

The reason the transgression, along with Guizac's ignorance
of English, disturbs Mrs. McIntyre so much is that it and the
Guizac/Gobblehooks themselves belie the conviction on which
her entire existence is based: that words bear an intrinsic resemblance to the things they name, and that this identity, the totality of word and thing, governs every kind of perception, including chromatic vision. Mr. Guizac's behavior shows that the
specific names of things have nothing whatever to do with the
colors or the things, but represent the most arbitrary enactments
of a fallacious closure. The danger lies in the lack of any real,
palpable difference between Mr. Guizac and Mrs. McIntyre. He
contaminates her. Her entire life is based on totalization in language, and he will not let her believe in it any longer.

"Well," Mr. Shortley said, "if I was going to travel again, it would
be either China or Africa. You can tell right away what the difference is between you and them. You go to these other places and
the only way you can tell is if they say something. And then you
can't always tell because about half of them know the English
language. That's where we make our mistake," he said, "—letting
all them people onto English. There'd be a heap less trouble if
everybody only knew their own language. My wife said knowing

20. *Ibid.*, 276.

two languages was like having eyes in the back of your head. You couldn't put nothing over on her.[21]

Indeed not.

"Gabble gabble gabble," *Gobble*hook—the Guizacs, a living transgression of the English language, are effectively no different from the peafowl. Certainly their Polish is, in Mrs. McIntyre's mind, reduced to a birdy gibberish. But the logical inference is that clean English is in fact just as dirty; neither is anyone else effectively different from the peafowl. Mrs. McIntyre does not like hearing Polish in much the same way that she hates to hear the peacocks scream in the middle of the night. But to the Guizacs, her English means no more and probably does not sound much better. With peacocks and displaced persons about, "You liable to hear most anything," says the old black man, Astor. But you are always "liable" to hear most anything, screams in the night or some other noise, equally unintelligible to you but nevertheless a language to somebody. Words are always at war, with each other and themselves far more than with other languages. But they are at love, too, and are alive and dead, clean and dirty, all at the same time. How can Mrs. McIntyre contain these birdpeople, give them names that will stick and that will anchor them firmly in her system, making them, like the tamed, named peacock, so many mouths to feed? The priest makes no effort to impose such a closure, to interpret the Guizacs or the peachickens, beyond his personal conviction, which he knows fully well to be an article of faith. "Christ will come like that," he says looking at the peacock's tail; that is, he will come as inexplicable, unnameable beauty.[22]

By a final act of violence, the murder of Mr. Guizac, Mrs. McIntyre attempts to preserve her faith in the authority of names, but the effect of this is to shatter the entire scaffolding of the poor woman's self. The equilibrium in which the physical and mental codes of her body had been fastened comes unstuck, and she proves unable to pass beyond its loss, as the priest has. Below is a schematic representation of the narrative.

21. *Ibid.*, 297.
22. *Ibid.*, 291.

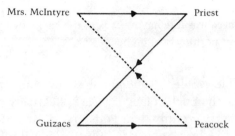

The story is articulated in the symbolic language of color and of language itself. It is an allegory of the Lacanian paradigm of the self.

O'Connor's well-known use of simultaneous thematic violence and rhetorical irony achieves a subversion of linguistic desire much like what we observed in Bataille. She takes the project of realism as her initial object, but she aims, by exhausting it, to arrive at an intimation of what is beneath the surface of the real: the sacred, poetic *manie*. This transgression of realism is articulated as violence and laughter, coincident thematic and rhetorical excess. The violence depicted by the story often, if not always, colludes with comic irony to elicit tenuous laughter (tenuous in the etymological sense of *stretched*, pulled in two directions) from the reader.

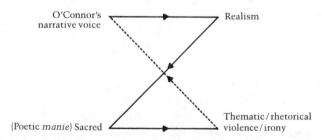

The sacred is for O'Connor the ego of literary language, but it can only be articulated in terms of its id: violent death, disease, maiming, and a rhetoric of displacement, parabasis.

In *A Confederacy of Dunces*, the only published novel of John Kennedy Toole, we find the most revealing confrontation of the novel with history since Faulkner. This novel combines the strategies of Bataille, Faulkner, and O'Connor, and for the first time, the narrative voice identifies itself with the raven's latest avatar: a mangy cockatoo. "Darlene put the cage on the bar and uncovered a huge, scrofulous rose cockatoo that looked, like a used car, as if it had passed through the hands of many owners. The bird's crest dipped, and it cried horribly, 'Awwk.'" The book engages a discourse of striptease and anachronism, in which the narrative voice, like the bird, becomes irreducibly emblematic of all its emblems. The fixed value arbitrarily placed at the dialectical terminus, to complete the circuit, is not the bird itself but, in order of abstraction, the protagonist Ignatius Reilly, not a character so much as a system of *ressorts*, valves (the pyloric, governing gas flow, most prominently—"his pyloric valve snapping shut indiscriminately and filling his stomach with trapped gas, gas which had character and being and resented its confinement"), an interconnected hydraulic system part of which is physical, exuding flatulence and excrement, and part of which is linguistic, excreting theories and plots and filling notebooks; the amateur stripper Darlene's costume, which her cockatoo pulls off her; and the reality of the French Quarter of New Orleans, which the narration itself strips.

> "Look Lana." Darlene took off her pea jacket and showed the manager the tiny rings attached to the side of her slacks and blouse with safety pins. "You see these things? That's what's gonna make the act smooth. I been practicing with it in my apartment. It's a new angle. He grabs at those rings with his beak and rips my clothes off. I mean, these rings is just for rehearsal. When I get my costume made, the rings are gonna be sewed on top of a hook and eye so when he grabs, the costume pops open. I'm telling you, Lana. It's gonna be a smash hit sensation."[23]

As in Bataille, the discourse of eroticism is defeated by its means, by its dialectic that confuses Darlene with the bird, and the discourse of realism is defeated by its confusion of the narrative voice with Ignatius. Ignatius is himself composing a novel, one that he intends to be most didactically moral. Ignatius J.

23. John Kennedy Toole, *A Confederacy of Dunces* (Baton Rouge, 1980), 146, 27.

Reilly might easily have been the author of *On Moral Fiction*, believing just as firmly as John Gardner in the pure anteriority of moral values and the depravity and inferiority of the present (literary) world in which he lives. Ignatius' mission, as historian and novelist, his morally conceived act of literary composition, is the object of the text. Ignatius, a medievalist as was Gardner, has appropriately set himself the most uplifting and righteous task of dragging the twentieth century five hundred years backwards. History here is not only confused with literature, but the two are identified with a lunacy that is defined in the symbolic language of anachronism, temporal parabasis.

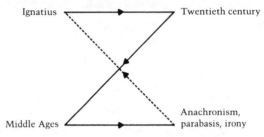

In the more palpable symbolic dialectic of striptease, the novel undresses history and literature, defeating the literary with the erotic desires, and vice versa, losing the projects of realism and of lust.

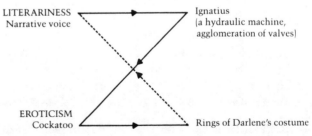

The costume itself is exposed as the real object of the strip. As Roland Barthes put it, "Only the duration of the undressing constitutes the public as voyeur."[24] Once the costume is gone, there

24. Roland Barthes, *Mythologies* (Paris, 1957): "Seule la durée du dévêtement constitue le public en voyeur" (147).

is nothing left to strip. The bird, in this double (vertical and horizontal) chiasmus, is confused with Darlene—it is losing feathers too; and the novel of realism is rendered ironic at the same time by taking its own (Ignatius') project as its object.

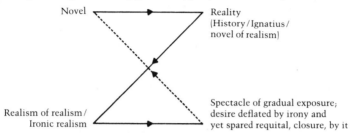

The language of undress reiterates in a graphic manner an important implication about the project of literature: it has no object, no terminus, no necessary conclusion. There is no reason why the cockatoo should stop with Darlene's costume.

> "Listen, Darlene, it was safer when you just had that goddam thing flying around your head or whatever it did."
> "But now it's gonna be a real part of the turn. It's gonna *pull . . .*'
> "Yeah, and it might pull your tits off. All I need in this place is a goddam accident and a ambulance to drive away my customers and ruin my investment. Or maybe this bird gets it in his head to fly out in the audience and pull out somebody's eyes. No, to be frank, I don't trust you and a bird, Darlene. Safety first."[25]

It could easily pull her "tits" off, flay and dismember her, carry the act to the grave. But that would not conclude either, would not totalize or reveal anything but death. By tearing its object to infinite pieces, the narration might hope to immobilize it at the cost of dispersal, undoing, and loss. We observed the result on Char's poetry. But Toole's novel does not attempt this. It saves the traditional narrative text to enact and reenact with ironic gusto its exposure, its undressing. In the dispersal of erotic and literary desires, foregoing possession, the novel celebrates loss,

25. Toole, *A Confederacy of Dunces,* 147.

does not mourn it. It has, like Bonnefoy's poetic voice, come out on the other side of losing: "Here is undone the knight of mourning."

Barry Hannah's bird is just as instructive in regard to history. A woodpecker, it does not talk like the raven but, like him, taps. And it is dispatched by an arrow (Zeno's?) that does not, however, arrest its motion but alters, while prolonging, it.

> There was one woodpecker going at it in the high branches of a dead tree. It was the only sign of life, and we'd been there two hours.
> Charlie looked up at the woodpecker. Then he loaded the bow.
> "Aw, Charlie," I said.
> "If I don't kill something, I'm going to kill my wife," he said.
> Says I, "Go ahead. You ain't going to hit it, anyway."
> But he did. The arrow rose from the bow as dead-sure as a heat-seeker and skewered the lovely redheaded thing, went on up into the air with the bird still on it.
> . . . .
> "I been having hate in me since my wife turned lesbian or narcissistic or whatever," Charlie says. "But look, I've killed this beautiful bird. Ray, you've got to do something for me.
> . . . .
> Now I am looking at the bird with arrow through it.
> And all it does is make me very sleepy.[26]

The muse of *Ray* does not talk, but pierces, taps, hammers, and finally is pierced. The novel is written in the symbolic language of piercing. And as always, that which does the piercing and that which is pierced are involved in a chiasmus.

Ray narrates his own story, but in the novel he is not a novelist but a poet and a doctor, and sexually rapacious. In all capacities, he modulates the dialectical systole and diastole of narrative and the body's poem of blood and the heart that cannot stop rhyming until it does. He dispenses drugs and words from "a zone of Edgar Allan Poe privacy." The problem of life is that "it is terribly, excruciatingly difficult to be at peace . . . when all

26. Barry Hannah, *Ray* (New York, 1981), 98–99.

our history is war." Literature struggles in a similar irresolution, tension, which it punctuates with violence, by piercing itself as it does here, to keep from disappearing. Like Char's poems, *Ray* is part aphorism, part story, part journalism, part poetry—pure generic irony. Mr. Hooch, the novel's exemplary poet, says, "I know life all round, up and down. I have become my dreams. I have entered the rear of Mother Nature and come out her mouth, and I am the sin that is not ugly."[27] The doctor, the poet, the soldier, the murderer, the hunter, the fornicator—all manipulate, modulate, or accelerate the tension of differences, the progressive defeat and loss of life. To live is to give shots or shoot bullets, do violence, if not to others then to oneself. The tension is life, or in literature, irony, the grotesque, and if not directed outward, it works on itself. It is symptomatic of English that Hannah, unlike Char, had to turn to narrative, rather than fragment, to enact that tension, which pierces the narrative all through, making its most salient feature ellipsis, the holes made by the ironic piercing.

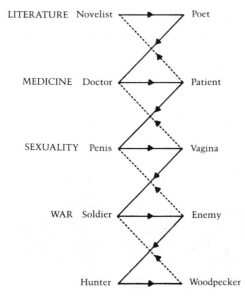

There is no piece of literary writing that does not deserve and cry out for irony, and no human who does not need to pierce and be pierced. Of course, this could not be any more grotesque. Many texts loudly decry the corrosive intrusion of critical, ironic scrutiny that they incite. The last thing most people want is to have needles or bullets put into them. What about penises? It depends. Is criticism bullet or penis? That depends, too. Probably it is both. But whatever it does redounds to it. Hannah's characters cry out for piercing. They need to, to suspend the text in that no-place from which we may not extract it by asking such questions as "What friends of yours do these characters remind you of?" or "How may you improve your personality with what you learned reading this novel?"—questions typically inscribed in the back of high school anthologies. Having frightened an old gentleman to death, DeSoto here craves a bullet:

> "Shoot me in the thigh," DeSoto said. "If you shoot me in the thigh, I'll get you a job," said DeSoto.
> "I don't need it. I got his will money."
> "Then just shoot me in the thigh. I need some of the pain."
> DeSoto put his foot on the desk. Wently shot off one low in his thigh.
> Wently went away with a new perspective.[28]

The reader, too, gains a new perspective. His faith in mimetic realism is stunned, if not exterminated—or rather, set moving in a different way, like the woodpecker or DeSoto. The grotesque needs to preserve mimetic expectations, for it is a tension with respect to them, a dissonance in their harmony. Irony must be able to feign totalization, to provide itself with an object, a center that it proceeds to shatter.

Hannah's use of the Civil War in his novel is evidence that it still works as a metaphor in the symbolic idiom of history. But Ray confuses the Civil War with Vietnam. His flashbacks from the latter are freely intertwined with the mythology of the former. "I live in so many centuries," he says, "everybody is still

28. *Ibid.*, 25–26.

alive."[29] Time is grotesque, incongruous, a perpetual catachresis, a convention whose mendaciousness everyone affects not to notice, and at length succeeds in forgetting. Cognition and memory are the same thing.

Hannah's melding of the Civil War with Vietnam in his novel's articulation of defeat alerts us to the dissolution of southern literature as a voice distinct, in the symbolic language of history, from that of the North. In the Agrarian poets and Faulkner, the South succeeded in overwhelming the rest of America literarily. But the consequence of southern literature having become the dominant literature of America has been that there are presently as many, or more, northern writers working in the mode of the grotesque—John Irving, for instance. And all of America has now known defeat in the symbolic language of history, as it had not before, in Vietnam. Southern literature may indeed, in its success, premised on defeat, have defeated itself. The French turn less and less to contemporary southern writers to nourish their own traditions. They still turn to Poe, however, as witness the work of Lacan and Derrida on "The Purloined Letter." They still read Faulkner, and they still read such contemporary southerners as Fred Chappell. Indeed, they give Chappell prizes. But they give the same prizes to John Updike.

Southern writers such as Chappell have learned all about poetic derangement, the grotesque, from the French and from Poe. What they have learned, finally, is that there is nothing more deranged or grotesque than what is utterly banal. All metaphors are mistakes, and classical theory notwithstanding, there is no qualitative difference between catachresis and the most demure trope. All knowing is derangement, whether named phenomenology or phantasmagoria. And so, let us follow Chappell's example, for

> . . . as my father said, "Fire's in the bloodstream."
> The groaning it cost my muse to take off my edge

29. *Ibid.*, 41.

Still sounds in my sleep, rasps my furious dream.
—Tell you what, Jim: let's grow old and sage;
Let's don't wind up brilliant, young, and dead.
Let's just remember.

He speaks for a whole age, perhaps the golden age of southern literature in saying, "That decade with Rimbaud I don't regret. / But could not live again. Man, that was *hard*."[30]

America, in embracing southern literature as its own, may have obliterated what fed that literature, the "sense of comprising some spiritual order of the outcast and benighted—a kind of perversely, left-handedly chosen people. . . . For the last decade or two, as the South has industriously undertaken to alchemize itself into a replica of Pasadena, its old simple passionate definitions of life have begun to wane and diffuse into the pleasant monotone coma of the rest of corporate American suburbia."[31] No one returning to the South after some years of self-imposed exile could fail to register shock at the change: car dealerships and jumboburger stands, all-night minimarkets where once were pastures, miniature golf concessions where once were woods. Even the benighted and bankrupt but ever puritanical Northeast begins to realize the consequences of its righteous project of socially redeeming the South. It is not the South anymore, but the Sun Belt. Its citizens have struck oil and are now able to afford being liberal. They can purchase indoor plumbing, finance sumptuous housing projects, and live off the fat of the land, as northern television announcers say they ought, in Lincoln Continentals and polyester suits. Many northerners are so pleased with the monster they have made that they have rushed off to be part of it. For the others, neck deep in the ruins of aspiration, there is somewhere a moral in the tale.

And, though pierced with the arrow of acceptance, the raven is not quite dead, in America or France. Where he will next make his home is not sure—perhaps in the bleak, rueful North, perhaps for a while longer among those southerners stricken with

30. Fred Chappell, *Midquest: A Poem* (Baton Rouge, 1981), 61.
31. Marshall Frady, *Southerners* (New York, 1980), viv.

dismay at their homeland's self-rape. But for the moment, in
Chappell and Hannah and other members of what may be the
last generation of truly southern writers, before the *literati*, too,
become ashamed of the very name and change it to Sun Belt, the
bird's black heart yet beats southward. High in some ancient
tree below the Mason-Dixon Line, one of the few not yet bull-
dozed or sold for timber, he still squats, inscrutable, persisting in
the face of encroachments, critical nest-plunderings such as my
own. Despite the many stakes, arrows, and writing pens driven
through his heart, he continues to croak, jabber, groan, flap, and
splatter his fecund hieroglyphics on the landscape. And across
the wide Atlantic, the ranting, gorgeous corpse still answers,
fainter than before, perhaps, but for the time being still audible:
"*Jamais plus. . . .*"

GLOSSARY

ALLEGORY   From the Greek meaning 'to speak figuratively'. The use of concrete imagery and description, not in the service of realism, but as metaphorical representation of an abstract meaning. Every term of an allegorical passage would have a double meaning, a literal one and a figural one.

ALTERITY   From the Latin *alter*, meaning 'other'. Describing all things experienced by the self as being different from it, rather than identical with it. This would include the self's concept or image of itself, insofar as the latter is conceived differentially, as characterized by a relation of difference (*see* DIFFÉRANCE/DIFFÉRENCE) rather than of identity.

ANALEPSIS   From the Greek meaning 'to take up, restore'. A narrative moment within a larger narration that is chronologically anterior to the context.

APORIA   From the Greek meaning 'difficulty, being at a loss'. An unresolvable equivocalness. For example, the situation in which neither of two or several possible meanings of a word can be decided upon as correct.

ARISTOTELIAN   *See* MIMESIS.

ASEITY   "Underived or independent existence" (*Oxford English Dictionary*). The manifest reality of a thing, its 'thingness'.

CATACHRESIS   From the Greek meaning 'misuse', also called *abusio* ('harsh use of tropes'). Extreme, wrenched metaphor. For example, a blind mouth, a livid silence, or even a loud color. A commonly cited example is Hamlet's "I will speak daggers to her."

CHIASMUS   From the Greek for 'crossing' and derived from the Greek letter *chi* (*X*), which represents graphically the rhetorical effect involved, for example, in the phrase "I do not live to eat, but eat to live."

CODE   Jonathan Culler (*Structuralist Poetics* [Ithaca, N.Y., 1975], 43) gives a simple example: "We might say . . . that in his sonnet 144,

'Two loves I have of comfort and despair,' Shakespeare takes the basic opposition good/evil and explores it in a number of codes: the religious (angel/devil, saint/fiend), the moral (purity/pride), and the physical (fair/coloured ill)." A code then is a set of relationships among signs according to which certain signs in a particular context connote particular meanings, a particular network of significations. We might speak of an "underwear" code according to which black or bright red underwear means something other than white underwear, and in which other factors such as brevity assume importance. Neither color nor brevity would have the same significance if we were speaking of hats or belts or tablecloths. This would be due to the impingement of various sexual/gonadotrophic codes on the underwear code because of the proximity of underwear to the genitals and (in women) the mammary glands, making it a kind of covering signifier to the gonadal signified.

DIACHRONIC   The chronological, historically determined aspects of an entity, by contrast with its synchronic dimension, which would be defined as not dependent on temporal factors.

DIFFERENCE/DIFFÉRENCE/DIFFERENTIAL   Jacques Derrida is responsible for the great importance of this term. In his use, a play on French *différer* is essential—the word means 'to differ', but also 'to defer', that is, to defer meaning. Drawing on Saussure's assertion that the relation between signifier and signified is always arbitrary and that each sign has meaning only by apposition, contrast, and resemblance with other signs, Derrida deconstructs the notion of an intrinsic meaning present within a given sign or text. Instead, each signifier appears to have a meaning that is dependent on all the other signifiers around it, and all the interpretants, or other signs, that it implies and that must be used to understand it. The text is defined as a purely formal absence of any signified, which the reader must supplement in the act of reading, in which he projects a signifier responding to the text's deferment of meaning even as he defers to the text and to other readers. Derrida has altered the spelling of the French word (from *différence* to *différance*) to specify his particular use of the word.

DISCOURSE   As applied by Michel Foucault (*L'Archéologie du savoir* [Paris, 1969]) and Edward Saïd (*Orientalism* [New York, 1978]), a system of superimposed and interlocking codes (*see* CODE), comprising among their aspects the cultural, the historical, and what is referred to as tradition, literary and otherwise, which determine the possibilities of articulating, and therefore of perceiving, a given object. This has little to do with Emile Benveniste's use of the same term. One might speak of the discourse of Poe, or of the discourse of the Raven, referring to the various codes that have generated and been generated by the articulation of Poe and his text. The fallacy into which Foucault and Saïd seem at times to lapse is the treatment of these codes as though they were objects, which one could pretend to distance oneself from and describe, objectively. This must be impossible, for to address a discourse at all is to become entangled in it. (*See* Jean Baudrillard, *Oublier Foucault* [Paris, 1977].

DISCOURSE OF THE OTHER   For Jacques Lacan, "the unconscious is that discourse of the Other where the subject receives, in the inverted form suited to the promise, his own forgotten message" (Lacan, *Speech and Language in Psychoanalysis*, 145). At its very simplest, then, discourse of the Other could be defined as the unconscious.

ECPHRASIS (EKPHRASIS)   From the Greek meaning 'description'. Description, often for its own sake, or to display eloquence—the translation of image into verbal representation, of painting into poem or narration. It is *literary*, fortuitous description, by contrast with *evidentia*, which is descriptive language in the service of persuasion.

ELLIPSIS   Omission of a word or words.

FIGURE/FIGURATIVE   A figure calls an object by name other than that commonly assigned to it, other than its own. It calls a thing by the name of something else in order to emphasize a property or properties shared by the object referred to and the object by whose name it is called.

HYPERBOLE   Deliberate figural exaggeration for the purpose of emphasis.

IMAGINARY ORDER   "In the sense given to this term by Jacques Lacan (and generally used substantively): one of the three essential orders of the psycho-analytic field, namely the Real, the Symbolic and the Imaginary. The imaginary order is characterized by the prevalence of the relation to the image of the counterpart (le semblable)" (Laplanche and Pontalis, *The Language of Psychoanalysis*, 210). In terms of my own paradigm, this describes the relations between the symmetrical self and the symmetrical other. *See* SYMBOLIC ORDER.

LITOTES   Deliberate figural understatement for the purpose of emphasis—the reverse of hyperbole. *See* HYPERBOLE.

METALEPSIS   A figure of a figure, or an extended comparison in which the central, or grounding, figure (comparison) is omitted. A comparison that depends on a prior, omitted comparison. For example, a

bird is like an airplane, and an airplane is like an automobile (both are
vehicles of transportation); therefore a bird is like an automobile.
This may appear to be a non sequitur but it is not necessarily. One
can fly (travel at much greater speeds than on foot, a figurative use of
fly) in an automobile. The otherness of the machine and the otherness of flight are thus figures for one another. In Latin, this trope is
called *transumption*.

METAPHOR   The comparison of objects by substitution of the name of
something else for the usual, commonly accepted name of a thing.
For practical purposes, it is the same thing as *simile*.

METONYMY   The substitution of the name of one of the properties,
attributes, possessions, parts, causes, or effects of a thing for its usual,
commonly accepted name.

MIMESIS   Imitation. A mimetic reading takes literary language as
purely representational, assuming a direct and immediate relation
between words and things, signifier and referent (*see* SIGN). This
would contrast with a semiotic reading, which moves from sign to
sign, signifier to signifier within a system of codes in which each sign
defers to others (*see* DIFFERENCE). The distinction made herein between the Aristotelian and the Platonic would correspond roughly to
that between mimesis and semiosis, respectively.

OTHER (UNSYMMETRICAL)   The hypothetical locus of the unconscious,
the gap or 'omission' that must be supplemented by interpretation.
According to Lacan, "the subject has to emerge from the given of the
signifiers which cover him in an Other which is their transcendental
locus: through this he constitutes himself in an existence where the
manifestly constituting vector of the Freudian area of experience is
possible: that is to say, what is called desire" (Lacan, *Speech and
Language in Psychoanalysis*, 106). The symmetrical other describes
everything perceived by the self as not identical with itself, including
certain aspects of itself, everything within the realm of the conscious
that is characterized by a relation of difference with the self.

OVERDETERMINEDNESS/OVERDETERMINATION   The phenomenon that
signifiers of the unconscious—of Otherness (*see* OTHER)—may be attached to several signifieds or causes (*see* SIGN). This is because "the
formation is related to a multiplicity of unconscious elements which
may be organised in different meaningful sequences, each having its
own specific coherence at a particular level of interpretation"
(Laplanche and Pontalis, *The Language of Psychoanalysis*, 292). The

concept does not mean that a given signifier has infinite meanings, or that it has no positive meaning (which would be the same thing).

PARABASIS   The intrusion of the author's voice within the text. In classical Greek drama, the term refers to a moment in a play at which the chorus steps forward and speaks in the author's name. Schlegel called irony (his "irony of irony," or "irony to the second degree" a "permanent parabasis," or distancing from the text within the text.

PARADIGM/PARADIGMATIC   In linguistic usage, these terms refer to the system of relationships linking a word within a given text to other words in the language outside that text—synonyms, antonyms, cognates. The opposition paradigm/syntagm is related conceptually to that of diachrony/synchrony in that both set up distinctions of inside and outside, the former with respect to a textual/grammatical/spatial unit, the latter with respect to a temporal one. *See* SYNTAGM/SYNTAGMATIC, and DIACHRONIC.

PHONEME/PHONEMIC   An aural unit of meaning, by contrast with a grapheme, which is a written unit of meaning.

PLATONIC   *See* MIMESIS.

POETICITY   The discourse of poetry or of a particular poetic practice. *See* DISCOURSE.

PRIMAL SCENE   Freud uses this term to designate a child's first apprehension of sexual activity by his parents. It is used herein in a metaphorical sense.

PROLEPSIS   A moment in which a narration looks ahead of itself—a narrative digression that is chronologically posterior to the larger narrative context.

REFERENT/REFERENTIAL   *See* MIMESIS.

SEMIOSIS/SEMIOTIC   *See* MIMESIS.

SIGN   As defined by Saussure, a sign comprises three parts—the signifier, the signified, and the referent. The signifier would be the form (phonemic and graphemic) to which a given signified is arbitrarily attached. The referent is the object (the image) referred to. C. S. Peirce has proposed a more elaborate definition, according to which the sign comprises an object, an interpretant, and a ground: an object to which the sign refers, an interpretant that it generates in the mind of the subject, and a ground that mediates between object and interpretant, on which the interpretant is based. There are three basic types of sign: the icon, in which the sign and its object are associated by actual resemblance (for example, a realistic portrait of a person); the index, in which the relation between sign and object is causal (for example, smoke as a sign of fire); and symbol, in which the relation between sign and object is entirely arbitrary. The use herein of the terms *sign*, *signifier*, and *signified* is based much more on Saussure than on Peirce.

SYMBOLIC ORDER   For Lacan, this term refers to those phenomena of the psyche that are structured like language. For example, the discourse of the Other (the unconscious).

SYNCHRONIC   *See* DIACHRONIC.

SYNECDOCHE   The figural substitution of part for whole. Very closely related to metonymy. For example, "the *eyes* of Texas are upon you."

SYNTAGM/SYNTAGMATIC   The relation of a word to the other words within a given textual or semantic unit, real or hypothetical. *See* PARADIGM/PARADIGMATIC.

TAUTOLOGY/TAUTOLOGICAL   From the Greek meaning 'saying the same things'. Repetition, through restatement, of an idea; a verbal or semiotic equation of the form $x = x$.

TRANSUMPTION   *See* METALEPSIS.

TROPE   From the Greek meaning 'a turn'. A substitution of one word or words for another word or words, which has the effect of altering the meaning of the word(s) substituted.

BIBLIOGRAPHY

Primary Works

Apollinaire, Guillaume. *Calligrammes*. Paris, 1966.
———. *Oeuvres en prose*. Edited by Michel Decaudin. Paris, 1977.
Bataille, Georges. *Madame Edwards/Le Mort/Histoire de l'oeil*. Paris, n.d.
Baudelaire, Charles. *Oeuvres complètes*. Edited by Marcel Ruff. Paris, 1968.
Beauvoir, Simone de. *L'Amérique au jour le jour*. Paris, 1948. *America Day by Day*. Translated by Patrick Dudley. New York, 1953.
Bloom, Harold, and Lionel Trilling, eds. *Romantic Poetry and Prose*. New York, 1973.
Bonnefoy, Yves. *Poèmes*. Paris, 1978.
Breton, André, and Philippe Soupault. *Les Champs magnétiques*. Paris, 1971.
Carlson, Eric W., ed. *The Recognition of Edgar Poe*. Ann Arbor, Mich., 1966.
Carr, John, ed. *Kite-Flying and Other Irrational Acts: Conversations with Twelve Southern Writers*. Baton Rouge, 1972.
Chappell, Fred. *Midquest: A Poem*. Baton Rouge, 1981.
Char, René. *Fureur et mystère*. Paris, 1967.
Core, George, ed. *Southern Fiction Today: Renascence and Beyond*. Athens, Ga., 1969.
Desnos, Robert. *Domaine public*. Paris, 1953.
Eluard, Paul. *Oeuvres complètes*. Edited by Marcelle Dumas and Lucien Scheler. Vol. I of 2 vols. Paris, 1968.
Faulkner, William. *As I Lay Dying*. New York, 1964.
———. *Early Prose and Poetry*. Edited by Carvel Collins. Boston, 1962.
———. *Sartoris*. New York, 1929.
———. *Selected Short Stories of William Faulkner*. New York, n.d.
———. *The Sound and the Fury*. New York, 1954.
Fowlie, Wallace, ed. and trans. *Rimbaud. Complete Works, Selected Letters*. Chicago, 1965.

The Greek Anthology. Translated by W. R. Paton. London, 1916.
The Greek Bucolic Poets. Rev. ed. Trans J. M. Edmonds. Cambridge, Mass., 1977.
Green, Julian. *Léviathan.* New ed. Paris, 1973.
————. *Oeuvres complètes.* Edited by Jacques Petit. Vol. V of 5 vols. Paris, 1977.
Hannah, Barry. *Ray.* New York, 1981.
Leiris, Michel. *Mots sans mémoires.* Paris, 1969.
Mallarmé, Stéphane. *Oeuvres complètes.* Edited by Henri Mondor and G. Jean-Aubry. Paris, 1945.
Montaigne, Michel de. *Oeuvres complètes.* Edited by Albert Thibaudet and Maurice Rat. Paris, 1962.
O'Connor, Flannery. *Three by Flannery O'Connor.* New York, 1962.
O'Neill, E. H., ed. *The Complete Poems and Stories of Edgar Allan Poe, with Selections from his Critical Writings.* 2 vols. New York, 1967.
Percy, Walker. *Lancelot.* New York, 1977.
Perse, Saint-John. *Eloges, suivi de La Gloire des rois, Anabase, Exil.* Paris, 1960.
Plato. *The Collected Dialogues.* Edited by Edith Hamilton and Huntingdon Cairns. Princeton, 1961.
————. *Republic.* Translated and edited by Desmond Lee. New York, 1974.
————. *The Symposium.* Translated and edited by Walter Hamilton. New York, 1951.
Poe, Edgar Allan. *Complete Works.* Virginia ed. New York, 1979.
————. *Works.* 2 vols. New York, 1876.
Ponge, Francis. *Le Parti pris des choses, suivi de Poèmes.* Paris, n.d.
Price, Reynolds. *The Annual Heron.* New York, 1980.
————. *The Names and Faces of Heroes.* New York, 1973.
Rabelais, François. *Oeuvres complètes.* Edited by Jacques Boulenger and Lucien Scheler. Paris, 1955.
Reverdy, Pierre. *Main d'oeuvre, poèmes 1913–1949.* Paris, 1949.
Rimbaud, Arthur. *Oeuvres complètes.* Edited by Rolland de Renéville and Jules Mouquet. Paris, 1954.
Robbe-Grillet, Alain, and René Magritte. *La Belle Captive.* Lausanne-Paris, 1975.
————. *L'Immortelle.* Paris, 1963. *The Immortal.* Translated by A. M. Sheridan-Smith. London, 1971.
————. *Instantanés.* Paris, 1962. *Snapshots.* Translated by Bruce Morrissette. New York, 1968.

Sarraute, Nathalie. *Tropismes*. Paris, 1957.
Styron, William. *The Long March*. New York, 1952.
Tate, Allen. *Collected Poems: 1919–1976*. New York, 1977.
Toole, John Kennedy. *A Confederacy of Dunces*. Baton Rouge, 1980.
Valéry, Paul. *Leonardo Poe Mallarmé*. Translated by Malcolm Cowley
and James R. Lawler. Princeton, 1973. Vol. VIII of *The Collected
Works in English*. Bollingen Series XLV. 15 vols. to date.
———. *Oeuvres*. Edited by Jean Hytier. Vol. I of 2 vols. Paris, 1957.
Verlaine, Paul. *Oeuvres complètes*. Edited by Y.-G. Le Dantec and
Jacques Borel. Paris, 1962.
Warren, Robert Penn. *Selected Poems 1923–1975*. New York, 1976.

Secondary Works

Annas, Julia. *An Introduction to Plato's Republic*. Oxford, Clarendon,
1981.
Aristotle. *On Poetry and Music*. Translated by S. H. Butcher. In-
dianapolis, 1956.
Bachelard, Gaston. *L'Eau et les rêves*. Paris, 1942.
Bandy, W. T. Introduction to *Edgar Allan Poe, sa vie et ses ouvrages*, by
Charles Baudelaire. Toronto, 1973.
Barthes, Roland. *Mythologies*. Paris, 1957.
Baudrillard, Jean. *Oublier Foucault*. Paris, 1977.
Beaujour, Michel. "Some Paradoxes of Description." In *Towards a The-
ory of Description*. Yale French Studies No. 61 (1981).
Bleikasten, André. *The Most Splendid Failure: Faulkner's "The Sound
and the Fury."* Bloomington, Indiana, 1976.
Bloom, Harold. *The Anxiety of Influence: A Theory of Poetry*. New
York, 1973.
———. *A Map of Misreading*. New York, 1975.
———. *Poetry and Repression: Revisionism from Blake to Stevens*.
New Haven, 1976.
Blumenthal, Henry. *American and French Culture, 1800–1900: Inter-
changes in Art, Science, Literature, and Society*. Baton Rouge, 1975.
Boltenhouse, Charles. "Poems in the Shapes of Things." *Art News An-
nual*, XXVIII (1959), 64–83.
Bonaparte, Marie. *Edgar Poe, étude psychanalytique*. New ed. 3 vols.
Paris, 1958. *The Life and Works of Edgar Poe: A Psychoanalytic
Interpretation*. Translated by John Rodker. London, 1949. .

Bonnefoy, Yves. *L'Improbable, suivi de Un Rêve fait à Mantoue*. Paris, 1980.

———. *Rimbaud par lui-même*. Paris, 1961. *Rimbaud*. Translated by Paul Schmidt. New York, 1973.

Booth, Wayne. *The Rhetoric of Irony*. Chicago, 1974.

Bowler, Berjouhi. *The Word as Image*. London, 1970.

Butor, Michel. *Les Mots dans la peinture*. Paris, 1969.

Culler, Jonathan. *On Deconstruction: Theory and Criticism After Structuralism*. Ithaca, N.Y., 1982.

———. *Structuralist Poetics: Structuralism, Linguistics and the Study of Literature*. Ithaca, N.Y., 1975.

Davidson, Donald. *Still Rebels, Still Yankees and Other Essays*. Baton Rouge, 1972.

de Man, Paul. "The Rhetoric of Temporality." In *On Interpretation*, edited by Charles S. Singleton. Baltimore, 1969.

———. "The Resistance to Theory." In *The Pedagogical Imperative*. Yale French Studies No. 63 (1982).

Deleuze, Gilles, and Felix Guattari. *L'Anti-Oedipe*. Paris, 1972.

Diderot, Denis. *Oeuvres esthétiques*. Edited by P. Vernière. Paris, 1968.

Felman, Shoshana. "On Reading Poetry: Reflections on the Limits and Possibilities of Psychoanalytic Approaches." In *The Literary Freud: Mechanisms of Defense and the Poetic Will*, edited by Joseph M. Smith. New Haven, 1980.

Fontanier, Pierre. *Les Figures du discours*. Paris, 1977.

Foucault, Michel. *L'Archéologie du savoir*. Paris, 1969.

Fowlie, Wallace. *Rimbaud: A Critical Study*. Chicago, 1966.

Frady, Marshall. *Southerners*. New York, 1980.

French-American Literary Relationships. Yale French Studies No. 10 (1952).

Friedlander, Paul. *Plato: An Introduction*. Translated by Hans Meyerhoff. Princeton, 1969.

Genette, Gérard. *Mimologiques, Voyage en Cratylie*. Paris, 1976.

Graves, Robert. *The Greek Myths*. 2 vols. New York, 1955.

Greene, Thomas M. *The Light in Troy*. New Haven, 1982.

Halpern, Joseph. Introduction to *Mallarmé*. Yale French Studies No. 54 (1977).

Havelock, Eric A. *Preface to Plato*. Cambridge, Mass., 1963.

Heidegger, Martin. *Being and Time*. Translated by John Macquarrie and Edward Robinson. New York, 1962.

Hillman, James. *The Dream and the Underworld.* New York, 1979.

Hollander, John. *The Figure of Echo.* Berkeley, 1981.

———. *Rhyme's Reason.* New Haven, 1981.

———. *Vision and Resonance.* New York, 1975.

Houston, John Porter. *French Symbolism and the Modernist Movement: A Study of Poetic Structures.* Baton Rouge, 1980.

Howe, Irving. "Southern Agrarians and American Culture." In *Celebrations and Attacks.* New York, 1979.

Irwin, John T. *American Hieroglyphics.* New Haven, 1980.

———. *Doubling and Incest/Repetition and Revenge: A Speculative Reading of Faulkner.* Baltimore, 1975.

Jakobson, Roman. "Language and Poetics." In *Essays on the Language of Literature,* edited by Seymour Chatman and Samuel Levin. Boston, 1967.

Johnson, Barbara. *The Critical Difference.* Baltimore, 1981.

Jonas, Hans. *The Gnostic Religion.* Boston, 1958.

Kaiser, Wolfgang. *The Grotesque in Art and Literature.* Translated by Ulrich Weisstein. New York, 1966.

Ketterer, David. *The Rationale of Deception in Poe.* Baton Rouge, 1979.

Kroupa, Adolph. "La Légende du Dernier Poème de Desnos." *Les Lettres françaises,* June 9, 1960, pp. 1,5.

Lacan, Jacques. *Ecrits.* 2 vols. Paris, 1966.

———. *Speech and Language in Psychoanalysis.* Edited and translated by Anthony Wilden. Baltimore, 1981.

Lanham, Richard A. *A Handlist of Rhetorical Terms.* Berkeley, 1968.

Laplanche, Jean. *Vie et mort en psychanalyse.* Paris, 1970. *Life and Death in Psychoanalysis.* Translated by Jeffrey Mehlman. Baltimore, 1976.

Laplanche, J., and J.-B. Pontalis. *The Language of Psychoanalysis.* Translated by Donald Nicholson-Smith. New York, 1973.

Maritain, Jacques. *Creative Intuition in Art and Poetry.* New York, 1974.

O'Connor, Flannery. *Mystery and Manners.* Edited by Sally and Robert Fitzgerald. New York, 1969.

Palmer, R. R., and Joel Colton. *A History of the Modern World.* New York, 1971.

Pearce, Richard. *William Styron.* Minneapolis, 1971.

Percy, Walker. *The Message in the Bottle.* New York, 1975.

The Princeton Encyclopedia of Poetry and Poetics. Princeton, 1974.

Quinn, Patrick F. *The French Face of Edgar Poe.* Carbondale, 1957.

Raser, Timothy. "The Poetry of Baudelaire's Art Criticism." Ph.D. dissertation, Yale University, 1982.

Regan, Robert, ed. *Poe.* Englewood Cliffs, 1967.

Ricardou, Jean. *Pour une théorie du nouveau roman.* Paris, 1971.

Riffaterre, Michael. *Semiotics of Poetry.* Bloomington, Ill., 1978.

Sarraute, Nathalie. *L'Ere du soupçon, essais sur le roman.* Paris, 1956.

Sartre, Jean-Paul. *Critiques littéraires (Situations I).* Paris, 1947.

Schlegel, Friedrich. *Kritische Friedrich-Schlegel-Ausgabe.* Edited by Ernst Behler. Vol. XVIII of 35 vols. to date. Paderborn, W. Germany, 1963.

Simpson, Lewis P. *The Brazen Face of History: Studies in the Literary Consciousness in America.* Baton Rouge, 1980.

————. "The Southern Republic of Letters and *I'll Take My Stand.*" In *A Band of Prophets: The Vanderbilt Agrarians After Fifty Years,* edited by W. C. Havard and Walter Sullivan. Baton Rouge, 1982.

Stonum, Gary Lee. "Undoing American Literary History." *Diacritics,* XI (1982), 2–12.

Symons, Julian. *The Tell-Tale Heart.* New York, 1981.

Tate, Allen. *Essays of Four Decades.* Chicago, 1968.

————. *Memoirs and Opinions 1926–1974.* Chicago, 1975.

Twelve Southerners. *I'll Take My Stand: The South and the Agrarian Tradition.* Baton Rouge, 1977.

Woledge, Brian, Geoffrey Brereton, and Anthony Hartley, eds. *The Penguin Book of French Verse.* Harmondsworth and Baltimore, 1975.

Woodworth, Stanley D. *William Faulkner en France 1931–1952.* Paris, 1959.

Zweig, Paul. *The Adventurer.* Princeton, 1981.

INDEX